Water Planning in Britain

Dennis J. Parker
and
Edmund C. Penning-Rowsell
Middlesex Polytechnic

London
GEORGE ALLEN & UNWIN
Boston   Sydney

First published in 1980

GEORGE ALLEN & UNWIN LTD
40 Museum Street, London WC1A 1LU

© Dennis J. Parker and Edmund C. Penning-Rowsell 1980

British Library Cataloguing in Publication Data

Parker, Dennis J
    Water planning in Britain. – (The resource
    management series; 1).
    1. Water resources development – Great Britain
    I. Title   II. Penning-Rowsell, Edmund
    III. Series
    333.9′1′00941   HD1697.G7   80-40825

    ISBN 0-04-711006-6
    ISBN 0-04-711007-4 Pbk

Typeset in 10 on 12 point Times by Red Lion Setters, London
and printed in Great Britain
by W & J Mackay Ltd, Chatham.

To all the girls back home:
  Anna, Annabel, Jacky, Katie, Rachel and Susie

Foreword

The Resource Management Series reflects the resurgence of interest in resource analysis that has occurred over the past twenty years in both the natural and the social sciences. This interest mirrors wide public concern about declining environmental standards, man's detrimental impact on the ecosystem, the spatial and temporal allocation of resources, and the capacity of the Earth to sustain further growth in population and economic activity.

Academic research should play a crucial role in policy formulation if informed decisions are to be made about resource use or about the nature and pace of technical and economic change. The need to assess the impact of technological developments on the environment is widely recognised; this cannot be done in physical terms alone but must involve social science research into the economic, social and political implications. Failing this, society may persist in trading off environmental gains for more easily definable economic advantages, an option which is particularly tempting in times of slow economic growth, high rates of inflation and rising unemployment. Furthermore, a planned approach to resource use makes the study of policy – its formulation and implementation – imperative; and this requires a sound understanding of the options available, the legal and administrative contexts, the decision-making behaviour of planners and managers, and the day-to-day realities of the decision-maker's environment.

Cost–benefit analysis, landscape evaluation, environmental impact assessment, systems modelling and computer simulation techniques have all advanced significantly in recent years as tools of resource analysis. Although none of these are without their deficiencies, they have undoubtedly improved our understanding of the effects of resource utilisation decisions and of the complex interrelationships that exist within and between the physical and economic systems. Moreover, their use has clearly indicated that effective inquiry in the resources field cannot be confined to any one discipline.

The *Series* has been planned as an interdisciplinary vehicle for major contributions from scholars and practitioners with a wide variety of academic backgrounds. The *Series* is unequivocally directed towards policy formulation and management in the real world, and it will not include contributions which merely describe an economic or physical resource system, or those which are entirely theoretical in nature. However, the subject area is defined widely to include the management of all natural resources, renewable and non-renewable, whether managed by private enterprise or public-sector agencies.

It is hoped that the books appearing in this *Series* will command the serious attention of all students, scientists, planners, resource managers and concerned laymen with an interest in understanding man–environment interactions and in improving our resource decisions. Each book draws on substantial research or practical management experience and all reflect the individual views and styles of the authors. The editors and publishers hope that the *Series* will not only encourage further research but will also play an important role in disseminating the results.

In the first book in the *Series*, Dennis Parker and Edmund Penning-Rowsell explain and critically evaluate the water planning system in Britain. They have produced what is undoubtedly the most comprehensive analysis so far undertaken. They point out that, whilst an understanding of hydrological processes and technological possibilities is clearly of importance, water planning today is essentially about the deployment of scarce capital resources and the allocation of available water between competing users. Planning decisions depend not only on public preferences, but also on the established legal framework, political pressures, economic constraints, the organisational structure of management and on the training or professional bias of the decision makers. The book exemplifies the stance taken in the whole *Series* that assessments of resource problems must take into account the complexity of, and the interrelationships which exist between, the natural environment and man's economic, social and political institutions.

Throughout, the authors adopt a critical evaluatory approach. They are not content merely to describe the current water planning system, and they attempt to assess the extent to which it is capable of dealing with demand pressures and capital constraints in an efficient and equitable manner. Attention is also paid to alternative policies, practices and administrative structures which could be adopted to improve the efficiency of the system and to make it more accountable to the public.

Both authors have been engaged in substantive research projects concerned with various aspects of water resource development. Not only do they draw on the results of this research throughout the book, but they also include material derived from a comprehensive review of the literature. Undoubtedly, the book benefits from the authors' experience as teachers, which has helped them to produce a text that is understandable and useful to students in a wide range of disciplines.

RICHARD MUNTON and JUDITH REES
March 1980

Preface

This book is one product of a decade of water research at Middlesex Polytechnic. The 1970s began with flood hazard research, focussing eventually
upon flood alleviation economics. This was followed by research in urban
water pollution, together more recently with administrative and institutional,
recreational and historical studies of water planning. Much of this work has a
planning- and management-orientated social science context, exploiting the
strengths of multi-disciplinary group effort. Research results have so far been
communicated through papers, books, consultancy projects and training
courses. The research has been funded by Middlesex Polytechnic, the Natural
Environment Research Council, the Science Research Council and the
Ministry of Agriculture, Fisheries and Food. The water industry itself has
contributed directly through the Central Water Planning Unit, the Water
Research Centre, the Water Authorities and British Waterways Board.

Within such a context this book examines, explains and evaluates the
broad scope of British water planning. The 1974 'revolution' in water
management in England and Wales, which generated much international
interest, created a new environment for water planning. Changes in Scotland
in 1975 followed a different course but have attracted much less attention.

Water provides many essential public services. The effective management
and planning of water is of vital national importance, especially as accessible
clean water becomes scarce. Britain's water industry has a proud tradition of
technical excellence based upon an engineering profession founded during
the last century. Nevertheless the water industry faces great problems in the
1980s – problems of environmental protection, finance, public accountability and equity – all of which must be overcome to maintain and improve
standards of service. How the new institutional arrangements – now more or
less stable after more than five years of operation – help to solve these problems at a time of national economic difficulty and changing social goals and
environmental conditions is fundamentally important to all concerned for
public health, for the environment and for their water bills.

We begin by examining the basic influences on water planning. This
conceptualisation views the water planning system – both its structure and
processes – as operating at the interface between environment and society
(Ch. 1). From this emerges a number of key evaluative questions, to which we
return in following Chapters, and the need to analyse water planning institutions (Ch. 2). The subsequent four Chapters (Chs 3–6) each examine the
resource base and social context of major functional areas of water planning,
examining the planning systems and techniques relevant to each. The

dominant themes are environmental, social, economic and political and in each Chapter the evaluation of a number of central policies and particular plans and schemes contributes to understanding the processes of water planning in Britain today.

Throughout we develop a framework for critical inquiry and analysis and the final Chapter (Ch. 7) adopts a critical stance and asks more fundamentally 'who is water planning for?' and whether the structure and processes of the water planning system effectively serve social goals. Few books on water planning deal with both Scotland and England and Wales. Although Scottish sources and data are particularly scarce we have attempted to present a balanced coverage of Scotland while capitalising upon the insights which Scottish comparisons provide.

This book has been written for a broad audience. The treatment is comprehensive and the book should appeal to a wide readership in universities, polytechnics and colleges. The text is appropriate to courses in planning, geography, public administration and environmental science and management. Engineers may also find it provocative. Annotated selected readings for each Chapter provide a guide to further reading for teachers and students alike. Finally this book should prove interesting and useful for many professionals in environmental planning – particularly planners in the water industry and in local and central government – and for those 'amateur planners' in pressure groups with strong environmental and water interests.

DENNIS PARKER and EDMUND PENNING-ROWSELL
Middlesex Polytechnic
January 1980

Acknowledgements

In writing a book of this kind the authors inevitably depend on the help and advice of many people. Stan Gregory and Roy Ward made valuable comments during the planning of this book. Ted Hollis and Tim O'Riordan provided important suggestions as well as detailed comments on parts of the manuscript. All writers need editors and we thank Judith Rees and Richard Munton for making suggestions, particularly on slimming an over-weight manuscript.

We also owe a debt to colleagues at Middlesex Polytechnic. Clive Gray deserves special mention for critically examining several draft manuscripts and for providing intellectual stimulation. Dennis Hardy, Iwan Davies, Bryan Ellis, Madeleine Wahlberg and Aram Eisenschitz all contributed in one way or another. Pauline Hollis, Laurie Greenfield and Andrew Martin provided indispensable bibliographical assistance. Thanks are also due to John Chatterton and Don Harding for their help and to Roger Jones of George Allen and Unwin for his patience and continual encouragement.

We would like to record our thanks to all those involved in water planning in one capacity or another who helped us generously. They include in England and Wales: G. Cundale, Brecon Beacons National Park Authority; E. Chmara and J. Darlington, Countryside Commission; R. Grove-White and E. Mack, Council for the Protection of Rural England; M. Stevenson, Borough of Brecknock Surveyor's Department; L. Pearson, Ashford District Council Planning Department; J. Casson, North West Water Authority; J. Rowbotham, Lancashire County Council; D. Phillips, The Water Companies' Association; A. Blenkharn, Water Space Amenity Commission; R. Hall, British Waterways Board; K. Ashbrook, Dartmoor Preservation Society; J. Rimmer, Country Landowners' Association; D. Burroughs, British Water and Effluent Treatment Association; J. Eno and D. Pollington, Northumbrian Water Authority; D. Newsome, Water Data Unit; P. Bray, Anglian Water Authority; A. Hughes, Ministry of Agriculture, Fisheries and Food; D. Stratford, Thames Water Authority; A. Hardy, former Wye River Authority; J. Haworth, National Water Council. We would also like to thank R. Smith, Department of the Environment, for making details of the Carsington public inquiries available and the helpful staff in the National Water Council library.

Those in Scotland who helped us include: D. Douglas and L. Deaton, Borders Regional Council; J. McGeoch, Tayside Regional Council; R. Davenport, British Waterways Board; S. Ross-Smith, Scottish Inland Waterways Association; M. Gray, Linlithgow Union Canal Society; J. Atkins and N. Semple, Scottish Development Department; D. Watson, Highland Regional Council; D. Parrish, C. Barbour and C. Clark, Department of Agriculture and Fisheries for Scotland; D. Buchanan, Highland River Purification Board; W. Devenay and W. Greer, Strathclyde Regional Council; F. Little, North East River Purification Board; J. Williamson, Scottish Association of Directors of Water and Sewerage Services; I. Brown, Grampian Regional Council; D. Hammerton and R. Smith, Clyde River Purification Board; I. Fraser, Scottish River Purification Boards' Association; C. James, Solway River Purification Board; J. Currie, Tweed River Purification Board; and W. Collett, Forth River Purification Board.

We are grateful to the following for permission to reproduce or adapt copyright material.

The Water Data Unit for the frontispiece map from p. 3 *Water Data 1975*, 1977; The Royal Town Planning Institute for Table 1.1 from p. 23 *Planning for the future*, 1977; North West Water Authority for Table 1.2 from p. 63 *Report on planning*, 1978; for an extract on p. 132 from p. 39 *Annual Report*, 1978; and for Table 5.3 from unpublished material; Tayside Regional Council for Table 1.3 from p. 120 *Regional Report*, 1978; Wessex Water Authority for Table 1.3 from p. 62 *The Wessex Plan 1978–1983*, 1978; and for Figure 6.2 from the *Avon and Dorset Land Drainage District Land Drainage Survey Report*, 1979; Fishing News Books Ltd for Figure 2.2 from *Salmon Fisheries of Scotland* by Association of Scottish District Salmon Fishery Boards, 1977; J. Rees for the map of Water Companies in Figure 2.2; Ministry of Agriculture, Fisheries and Food for the map of Internal Drainage Boards in Figure 2.4; National Water Council for Table 3.2 and Figure 3.2 from p. 24 and p. 27 *Water industry review 1978*, 1978; Northumbrian Water Authority for Figure 4.1 from *Annual plan*, 1978; Clyde River Purification Board for Figure 4.2 from pp. 35, 26 and 27 *Annual report 1976*, 1977; Scottish Development Department for Figure 5.1 from map 2 *A measure of plenty*, 1973; the Controller of Her Majesty's Stationery Office for Figure 5.1 from *MHLG Desk Atlas*; Controller of Her Majesty's Stationery Office and British Waterways Board for Figure 5.2 from *Waterways of the British Waterways Board, 1974;* Water Space Amenity Commission for Figure 5.1 from p. 19 *The recreational use of water supply reservoirs in England and Wales*, 1977; Countryside Commission for Figure 5.2 from *Conservation and recreation in England and Wales*, 1979; Welsh Water Authority for Table 5.2 from pp. 10 and 11 *A strategic plan for water space recreation and amenity*, consultation edition, 1978; Dartington Amenity Research Trust for Figure 5.3 from *Llangorse lake, a recreation survey*, 1973; Pergamon Press Ltd for Figure 6.3 from Planning for floods, by D. J. Parker and D. M. Harding in *Disasters*, **2, 1,** 47–57, 1978; and J. B. Chatterton for Figure 6.1 from *The benefits of flood alleviation: a manual of assessment techniques*, 1977.

We are indebted to Mary Prime who typed much of the manuscript with great accuracy and efficiency; thanks are also due to Mary Hayden and Marlene Mascarenhas for their invaluable help. For refreshment during hours spent hatching plans for the book we thank the proprietor of the Boomerang Cafe. Finally we owe a special debt of gratitude to our families for their help and patience.

Contents

Tables

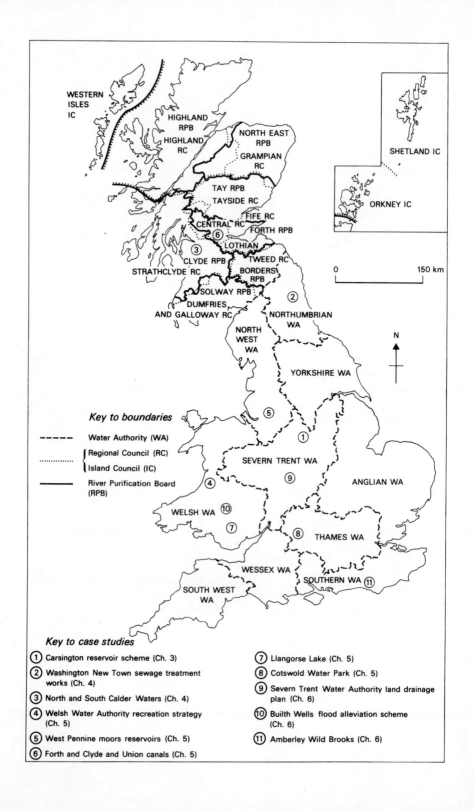

WESTERN
ISLES
IC

HIGHLAND
RPB

HIGHLAND
RC

NORTH EAST
RPB

GRAMPIAN
RC

SHETLAND IC

ORKNEY IC

TAY RPB

TAYSIDE RC

FIFE RC

CENTRAL RC

FORTH RPB

⑥

③

LOTHIAN

CLYDE RPB

TWEED RC

STRATHCLYDE RC

BORDERS
RPB

SOLWAY RPB

DUMFRIES
AND GALLOWAY RC

②

NORTHUMBRIAN
WA

0   150 km

NORTH
WEST
WA

N

YORKSHIRE WA

⑤

①

Key to boundaries

- - - - - Water Authority (WA)

.... Regional Council (RC)

{ Island Council (IC)

——— River Purification Board
(RPB)

SEVERN TRENT WA

⑨

④

ANGLIAN WA

WELSH WA ⑩

⑦

⑧ THAMES WA

WESSEX WA

SOUTHERN WA ⑪

SOUTH WEST
WA

Key to case studies

① Carsington reservoir scheme (Ch. 3)

② Washington New Town sewage treatment
works (Ch. 4)

③ North and South Calder Waters (Ch. 4)

④ Welsh Water Authority recreation strategy
(Ch. 5)

⑤ West Pennine moors reservoirs (Ch. 5)

⑥ Forth and Clyde and Union canals (Ch. 5)

⑦ Llangorse Lake (Ch. 5)

⑧ Cotswold Water Park (Ch. 5)

⑨ Severn Trent Water Authority land drainage
plan (Ch. 6)

⑩ Builth Wells flood alleviation scheme
(Ch. 6)

⑪ Amberley Wild Brooks (Ch. 6)

1 *Water planning*

A rationale for water planning

There is every reason to expect the use of water in Britain today to be planned.
Water is a commodity essential to life, community welfare and the function-
ing of the economy and is, therefore, of truly national importance. Water use
has become completely interrelated with all other activities, to the extent that
we now depend upon water even when its use is not strictly essential. With
steady intensification in the use of Britain's water and associated land resources, decisions about water impinge more and more upon the lives of everyone, from the householder to the farmer and to those concerned about
environmental quality.

The characteristics and roles of water in society make its planning essential. Water is a renewable resource, but in specific locations at a given time the
supply of fresh water is finite, imposing what can be a severe limit upon all
activities. The flow of water is variable over time creating shortages and
excesses which lead to uncertainties needing careful assessment and planning
to prevent serious economic and social disruption. In addition water is a
measurable resource with a measurable demand little affected by the whims
of fashion and is, therefore, fundamentally susceptible to planning.

Private enterprise provides some water services in Britain, such as some
sport fisheries, and has an impressive record of providing public water
supplies. However, the effectiveness of private enterprise in providing water
services is limited in several ways. Some water services, such as recreational
opportunities and environmental protection, are not fully marketable,
having a public value beyond that measured by market prices. Others, such as
flood protection, may be indivisible meaning that they cannot be marketed in
discrete units. It is not normally possible to build a flood alleviation scheme
to protect the land of a single owner. Others will benefit too making public
guidance necessary.

The water cycle is characterised by physical interdependencies which
favour public intervention and planning. Water has multiple-use potential
but private enterprise often leads to single-purpose use ignoring interdependency of uses and producing sub-optimal social benefits. Developments at
one location have important consequences at another: river water abstractions may reduce downstream navigation possibilities and effluent disposal
may increase the costs of water treatment to a downstream industrial water
abstractor. Public intervention and planning may have several other advantages over private enterprise. Private water developments may not be of

sufficient size to capture economies of scale which a public monopoly may be able to achieve. Private enterprise cannot be relied upon to ensure that the distribution of fundamental water services in society is fair but equity can be sought through central guidance. All these factors favour public intervention and planning (Fox and Craine 1962, Craine 1969).

Water is a life-supporting medium not only for humans but for aquatic and terrestrial communities most of which we depend upon either directly or indirectly for our existence. Unless planned, the impact of waste disposal can be detrimental for such life-forms. Resolving conflict and calculating the consequences of alternative actions are fundamental parts of planning. When competing demands arise, as they often do, for example between the domestic water consumer and the industrial water user, these conflicts have to be resolved. A decision in favour of a particular use at the expense of another involves some people forgoing opportunities, and produces both losers and gainers in society.

Some water policy decisions and projects are of national importance making central guidance essential. In achieving national goals water planning is an essential factor, for example in social and economic developments and in maintaining and improving the quality of the environment. Because there are competing demands for water and associated land resources, it is essential that national interests are identified and represented in decisions about the use of water, or in decisions about the use of other resources such as land, which may predetermine future use of water.

Planning is fundamentally about deciding how to spend money. In Britain the water industry spends annually over £1800millions, reflecting the large-scale applications of technology and capital required to provide the nation's water services and indicating the importance of financial decisions. Within this budget the best value for given expenditure has to be gained, whether it is upon sewer renewal or water quality improvement. Achieving the best value for money requires careful comparison of alternatives, control of expenditure and meeting of deadlines, all of which require planning.

These reasons all add up to the need for a properly planned approach to the development of water services and the use of water. The purpose of this book is to examine, explain and evaluate water planning in Britain. To this end we consider the social context and the resource base of water planning and the water planning system. Here this system includes the water planning institutions, the decision-making process and the resulting policies, plans and schemes. These policies, plans and schemes are considered both through a discussion of overall water planning policy and through individual examples.

A conceptual framework for water planning

Before particular aspects of water planning, such as the water planning system, water supply, effluent disposal, pollution control, water recreation

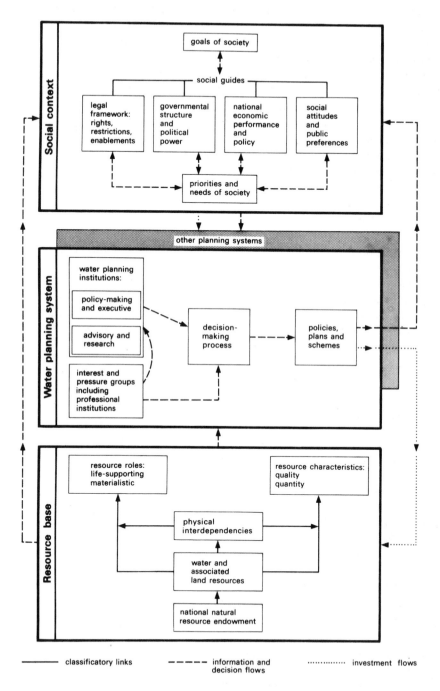

Figure 1.1 The water planning environment: a conceptual framework.

and land drainage, are considered in detail, it is useful to examine the basic influences on water planning in Britain. This can be achieved through a conceptual framework which serves to identify important aspects of the water planning system and its resource base and social context, and to guide and structure an examination of water planning. In this conceptual framework water planning is viewed as an activity which occurs at the interface between society (the social context) and environment (the resource base), being affected by, and in turn affecting, both (Fig. 1.1).

Above all planning is a social activity with immense social implications: indeed planning is a prime mechanism for progress and social change. The organisation of planning cannot be divorced from the organisation of society and planning is 'an activity by which man in society endeavours to gain mastery over himself and to shape his collective future consciously by power of his reason' (Friedmann 1959). The planning of water is no exception to these conditions. It is clear, therefore, that the major characteristics of society provide a context within which the goals and priorities of water planning must be set. Society's aims alter over time as attitudes and needs change, and water planners should be sensitive to shifts in the social context of their work. This profoundly influences all forms of public planning. Although only water planning is shown in Figure 1.1 all forms of planning, whether they be housing, land or water planning, are interrelated and none can be performed in isolation from the others. Water planning cannot be viewed as self-contained but a growing criticism of it in some countries is that it tends to be partially isolated from the rest of society (Burke and Heaney 1975, Swainson 1976, Beaumont 1977). The critics argue that water planning is, to some extent at least, out of touch with society's changing needs and fails to reflect public preferences, as should be expected in democratic societies.

The social context of water planning, and other forms of planning, is as complex as society itself and is almost completely pervading. The identification of the need for planning, for organisational arrangements, legal duties and powers and support for planning, all of which make planning possible, are derived from the social context. Water planning needs to be legitimised by society for water planners to exert power and execute decisions. It must seek public support for decisions and actions. The extent of legitimisation may vary but is achieved through mechanisms such as public consultation, the employment of independent consultants, through public inquiries and by the adoption of professional standards and planning practices (O'Riordan 1976a). Water planners must also be accountable to society for their decisions, although in practice planning systems vary considerably in their degree of accountability. In Britain, ensuring accountability involves fitting into the concept of democratic organisation and adopting organisational arrangements and methods which are responsive to social needs. Organisational arrangements may be rendered obsolete by the fast pace of social development and the planning system may be altered to suit society's new requirements. Society's attitudes towards wealth generation and its ability to create wealth to provide sources of finance, without which the effectiveness of planning is limited, are further fundamental social influences on water planning.

The resource base represents that part of the environment which is recognised and evaluated by society, aided by water planners using specialised evaluation techniques, as having utility. As attitudes, needs and technology change over time society's evaluation of the resource base alters, sometimes with organisational ramifications. For example, the growing recognition of the importance of lowland river sources for drinking water is related to our growing water needs. However this recognition emphasised the importance of lowland river pollution control which led in part to the reorganisation of water management in Britain in 1974 (Chs 2 and 3). The resource base provides society with opportunities and limitations which water planners seek in turn to maximise and to overcome.

Water planning seeks to make adjustments to both the social context and the resource base in order to sustain the yield of the resource base and to provide for society's needs. Water plans may involve adjustments to the resource base, such as installing manmade storage capacity, and adjustments to the social context by, for instance, providing incentives for economy in water use and thereby changing attitudes.

This view of water planning, at the interface between the social and resource environments, emphasises the dependence of water planning upon the social context, and in turn the dependence of society upon the opportunities and limitations presented by the resource base. These relationships are elaborated below in relation to the overall analytical framework (Fig. 1.1).

The social context

The **goals of society** are its aims in general. These goals are complex and may be explicit or implicit and multiple and changing. They evolve continuously from a complex interplay of social and political forces and may be articulated for example in terms of public opinion, election and referendum results and ministerial statements. Society often fails to support a particular goal unanimously and competing interests in society articulate their views thereby attempting to influence public opinion, making goals the subject of endless debate. The goals of society are not predetermined by planners but rather planners should assist society to identify and clarify its goals, to make them more explicit and to work towards them. One important perception of the major goals of British society has been outlined by the Royal Town Planning Institute (1976) (Table 1.1). These goals form a framework within which water planning could identify its more specific goals and objectives.

The goals of society are influenced by, and in turn influence, **social guides**. These are the major forces and elements in the structure and working of society which direct and guide social activities, including all forms of planning. They include the legal framework, governmental structure and

Table 1.1   One view of the major goals of society.

To respect the values of life and eliminate the causes of unnecessary physical and mental suffering

To foster personal freedom and reconcile it with the need for collective freedom

To increase personal involvement in decision making on economic and environmental issues

To safeguard the long-term interests of society and its environment against exploitation for short-term gain

To reduce inequalities, not merely of opportunity, but of material conditions of life

To reduce dependence on wasteful forms of production, development and living

To develop greater social responsibility by government, private institutions and individuals alike

---

Source: Royal Town Planning Institute 1976.

political power, national economic performance and policy and social attitudes and public preferences. All of these social guides interact with each other, although for simplicity's sake this is not shown in Table 1.1.

Planning, including water planning, is both facilitated and constrained by society's **legal framework** which consists of rights, restrictions and enabling legislation. In Britain legislation is passed by Parliament with reference to the constitution and the goals of society. English law, and the Scottish equivalent which is different, form the legal basis for all planning, including water planning.

Unwritten common law, which has evolved over centuries, is a part of the constitution which influences water planning. Under English common law all land belongs to someone including land covered by water so that, for example, the bed of a river to the centre line belongs to the owner of the adjacent bank. Whilst this common law has protected the rights of landowners in the past it has also restricted the control of water planning agencies over water resources.

Statute law includes written enactments, passed by Parliament, which can override any part of the common law. Through new statute laws water agencies in England and Wales have, for instance, gained more control over water resources by altering common law rights (Ch. 3). Byelaws are local laws needed because local conditions vary. They may be made by local authorities, water agencies or by the central government. Legislation enables planning agencies to be established as well as altered and also provides planners with tools for planning. Through the Water Act 1973, for example, the administrative structure of water planning in England and Wales was changed, thereby establishing a new water management structure with extended responsibilities (Okun 1977). The Control of Pollution Act 1974 enables water management institutions to enforce certain conditions upon water polluters which hitherto did not exist (Ch. 4). An important role of planning is thus to enforce rules democratically made.

For social progress to occur society needs a **governmental structure** which has the power to help identify and set goals, to review courses of action, to mobilise resources and to coordinate action. Through the British concept of democratic organisation a process has evolved whereby decisions are made by Parliament and local government. These decisions are the result of a complex synthesis of views, compromise, bargaining and concession-trading and the distribution and exercise of **political power** determines the outcome. Three main groups are involved. The electorate is represented by Members of Parliament who are responsible for articulating the views of their constituents or the public as a whole. In practice the electorate's views may be poorly represented if it chooses to be passive or is so through ignorance.

Specialised interests are articulated by groups within society which seek to influence policy in the direction of their own interests which often do not coincide with the public interest. Whilst some groups in society only have a marginal interest in water planning, others are more directly involved and may even become internalised into the water planning system, provision being made for their systematic involvement in policy making. Finally, policy advisers such as civil servants, and members of central or local government who are ultimately responsible for decisions and their implementation, also have their influence upon policy (O'Riordan 1976a).

Water planning is profoundly influenced by **national economic perform-ance and policy**. The nature, effectiveness and speed of water planning is dependent upon the amount of money available to finance both the planning process, in that staff are required for this, and the subsequent policies, plans and schemes. The availability of money for water planning is itself heavily dependent upon the performance of the national economy and government finance policy. During periods of economic stringency, such as the mid-1970s recessions, public sector spending may be 'squeezed' by the government which may impose a ceiling upon water agency expenditure or a moratorium upon new schemes and plans to appoint more planning staff. Government anti-inflation measures involving 'freezing' charges for water services may also reduce the real income of water planning agencies. Poor national econo-mic performance also constrains change and the government might, for example, be reluctant to impose extra pollution control costs on firms. National economic performance also affects the demand for water services which may not continue to grow or may even fall during a recession.

On the other hand, economic circumstances or government economic policy may increase the amount of money available for water planning, for instance during periods of economic progress more money may be available to accelerate the implementation of policies to improve river water quality. Central government also uses the flow of money through the nationalised industries, including the water industry, to try to regulate the national economy.

Public opinion may well affect national economic policy, and therefore water planning. Public opinion on private enterprise, nationalisation of industry, social inequality or the problems of lagging regions, have all influenced British government policy and the financial allocations for water planning in the past. For example, Scottish economic development policy since the 1930s has increased the amount of money available there for water services.

Social attitudes and public preferences influence the goals of society and guide the judgement of political representatives. Social attitudes towards water and planning are conditioned by social values, education and previous experience. Policies to increase water charges substantially might well generate an unfavourable public response which might be conditioned by society's traditional view of water as a basic necessity, by insufficient appreciation of the true costs or scarcity of water and by a history of cheap water supplies (Ch. 3). Although social attitudes and public preferences may well influence water planning in this way, the links between public attitudes and preferences and policy making may not always be as strong as the theory of the democratic organisation of society suggests. Public opinion is often vaguely expressed. People are often indifferent to policy issues unless they are directly affected. Only where common interests appear to be threatened are preferences explicitly articulated, commonly resulting in sectional viewpoints. In addition, methods for gauging public opinion and for involving the public in decision making may be poorly developed (O'Riordan 1971).

Table 1.2   Ministerial guidance on water planning priorities given to Water Authority chairmen in 1973.

First priority	Public health and safety
Second priority	New housing development
Third priority	Industrial development
Fourth priority	Control of pollution for improvement of water quality in rivers and estuaries
Fifth priority	First-time rural sewerage for existing houses

In assessing the priority of need for any particular scheme the above priorities were to be taken into account

Source: North West Water Authority 1978a.

Society's **priorities and needs** are formed by this complex matrix of social guides, including legal, governmental and political, economic and public opinion guides. The planner must identify the social guides and synthesise the flows of information and decisions emanating from them. Sometimes, as in 1973, the government may give explicit guidance upon water planning priorities (Table 1.2). Policies, plans and schemes should be formulated to reflect society's priorities and needs expressed in this and other ways.

The resource base

It is not the purpose of this book to explain the hydrological cycle and its workings in Britain: such explanations are given elsewhere (Rodda, Downing and Law 1976, Smith 1972, Ward 1975). Although we recognise the fundamental importance to water resource planning of understanding and measuring hydrological processes, we concentrate here upon identifying and classifying the main qualities and functions of the resource base (Fig. 1.1). In the Chapters which follow, for the areas of water planning including water supply, effluent disposal and pollution control, recreation and amenity and land drainage, we provide a detailed explanation of the principal features of the resource base appropriate to each.

The **national natural resource endowment** includes land, minerals, water and air resources. Water planning is very closely related to land use planning because most modifications and uses of the hydrological cycle have land use implications and because water planning often involves raising the value of associated land resources. On the other hand the construction of a new reservoir in an upland area may lead to the loss of agricultural land through flooding (Ch. 3). A reservoir which is to be used for water sports can hardly be so used without adjacent land also being used for access and land-based facilities (Ch. 5). Land drainage, including protecting land from flooding and improving soil drainage for agricultural purposes, is an important part of water planning with more emphasis on enhancing land than water resources (Ch. 6). Britain's water planning agencies are in fact important landowners in their own right and they effectively have to plan both **water and associated land resources**.

Apart from the interrelatedness of water and associated land, the resource base is characterised by other important **physical interdependencies** which reflect the nature of water and the hydrological cycle and which must be recognised by society and the water planning system if resources are to be successfully utilised. The first interdependency is that at a particular site water has a multi-purpose potential which can produce positive or negative consequences. For example, a reservoir built to provide water supplies may also automatically provide possibilities for controlling floods and for recreational development. Alternatively, one use of water may have a detrimental impact on others, as in the case where enlargement of a river channel to reduce flooding damages fisheries and destroys bankside vegetation which supports wildlife, so conflicting with angling and nature conservation interests. During its passage from source to sea, river water also has re-use potential and may, for instance, be used many times for industrial cooling, navigation and recreational purposes.

A second interdependency arises from the nature of water as a fluid which, under gravity, moves from high to low ground and which circulates in the hydrological cycle. Uses of water at one place have important physical and economic consequences elsewhere. For example, extraction of groundwater for water supplies at one place may lead to diminished stream flow and therefore reduced navigation opportunities at another, because the underground and surface water systems are a single hydrological unit.

Because water has multi-purpose potential and because uses of water are spatially interdependent, hydrological systems and especially river basins are often considered to be the most appropriate areal management units for water resources (Fox and Craine 1962).

For society, the most important resource characteristics of water and associated land are **quality** and **quantity**. These are interdependent and society is often concerned about ensuring a sufficient quantity of water of satisfactory quality. For both water and land resources, quality and quantity vary naturally over time and space and both can be enhanced or depleted by society. In Britain, as in most other countries, there are quite marked daily, seasonal or annual variations in stream flow and groundwater availability which are related to meteorological and possibly climatic variations. These may result in water surpluses, manifested as floods, or water shortages in times of drought. Water availability also varies over space, due to the interaction of meteorological, climatic, geological and topographical factors, so that the north and west of Britain, particularly Scotland, generally yield more water resources than the south and east. Society can and does manipulate water availability in time and space and this is one function of water planning (Twort, Hoather and Law 1974). Water resources can also be depleted if the rate of exploitation exceeds the rate of natural replenishment and the principles of sustained yield management of renewable resources are thus ignored.

Water quality varies considerably between different parts of Britain according to the characteristics of rock, soil and vegetation in the source area. Water from peat areas is usually coloured yellow-brown whereas water from groundwater sources in Britain is usually colourless. Water quality is not so much enhanced by society as depleted, since nearly all of the uses of water have some unfavourable side-effects. The disposal of sewage effluents into rivers is a common example of how water quality can be lowered so reducing the quantity of clean water available for water supply abstraction (Ch. 3).

The quality of land resources, including its agricultural, urban development, landscape and amenity value, is often dependent upon its proximity to water and in specific localities affects the availability, or quantity, of land for different purposes. A manmade lake may either enhance or detract from the landscape and amenity quality of an area, or the threat of flooding in an urban area may depress land values whilst flood protection may increase them.

Water and associated land have two important and interdependent **resource roles** in society. The first is the essential **life-supporting** role and the second is the **materialistic** role which, in strict terms, is the use of resources beyond the essential (Freeman, Haveman and Kneese 1972). The life-supporting services of the water environment come under considerable pressure from society itself. As the production and consumption of industrial and agricultural products grows so wastes are released into the water environment which becomes less able to provide satisfactorily the life-supporting services it offers. For example, as the demand for land drainage increases in response to needs to increase home-grown food production, so rich wetland wildlife habitats may be destroyed (Ch. 6).

The materialistic roles of water in society are almost as numerous as society's activities. Water provides society with a medium for assimilating and dispersing wastes which are the by-products of domestic, industrial and agricultural activity not all of which are essential. It provides a source of material inputs into the economy – water is used for industrial production, cooling and irrigation (Rees 1969). It provides an important medium for transportation, power generation and leisure activity. Any or all of these materialistic uses of water have implications for each other and for the life-supporting role. The greater the waste load placed upon a water resource, the more limited will be the life-supporting or amenity role.

Society is so complex that many strictly materialistic uses of water have become viewed as essential and even life-supporting. For example, many of the uses of high quality water in the home for personal hygiene and sanitation are considered by many in society to be essential when in reality water use here could, with some ingenuity, be substantially reduced. In many cases pursuit of materialistic ends has taken place with no consideration or even recognition of the relationships with the essential life-supporting role of water.

The water planning system

The water planning system is only one of many **other planning systems** including those for community-based planning, such as transport, housing, recreation, social and economic planning, and resource-based planning such as fuel, mineral, food and land use planning. In common with water planning, each form of planning has a similar social context but a particular resource base – in the case of community-based planning 'social resources', such as houses or schools, form the resource base. Although water planning is inextricably part of the wider planning system, in practice there are faults in the way Britain's planning machinery is integrated. Some interrelationships are barely developed at all and coordination between water planning and other forms of planning, such as National Park planning, could be improved.

The water planning system has a management structure, reflected in **water planning institutions**, determined mainly by government through statute law. These institutions may interact with sections of society which have specialised interests in water planning, and these **interest and pressure groups** seek to influence decisions. Water planning is a **decision-making process** facilitated by the water management structure and which results in **policies, plans and schemes**. These are formulated by water planners, most of whom belong to **professional institutions**, and who work within the water planning institutions. The water planning system is guided and financed by society, with information and decisions being fed to the planning system, and flows of investment being made available to fund planning. Both society and the water planning system evaluate the resource base, deriving information from it, and allowing its characteristics and functions to be assessed.

The management structure of the water planning system determines the scale of responsibility and power of each water planning institution, each individual decision-maker and groups of decision-makers in the structure. This structure influences to some extent what is done, almost entirely by whom it is done, and ultimately how effectively it is done. In Britain, as in many other countries, water planning institutions can be divided into the **policy-making and executive** and the **advisory and research** agencies. The former have the statutory duty and power to make decisions and to implement them whereas the power of the latter agencies depends upon their ability to reason and to persuade the former, making their influence upon decisions variable. Advisory and research agencies are used particularly to guide the coordination of decisions and to promote innovations.

Interest and pressure groups include people with common interests, who aim to influence policy. Interest groups are very similar to pressure groups. The latter may be defined as groups which are normally continuously active in attempting to influence policy and the former may only try to apply pressure discontinuously or not at all. Some groups, such as the farmers and anglers, are well represented on British water planning committees, though these committees may only be advisory. Other groups maintain that their representation in, and the public accountability of, water planning institutions is inadequate. Interest and pressure groups seek to influence decisions in a variety of ways including through advisory committees, direct representation to water agencies, by parliamentary and ministerial lobbying and at public inquiries. **Professional institutions** are important in this respect.

Britain's water planning institutions are large organisations and, in total, employ about 80 000 staff, about half of which are manual workers. In Britain, as in many countries, water planning is dominated by the engineering profession, notably water, civil, and public health engineers. This dominance has arisen because engineers have traditionally been responsible for the design of water and sewage treatment works and water supply schemes. In general, society encourages professionalism and professional institutions such as the Institution of Water Engineers and Scientists. Society is willing to give professional bodies its support and monopoly powers in return for safeguards, such as the standards of training and professional competence which these bodies can ensure. Without professional standards there is little doubt that society would suffer, although at the same time it should be recognised that by their very nature as organisations whose purpose is the maintenance of standards, professional institutions tend towards established practice and conservatism which may fit uncomfortably into a changing world.

The **decision-making process** consists, in theory, of a sequence of steps leading from the setting of a planning goal or the identification of a problem through to the implementation and monitoring of the effectiveness of a policy, plan or scheme. In practice in water planning as in other forms of planning, the sequence of steps varies considerably. It may, for example, include an exhaustive discussion of goals at the outset, a comprehensive review of alternatives for the achievement of the chosen goal, careful setting of criteria for evaluating alternatives and their systematic application to produce a plan which is then implemented and monitored to determine its success in achieving the required goal (Mitchell 1971, 1979).

On the other hand, decisions may be made in a very different way. They may be made hurriedly in response to crisis or may merely involve muddling-through, whereby goals are not discussed at all and alternatives are narrowly defined and poorly evaluated. Sometimes decisions are influenced by the state of individual financial budgets with little evaluation of wider priorities. In practice, decision making tends not to conform to a perfectly rational and deductive process (Dror 1964, Lindblom 1959, Faludi 1973). Decisions are made according to prevailing perceptions, attitudes, pressures and constraints, such as lack of time or knowledge. How decisions are made, especially whether they are made systematically and are based upon a comprehensive review of alternatives, can sometimes be inferred from an analysis of the resulting policies, plans and schemes.

Policies, plans and schemes are the outcome of the decision-making process. A policy is an overall statement of intent or a course of action which is usually related, either explicitly or implicitly, to a goal. Policies reflect preferences, priorities and principles and are usually of longer-term signifi-cance than plans and schemes which are based upon them. A plan is a means by which policies are put into operation and is concerned with reaching objec-tives or targets and integrating a set of smaller scale schemes in order to meet them. Plans are also concerned with timing, phasing and coordination of schemes to match financial budgets; they may be written documents but in some cases they may simply comprise a rolling financial programme. A scheme is an individual project, such as a sewage treatment works, designed to contribute to the achievement of the objectives or targets of a plan.

Two examples of policy statements from British water planning documents are shown in Table 1.3. The Tayside water supply policies are all designed to achieve an objective which might also be called a goal. The Wessex water supply policy is stated differently and includes a brief rationale for the policy and a brief outline of the basis of part of a plan.

The theoretical relationships between policies, plans and schemes are rarely simple in practice. Schemes may somehow exist without plans or poli-cies, and plans may exist without a clear policy, particularly if decision making is unsystematic or in response to a crisis. Policies, plans and schemes may exist at several different levels in the planning process and planning documents sometimes refer to primary and secondary levels of policy, with the latter providing a more definitive statement than the former. What becomes labelled as a policy, plan or scheme not only depends in practice

Table 1.3 Examples of water supply objective and policy statements from regional water authority reports and plans.

Tayside Regional Council Regional Report 1978
'Objectives: to provide and maintain a wholesome supply of water to all residential development
Policies: The Regional Council will –
      1 Provide and maintain facilities for the storage, purification, treatment and distribution of the public water supply
      2 Attempt to maximise the use of spare capacity in existing services
      3 Attach a high priority to the maintenance of existing systems
      4 Provide for new developments only where these can be supplied at reasonable cost to the Regional Council
      5 Normally request refusal of planning applications where services cannot be provided within a period of four years'

Wessex Water Authority, The Wessex Plan 1978–1983
'In the Regional context the aggregate yield of developed public water supply sources exceeds the present total demand by a reasonable margin, but public supply systems are not fully integrated, therefore there are small margins of surplus or deficiencies of reliable yield in several areas. Current policy is aimed at developing systems to meet forecast increases in demand and improve the management of source and distribution systems through:
(a) linking existing independent systems to improve flexibility in the use of (existing and proposed new) sources;
(b) the replacement of plant and the strengthening of distribution systems by installation of booster pumps and service reservoir storage where appropriate;
(c) improving the operating efficiency of existing systems by expedients such as reducing losses of water from treatment works and distribution networks.'

Sources: Tayside Regional Council 1978.
         Wessex Water Authority 1978a.

upon the essential qualities of each, but upon the scale or level of planning.

All three – policies, plans and schemes – should reflect resource management principles based upon the nature of the hydrological cycle and the interdependencies associated with it and its use, already described above. Thus the overall organisational system for water planning may be based upon the concept of the river basin with water agency boundaries in accord with major watershed boundaries. Also plans and schemes may reflect the multi-purpose potential of water resources and the need for sustained yield management (White 1969).

Policies, plans and schemes are designed ultimately to change elements of the resource base and the social context. They may involve investment in reservoirs to store and supply more water or in environmental protection to maintain and enhance the life-supporting role of water. On the other hand they may instigate flows of information and decisions to society aimed, for example, at increasing awareness of flood risks or water shortages.

The legacy of history

In the interests of simplicity a time dimension is not shown in the conceptual framework (Fig. 1.1) although the legacy of the past is important in understanding water planning in Britain today. Britain's water planning institutions are largely the result of reorganisation which created Water Authorities in England and Wales in 1974 (Porter 1978) and Regional and Island Councils in Scotland in 1975. Although these institutions[1] are relatively new the influence of the past makes itself felt through the continuation of traditions and administrative practices which have their roots in previous planning systems which may date from the last century. For example, a Water Authority's outdated sewerage and sewage disposal facilities, which now represent a considerable financial burden because of the high costs of replacement, were inherited from a local authority planning system in which such replacements were given low priority (Ch. 4). Also the lack of a national policy for water in Britain is related to the lack of a central water planning authority. This situation has its roots throughout the past one hundred years during which *ad hoc* government committees and subsequent central advisory bodies, such as the Water Resources Board abolished in 1974, have existed. None of these committees or bodies had executive powers.

A framework for evaluation

The conceptual framework encapsulated in Figure 1.1 summarises an approach to analysing and explaining water planning in Britain today. Its value is that, together with much of the literature cited in this Chapter, it poses a series of questions and suggests directions of inquiry which are important in an appraisal of water planning in Britain, or for that matter any other country. The conceptual framework and the literature do in fact raise so many queries, some of which require further research beyond the scope of this book, that several key questions are selected below for further attention in the following Chapters.

The questions and lines of inquiry which the conceptual framework poses are related to its three main components and their interrelationships: the social context, the resource base and the water planning system. The questions are not meant to be a basis for definitive evaluation, rather more to lead to an analysis of key issues.

Key social context questions
1 Does society provide water planners with an adequate framework of legislation, institutions and financial provision?
2 To what extent do social attitudes and preferences towards water and associated land resources affect policies, plans and schemes?

Key resource base questions

3   How do the inherent characteristics of water in Britain influence the choice of alternative policies, plans and schemes?

4   To what extent are resource management principles incorporated into water policies, plans and schemes?

Key water planning system questions

5   How well is water planning integrated with other forms of public planning?

6   Is water planning comprehensive and systematic and are all the relevant interests adequately involved?

This book considers the whole of Britain. There are striking differences between the resource bases of Scotland and England and Wales which stem from differences in climate. The size of population relative to water availability and the different legal framework also means that water planning in Scotland has a different social context to that in England and Wales. These differences have led to the development of an alternative approach to the management and planning of water services in Scotland and produce some penetrating insights and comparisons.

[1]In this book 'Water Authorities' refers to the ten institutions in England and Wales; 'regional water authorities' refers collectively to Water Authorities, Regional and Island Councils and River Purification Boards. The term 'water authorities' is reserved for collective reference to past water planning institutions, such as River Authorities and water supply undertakings. The term 'water industry' includes all institutions with water planning responsibilities.

Selected further reading (for full bibliography see pp. 254–66)

For a provocative analysis of the social context of water planning, the characteristics of water resources and an evaluation of North American water management institutions see:

Fox, I. K., and L. E. Craine 1962. 'Organisational arrangements for water development.' *Natural Resources Journal* 2, 1–44.

This work is extended in an appraisal of pre-1974 water management in England only:

Craine, L. E. 1969. *Water management innovations in England*. Baltimore: John Hopkins Press.

For an evaluation of water management policy embracing both private and public sectors and single and multiple purpose development in a North American context see:

White, G. F. 1969. *Strategies of American water management*. Ann Arbor: University of Michigan Press.

A review of the post-1974 water industry in England and Wales only, with useful extended case studies is:

Porter, E. A. 1978. *Water management in England and Wales*. Cambridge: Cambridge University Press.

The environmental context of resource planning including environmental philosophy, politics and law and amenity protection are debated in:

O'Riordan, T. 1976b. *Environmentalism*. London: Pion.

The hydrological cycle and its workings in Britain are analysed in detail in:

Rodda, J. C., R. A. Downing and F. M. Law 1976. *Systematic hydrology*. London: Newnes-Butterworth.

For those unfamiliar with water and water engineering terms see:

Nelson, A., and K. D. Nelson 1973. *Dictionary of water and water engineering*. London: Butterworth.

For water planning the most relevant journals are:

Water Resources Research, Water Pollution Control, Water, National Water Council Bulletin, Water Supply and Management, Water Space, Surveyor, Water Services, Journal of Environmental Management, Journal of the Institution of Water Engineers and Scientists, Journal of Planning and Environmental Law, Journal of Water Resources Planning and Management Division (Procs. of the American Society of Civil Engineers), *Natural Resources Journal. The Water Planning Journal*, published by Thames Water Authority, has a restricted circulation in the water industry.

2 The water planning system

Introduction: the significance of institutional arrangements

The framework for evaluation at the end of the previous Chapter poses questions concerning the institutional arrangements for water planning. Many aspects of these questions cannot be considered fully until we examine the different functional areas of water planning (Ch. 3–6). However, those aspects concerning the structure and financing of the water planning process, the integration of this process with other areas of public planning and the structure's appropriateness for the resource being planned can be separated for initial discussion in this Chapter. The separation allows us to analyse the division of responsibility between organisations, some of which have many functions, the conflicts these divisions create and the degree of public involvement in decision making. Also we can begin to evaluate the structure of the whole water planning system before examining its performance in the separate water planning areas against the full range of evaluative questions developed from the conceptual framework in Chapter 1.

In this institutional analysis, then, we are concerned primarily with the effectiveness of organisational structures. The greater the effectiveness and therefore the efficiency of the system the more appropriate should be the policies, plans and schemes which result for solving water planning problems and achieving the goals of society in this field with minimum economic cost and political conflict. Analysing effectiveness involves examining the patterns of responsibility and the locus of power within the planning system and the appropriateness of the areal units within which the water planning system operates (Barr 1973).

Evaluating the **pattern of responsibility and the locus of power** within the water planning system requires analysing the duties and powers of the policy-making and executive agencies within the system, the role and influence of the advisory and research organisations and the power of interest and pressure groups. Such an analysis needs to identify the level at which decisions are made, both within organisations and the division of such decision-making responsibilities between the organisations in the formal structure of the water industry as a whole. Inappropriate division of responsibility will result in conflict between or within organisations. If unresolved, this is likely to produce inadequate policies or plans, for example where the potential for multi-purpose use of water or associated land resources is not realised because different organisations are responsible for the different water uses. To understand and evaluate such policies and plans necessitates analysing existing roles and responsibilities; to improve these policies may necessitate re-structuring the planning system from which the problem originates.

Of central importance to this analysis is the influence of legislation and patterns of representation and public accountability in moulding the many institutions comprising the water planning system. Financing arrangements, public participation, the relationships with other fields of planning and social goals are also important in influencing the processes of formulating policy, plan making and scheme design. The major contrast between the water planning system in Scotland and England and Wales facilitates this analysis. Also of significance is the character of the water planner; the planning agencies are staffed by professionals with their own beliefs, prejudices and expertise. These all affect the definition of water resource problems, the perception of social goals and the means adopted for solving these problems and achieving those goals. Furthermore, despite far-reaching reorganisations, the agencies are inseparable from their history and traditions. These traditions influence the type of professionals employed in the planning system and the organisational structures within and the relationships between institutions.

Structural arrangements of water planning systems which are as comprehensive as are needed today are continually being pulled in two opposite directions. First, there is pressure for fewer but larger organisations responsible for many or all water functions. Such organisations aim to minimise conflicts between functions and maximise both the potential for multipurpose use of water and the economies of scale from exploiting water and associated resources at a regional or larger scale. However, the fewer and the larger the water planning organisations the greater the potential for inflexibility and the less the public is protected from excessive concentrations of economic and political power. Herein arises the second pressure which is for greater local public accountability of the water planning system, to ensure effective satisfaction of local needs and specialist agencies to promote particular functional areas. This pressure can result in a proliferation of organisations, both local and regional, with divided responsibility for any one function and greater potential for conflict both between and within organisations than with large multi-functional agencies. Whichever arrangement or compromise dominates the way that society and government views and values the water planning system is illuminated by the systems which result. Debate on the merits of the different approaches will be endless since there is no perfect solution which maximises all aspects of effectiveness yet is sufficiently flexible to accommodate the shifting public expectations of water planning which, in Britain since 1945, could not be accommodated without radical changes to the planning system itself.

Related to this debate about the scale of organisations is that about the **appropriate areal unit** for the major water planning institutions. Two basic alternatives emerge: catchment-based organisations or those based on local or regional government units such as counties or economic planning regions.

The case for multi-functional catchment-based units rests with the need to internalise many of the externalities of water use, which means accounting for the 'external' costs of one water use on another within the same organisation, to reduce cross-subsidisation and conflict between water planning functions. For example, any adverse effects of flood alleviation schemes on fisheries and recreation provision should be felt within the organisation planning the flood alleviation scheme rather than passed on to a separate – and perhaps weak – fisheries protection agency. Similarly it is important that any consequences and costs of pollution treatment and effluent disposal should fall on the same organisation as that concerned with water supply. A single administrative unit extending from river source to mouth should encourage appreciation of the physical interdependence in water planning functions and prevent one authority passing pollution and associated treatment costs downstream to another. Resolution of conflicts between water planning functions can thereby occur within rather than between organisations.

These are, however, strong arguments against catchment-based water planning units. Using political units of local or regional government allows maximum integration between water planning and other areas of public planning such as transportation, housing development and industrial location. Also the demand patterns of certain water uses cut across catchment boundaries. For example, the demand for water-based recreation is rarely catchment-based in any simple way and water demands may exceed the supply from single catchments so that planning water supplies and water space for recreation does not necessarily benefit from catchment-based organisational units. Choosing the appropriate areal unit is not simple but the subsequent analysis of water planning institutions both in Scotland and in England and Wales again allows a useful comparison of different approaches.

There are, therefore, many options in the arrangement of the water planning system and differences are often reflected in the policies, plans and schemes emanating from the planning process. In general the nature of the policy-making and executive institutions is reflected in the characteristics of the associated research and advisory agencies, and the arrangement of both will affect the way interest and pressure groups operate. All these parts of the water planning system are powerful, but in different ways. Public water planning institutions have the power that legislation, expertise and financial resources can bring, while interest and pressure groups can have the political power that comes from close association with the public or, in the case of professional bodies, through close association with the personal and professional interests of the water planners themselves. This Chapter reviews the role of the many individual agencies within the system and concludes with a brief initial evaluation of the effectiveness of the structure of the water planning system in Britain.

Policy-making and executive institutions

The policy-making and executive agencies within the water planning system are responsible for determining policies within which individual plans fit, for making decisions which produce plans, and for implementing these plans in the form of individual schemes. As they have the ultimate responsibility for planning decisions these agencies are subject to the most political pressure for public accountability.

In Britain the majority of the executive responsibilities in the water planning field are laid down in two quite separate pieces of legislation which dominate the water planning system today: the Water Act 1973 relating to England and Wales and the Local Government (Scotland) Act 1974. This legislation resulted in reorganisations in 1974 and 1975 respectively and has defined the roles of the different agencies by establishing rights, restrictions, duties and powers for both customers of water and water services and the water planning agencies themselves (Okun 1977).

Those government departments with responsibilities in the water field are the national focus of policy-making and executive agencies (Fig. 2.1). In England and Wales the Department of the Environment, the Ministry of Agriculture, Fisheries and Food and the Welsh Office, with their government ministers, have the responsibility of determining through Parliament national objectives in the water field and ensuring implementation of legislation. In Scotland the same functions are carried out by the Scottish Office, headed by the Secretary of State for Scotland. Therefore, for example, decisions on the nature and timing of major water pollution control policies like those in the Control of Pollution Act 1974 are made at this government department level. The other national policy-making and executive agency is the British Waterways Board which is concerned mainly with navigation on canals. The Board operates largely independently of other parts of the water planning system and is directly accountable to the Department of the Environment.

The main policy-making and executive activity in Britain, however, is decentralised at the regional level, with large and powerful agencies spending very sizeable budgets and employing a large staff, in contrast to the small local agencies operating prior to the 1974 and 1975 reorganisations (Andrews 1979). In England and Wales ten Water Authorities have had since 1974 the power and responsibility to meet their regional demands for water and those water-related services such as sewerage, land drainage and recreation; these functions, powers and responsibilities are fully codified in the Water Act 1973. In Scotland the structure is different; the same functions are carried out by two separate sets of organisations. First, there are the nine Regional and three Island Councils which form part of the local government structure set up in 1975 by the Local Government (Scotland) Act 1974 and they therefore are also concerned with education, housing and other local authority responsibilities. Secondly, seven River Purification Boards are responsible solely for water pollution control.

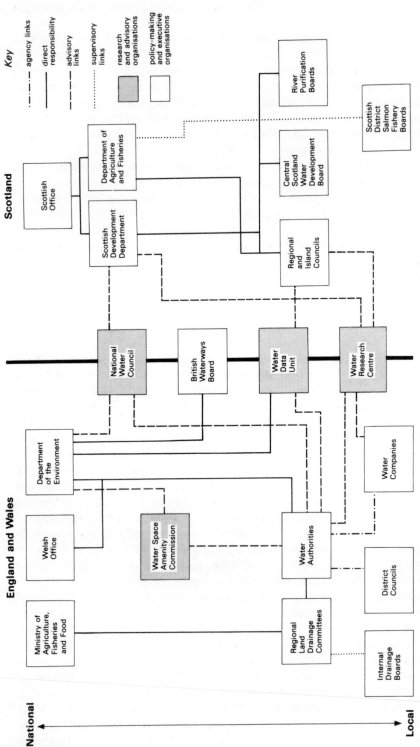

Figure 2.1 Basic elements of the policy-making and executive, advisory and research organisations in the British water planning system.

Although the structure of the water planning agencies differs in Scotland and England and Wales, and these differences influence water planning practice as we shall see in later Chapters, within both structures the authorities are regionally based and have considerable autonomy. In general they approach the task of meeting regional needs through policies, plans and schemes of their own, rather than simply implementing policies passed down by central government. However, this decentralisation in England and Wales has resulted in an imperfect system of public accountability, being neither at a national level through Parliament or locally through local government.

The organisation in Scotland

The Regional and Island Councils. In contrast to the creation of the independent Water Authorities in England and Wales, partly out of water departments within local government, the 1975 Scottish reorganisation created water departments within the local government structure and replaced the thirteen independent catchment-based regional Water Boards! Therefore the Scottish reorganisation was to some extent the very reverse of that south of the border.

The Water (Scotland) Act 1967 had created from some 200 small water undertakings, most of which were too small or financially weak to employ specialist staff, these thirteen regional Water Boards responsible for water supply, drainage and sewage treatment (Greer 1976). The requirement of local government reform, rather than the inadequacy of the Water Boards, led to the further reorganisation of the water planning system in 1975. The Wheatley Report (Royal Commission on Local Government in Scotland 1966–69) recommended incorporating water planning into local government to prevent what the Commission saw as the proliferation of *ad hoc* government as exemplified by the independent Water Boards. The Commission concluded that hardly any function seemed more suitable for being controlled by directly elected local authorities, particularly because of the influence that water supply and sewerage provision has on constraining new development. After much debate on the need for change, during which major alterations were made in Parliament to the Bill leading to the reorganisation including establishing nine rather than eight regions, the Water Boards were disbanded and water departments or directorates were created within the new regional government structure. As a result there are water planning functions within the nine regions and three all-purpose island areas (Fig. 2.1), a tier below which there are 53 districts, as in England and Wales, but these have no water supply, sewerage or sewage treatment functions but are responsible for detailed planning of recreational water space in their areas.

The Regional Councils, like the County Councils in England and Wales, have the power to collect rates based on property values and they are governed by elected representatives. Their expenditure has two main components:

capital and revenue. Capital is used to finance the construction of projects such as schools, libraries and sewage treatment works and revenue expenditure covers the local authority running costs including staff salaries and supplies. Capital projects are financed mainly by borrowing and the right of local authorities in Scotland to incur capital expenditure is controlled by central government through Section 94 of the Local Government (Scotland) Act 1974 which states that 'it will not be lawful for a local authority to incur any liability to meet capital expenses except with the consent of the Secretary of State'. The current pattern of allocation is for the Secretary of State to give block consent for a programme of capital works with annual adjustment for inflation to give 'cash limits' within which capital expenditure must be contained.

Revenue expenditure of the Regional Councils is financed from the rate support grant, from rent and rates, and from miscellaneous other income from local authority services. The rate support grant dominates this expenditure in Scotland and is allocated by central government to ensure provision of services of a broadly comparable standard throughout the country.

Revenue and capital expenditure are closely linked since capital borrowings incur interest payments which are a charge on revenue, as also are recurring costs from capital projects such as the staff salaries for new sewage treatment works. Therefore although local authorities are in theory autonomous and have powers to raise revenue through rates, in practice their activities are closely controlled by the Secretary of State either through the cash limit system in capital borrowings or through the size of the annually determined rate support grant.

Because of their widely differing sizes, there are different departmental structures within each Regional Council to cover water supply, flood protection and sewerage or drainage (terms which in Scotland include sewage treatment). The two largest Regional Councils, Lothian and Strathclyde, have separate directorates for water supply and sewerage although the Directors report to joint water and sewerage committees of elected Council members. Three regions, Grampian, Highland and Tayside, each have one directorate for both water and sewerage. The Fife region, which was added during the parliamentary debate, has included water supply and sewerage with other engineering functions such as roads, as have the three Island Councils, owing to the more economic organisation of pooled design staff and other specialists in smaller authorities. The remaining three regions (Borders, Central and Dumfries and Galloway) each have a Directorate overseeing both water supply and drainage, and separation of these services at the lower level of Assistant Director. Each Regional Council water department has a number of operational divisions, based on sub-regions, responsible for implementing plans and carrying out day-to-day maintenance.

The main potential advantage of incorporating water and related functions within local government is the opportunity for a truly corporate or integrated approach to water planning, fitting in with education provision, housing development and plans for recreation and public transport, particularly through the joint development of structure plans. The fundamental disadvantage of local government based water planning is that local government boundaries do not coincide with catchment boundaries. The main potential disadvantage as seen by water planners is that the Chief Engineer is no longer his own master as he was within the Water Boards, but is placed some distance away from sources of finance, decisions about which are made in competition with education and housing which are traditionally more politically significant at a local level.

Within local government, water planning is therefore more explicitly within the political forum. Such an arrangement is perhaps to the benefit of the public at large but is not always to the satisfaction of the engineers in charge. To these professionals decisions appear to be made for purely political reasons, over-ruling engineering judgement to the detriment of the efficient planning of water development. Such a view demonstrates the narrow perspective on water planning of many engineers since, with limited resources, all decisions about resources are 'political' in the sense of being concerned with value judgements about the relative merits of different expenditure patterns.

The River Purification Boards.   One major distinguishing characteristic, and many would say advantage, of the Scottish water planning system is that the Regional Councils are *not* fully multi-functional. Whereas the Island Councils do have full water responsibilities, pollution control is separated from the sewage treatment function of the Regional Councils into seven separate and independent River Purification Boards, although the boundaries of the areas concerned more or less coincide. The Boards have the duty to promote the cleanliness of rivers and specified estuaries. They do not have the responsibility for pollution treatment, which lies with the Regional Councils. The River Purification Boards are the 'gamekeepers' trying to stop the polluting 'poachers' and as such could be termed non-executive but this is an over-fine distinction as they do have real power, such as that of prosecution.

The reason for this separation of pollution control and pollution treatment functions in Scotland lies partly in history. The Wheatley Commission advocated amalgamating the pre-existing nine River Purification Boards into the local government structure, again for fear of *ad hoc* government. This move was bitterly opposed by the Association of River Purification Boards on behalf of its members and also by a large number of other interested parties articulated by Scottish Members of Parliament. The main pressure for the retention of the Boards came from those who pointed to the efficiency of their operation before 1973 and who saw inevitable problems in combining the pollution control function, with its need for objectivity and honesty, with the pollution-creating sewage treatment and effluent disposal function. In the event the government was forced to change direction during the debate on

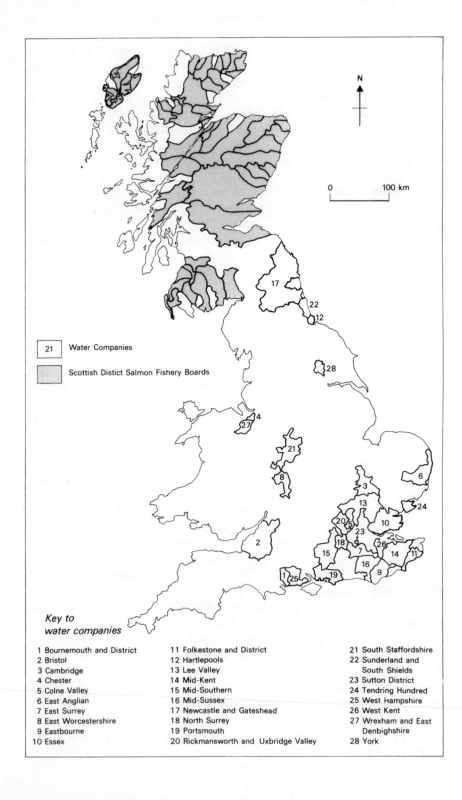

N

0   100 km

21 Water Companies

☐ Scottish Distict Salmon Fishery Boards

17

22

12

28

4

27

21

8

6

3

24

13

10

20 5

23

18 9

26

15   7

14

11

16

2

9

1 25

19

Key to
water companies

1 Bournemouth and District
2 Bristol
3 Cambridge
4 Chester
5 Colne Valley
6 East Anglian
7 East Surrey
8 East Worcestershire
9 Eastbourne
10 Essex

11 Folkestone and District
12 Hartlepools
13 Lee Valley
14 Mid-Kent
15 Mid-Southern
16 Mid-Sussex
17 Newcastle and Gateshead
18 North Surrey
19 Portsmouth
20 Rickmansworth and Uxbridge Valley

21 South Staffordshire
22 Sunderland and
   South Shields
23 Sutton District
24 Tendring Hundred
25 West Hampshire
26 West Kent
27 Wrexham and East
   Denbighshire
28 York

the Local Government (Scotland) Bill 1973 and re-instate the Boards within the Scottish water planning structure, although their number was reduced to seven.

The River Purification Boards are financed by requisition from the Regional Councils covered by the Boards, in proportion to the rateable value of those parts. The composition of Boards is arranged to allow for special expertise and local interests. As such membership is divided equally between those appointed by the appropriate Councils or District Councils from among their Councillors and members appointed by the Secretary of State for Scotland to represent the interest of anglers, commercial fisheries, agriculture, private and nationalised industry, navigation, landowners and trade unions.

The Central Scotland Water Development Board. Like the River Purification Boards the Central Scotland Water Development Board was a survivor of the 1975 reorganisation. The Board was created under the Water (Scotland) Act 1967 to supply water in bulk to the densely populated central area now covered by the Central, Lothian, Tayside and Strathclyde Regional Councils. The Board has power to retain reserves under its own control to ensure that substantial contingency water resources are available at short notice particularly for unpredictable industrial developments. The Board's membership includes the directors of the Regional Council water departments, it is financed by contributions from these Councils, and operates as a forum for consultation and cooperation between Regions and to allow discussion of relative priorities in water supply (Greer 1976). In essence it is a structural anomaly reflecting the substantial water demands in central Scotland, with some 80% of the country's population, and the difficulty of realising the possible scale economies of very large water supply schemes with the relatively small size of some of the Scottish Regions. Apart from the Water Companies in England and Wales the Board is the only organisation in Britain concerned solely with water supply.

The District Salmon Fishery Boards. Scottish salmon fishings in rivers, estuaries and along the coast are private heritable property and the Salmon Fisheries (Scotland) Acts 1862 provide for the establishment of District Salmon Fishery Boards (Fig. 2.2) by the proprietors of the rivers concerned to protect their rights. Although there are 108 Salmon Districts only 48 Boards exist, mainly in the Districts with valuable fishings. These Boards are completely autonomous and financed by the salmon proprietors themselves through their own internal rating system to protect, preserve and improve fishings. In 1962 the Hunter Committee suggested that these Boards be replaced by 13 elected area boards covering the whole of Scotland and

Figure 2.2 Location of the Water Companies and the Scottish District Salmon Fishery Boards.

financed by local fishery rates and rod and net fishery licence fees. Although the suggestion was accepted in principle by the government the required legislation has not been forthcoming and the existing Boards continue (Association of Scottish District Salmon Fishery Boards 1977).

The organisation in England and Wales

The Water Authorities.   The nine English and one Welsh Water Authorities were created as from 1 April 1974 by the Water Act 1973. Considerable controversy surrounded the passing of the legislation and the complexities of this bargaining process between all interest groups are described by Okun (1977). The new authorities were created from the 29 pre-existing River Authorities, created by the Water Resources Act 1963, and from the 1393 sewage treatment and sewerage departments of the local authorities in England and Wales together with 157 statutory water supply undertakings. This massive reorganisation brought together all aspects of water planning for the first time: both the 'clean' water supply side and the 'dirty' effluent disposal function (Andrews 1979).

The geographical areas of the Water Authorities are not based on administrative units, as are the Regional and Island Councils, but on groups of river basins so potentially minimising problems arising from physical interdependencies within hydrological systems. The Authorities are multi-functional in that they are responsible for all aspects of water planning and management, in contrast to previous authorities which were each responsible for only part of the hydrological cycle. These full responsibilities include the development of water resources (sometimes termed water conservation) and water distribution to domestic, commercial, industrial and agricultural premises. The Authorities are also responsible for pollution prevention in contrast to the separate River Purification Boards in Scotland, and also sewerage and sewage treatment. Duties taken over directly from the River Authorities include river management, flood protection, land drainage and sea defences.

The Water Authorities are also responsible for promoting fisheries on inland water and estuaries. In addition 'every Water Authority ... may take steps to secure the use of water and land associated with water for the purpose of recreation' and it is their duty to develop water and associated land resources for the best recreational use (Water Act 1973, Section 20). Furthermore the Authorities and the appropriate government Ministers 'shall have regard to the desirability of preserving natural beauty, of conserving flora, fauna and geological or physiological features of special interest' and 'to the desirability of preserving public right of access to ... places of natural beauty' (Water Act 1973, Section 22). It is the duty of the Nature Conservancy Council to notify Water Authorities of areas of special conservation or amenity interest.

Like the Scottish River Purification Boards the membership of Water

Authorities combines local representation and government appointees. A majority of each Authority comprises local representatives appointed from their councillors by County and District Councils in the area concerned, but the chairman is appointed by the Secretary of State for the Environment. Although the local government members are appointed to give public accountability they are encouraged not to consider themselves as delegates from their electorate but as members of the Water Authority. This distinction may appear trivial but in fact it was designed to encourage a corporate identity for the Authorities rather than replicate the party political divisions of local government (Okun 1977). Whether this unity within the Authorities encourages genuine search for all alternatives within the planning process must be open to doubt, but the reorganisation was undertaken at a most difficult time of rampant inflation and rising water charges, which Authorities interpreted as requiring a united approach to policy formulation rather than a full political debate. It is doubtful, however, if such indirect local authority representation promotes sufficient democratic control over water planning. Only the lowest level of public accountability is provided by this type of indirect representation, in contrast to full public control in the Scottish water planning system.

One of the aims of reorganisation was for Water Authorities to provide the various water services 'with due regard to both cost and economy' (Department of the Environment and Welsh Office 1973). Water Authorities derive their finance from charges to householders, business and farmers for both water supply and other services such as sewerage and sewage treatment, and the average bill per household for Water Authority activities is £38 per year (National Water Council 1978a). In addition, Authorities charge industry for water abstraction, effluent disposal and treatment. They charge a precept on the County Councils for land drainage and also from individuals who receive particular benefit by living within an Internal Drainage District (Ch. 6). The pattern of income and expenditure, both capital and revenue, demonstrates the primary importance of revenue from households for unmetered water supply and sewerage, and the predominance of expenditure on water supply, sewerage and sewage treatment (Fig. 2.3).

A very high proportion of revenue is used to finance the interest on capital borrowed. The water industry is highly capital intensive, employing nearly £40 000 per employee amounting to £538millions against a revenue total of £938millions (1976/7), a capital/revenue ratio of 0·57 against 0·25 for the gas and electricity industries and 0·05 for manufacturing industry (Jenking 1976). This capital can only be borrowed with government approval, either from the National Loans Board, along with other nationalised industries, or from overseas. This borrowing is closely controlled by the Treasury through the Department of the Environment, imposing cash limits as a means of attempting to control the national economy. The Water Authorities have to pay interest at market rates on borrowed capital and this interest has to be raised from the public through water rates and other charges.

The charging for water and related services by Water Authorities is intended to be on an equitable basis with no discrimination between different classes or types of users. In this way the water industry has set itself against welfare objectives within charging schemes of redistributing wealth from the rich to the poor in our society (National Water Council 1976). Charging for

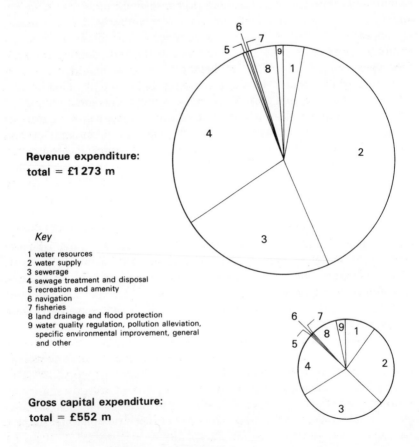

Revenue expenditure:
total = £1 273 m

Key

1 water resources
2 water supply
3 sewerage
4 sewage treatment and disposal
5 recreation and amenity
6 navigation
7 fisheries
8 land drainage and flood protection
9 water quality regulation, pollution alleviation,
  specific environmental improvement, general
  and other

Gross capital expenditure:
total = £552 m

Figure 2.3   Water Authority expenditure 1978–9.

services is supposed to be on a full cost basis with no cross-subsidisation between different areas of expenditure in the belief that economic efficiency is greatest when each type of activity is at least self-financing or makes a profit, although the criterion used to judge economic efficiency in a publicly-owned monopoly industry is problematic (Newbury 1977).

The introduction of these principles in 1974 was a major departure from established practice under which local government water services were subsidised through rate support grants and no proper allowance was made for the renewal of aging assets. The initiation of the principle of profitability was partly to force economic efficiency but also to generate surpluses, and the Secretary of State was given the power – as yet unused – to direct Water Authorities to achieve a specified minimum rate of return on assets employed, so as to reduce the need to borrow capital to finance new schemes. The proportion of Water Authorities' capital expenditure financed through revenue surpluses is very low at about 33% (National Water Council 1978a) and government policy is to increase this to reduce Authority borrowing. The policy of all services being self-financing becomes problematic in certain fields such as recreation where services may involve substantial cost yet the public is unused to paying for swimming in reservoirs or walking on moorland water gathering grounds (Ch. 5) and therefore other activities will be required to be even more profitable to compensate for this.

The self-financing directive had an immediate and dramatic impact in forcing increased water charges following removal of the rate support grant subsidies (Ch. 3). To compound problems, treatment of the water industry as a nationalised industry also led to ceilings being placed on capital expenditure, and during the mid-1970s recession large cuts were imposed by government making new capital investment more limited and emphasising the need for careful planning. Also in 1974 for the first time sewerage, sewage disposal, river pollution control and other expenses were shown as a 'general service charge' in rate demands. This attracted criticism of the service charge and led to the celebrated Daymond case. Mr Daymond of Plymstock, Devon, owned a house not connected to main drainage and 365 metres from the nearest sewer yet was charged sewerage services. He took the South West Water Authority to the High Court in a test case and won a ruling that Water Authorities have no power to demand payment for sewerage and sewage disposal from householders not receiving these services. Apart from throwing Water Authority charging schemes into disarray the Daymond case illustrates the local accountability problems of Water Authorities. Mr Daymond gained no satisfaction from his local Council acting with his Member of Parliament, and so had to resort to legal action.

The internal organisation of the Water Authorities involves two tiers (Van Oosterom 1977). First, in England and Wales regional headquarters' staff are organised around a corporate management team (Hender 1975) including Directors of Resource Planning, Operations, Finance, Scientific Services and Administration. Over these Directors sits a Chief Executive directly responsible for personnel and public relations (Department of the Environment 1973). The multi-functional nature of the Water Authorities is immediately apparent: the headquarters are not organised as in the Scottish Regional Councils with departments dealing with water supply, sewage treatment, land drainage and sea defences. Indeed all these functions are the responsibility of the Director of Operations (Reeve 1975) while the Director of Scientific Services supplies common services to all other sections of the Authority, dealing with quality control of water supply and effluents and being thus responsible for laboratories, medical services and fisheries (Fish 1975). The Director of Resource Planning has the crucial responsibility for allocating

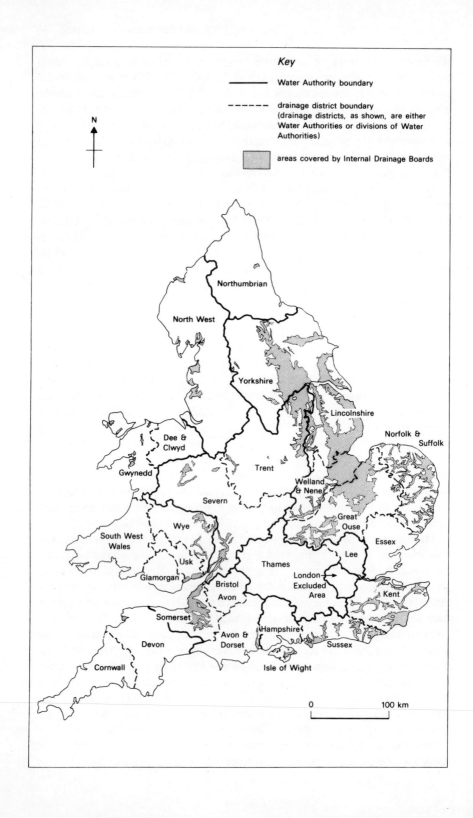

N

Northumbrian

North West

Yorkshire

Lincolnshire

Dee &
Clwyd

Norfolk &
Suffolk

Gwynedd

Trent

Welland
& Nene

Severn

Great
Ouse

Wye

South West
Wales

Essex

Lee

Usk

Thames

Glamorgan

London→
Excluded
Area

Kent

Bristol
Avon

Somerset

Avon &
Dorset

Hampshire

Sussex

Devon

Isle of Wight

Cornwall

0   100 km

resources between the different water services and for research and data collection as an aid to forward planning (Lloyd 1975). The rationale for this corporate approach is that regional water planning problems can thus be viewed in totality, reflecting the interdependencies inherent in the hydrological cycle. Budgets can be planned accordingly, rather than expenditure on pollution prevention being planned in isolation from provision for sewage treatment and water supply separate from sewerage installation.

The second tier within the Water Authorities is at divisional level. The working party on reorganisation in England and Wales (Department of the Environment 1973) advocated further multi-functionalism at this level, so that divisions would take all responsibilities for water throughout their areas. This has happened in some Authorities so that, for example, all eight divisions of the Severn Trent Water Authority are multi-functional, based on sub-catchments within the two main Severn and Trent basins. However in other Authorities the divisions are not fully multi-functional so that, in particular, the Anglian Water Authority has 12 water supply divisions, six sewage divisions and five river divisions (National Water Council 1978a). The Southern Water Authority has four combined divisions for rivers and water supply, three divisions for just rivers (termed drainage divisions), one single purpose water division and four river and water supply divisions. These structural differences in part reflect catchment characteristics but also were arranged to allow key professionals to remain in senior positions following reorganisation and as such may change as these staff retire.

The rationale for multi-functionalism at divisional level is that sharing essential design services, manual and professional staff and accommodation across all functional areas allows for a more efficient and economic operation and a single 'line management' link with headquarters. Potential disadvantages of divisional sub-catchment multi-functionalism are that pre-existing water supply or sewerage systems may not follow sub-catchment boundaries (Thames Water Authority 1978). Also links between divisional and headquarter professionals are indirect. Therefore liaison between the divisional chemists and the Director of Scientific Services are through the Divisional Engineer and therefore may be sub-optimal. However, multi-functionalism should promote the integration of water services so that treated sewage can become a source of water supply and recreation development can be incorporated with both (Pullin 1976a).

One significant anomaly in the internal structure of the Water Authorities occurs with the land drainage function. Here the Authorities have a duty to exercise only a general supervisory role and in London the Thames Water Authority has no responsibilities. The main executive agency in this field is the Regional Land Drainage Committee, composed of nominees of the Ministry of Agriculture, Fisheries and Food and County Councils. Only the

Figure 2.4 Drainage districts and areas covered by Internal Drainage Boards.

responsibility for finance lies with the Water Authority which is required to levy drainage charges, precepts and borrow money. Furthermore, the evaluation of land drainage schemes and the allocation of government grants is carried out by the Ministry, and many other organisations such as Internal Drainage Boards (Fig. 2.4) have important responsibilities, so the autonomy of Water Authorities in this field is strictly limited (Ch. 6).

The heart of the planning process: the Water Authority annual plans.   As obliged under Section 24 of the Water Act 1973 every Water Authority prepares annually a single 'annual plan', covering for the next five years the corporate responsibilities of the whole Authority.

The Department of the Environment (1977a) issued guidance notes on the form and content of these annual plans which, initially, were envisaged as embracing the next 20 years. Each Water Authority was to present its objectives, policies and programmes for the 20-year period, covering the whole range of its functions. Individual annual plans were supposed to fit into the national water strategy to be developed from the early plans submitted to the Department. This strategy would then form the basis of subsequent annual plans. Each plan was to detail existing water use and management, and provide a comprehensive 20-year regional overview with future demand estimates and related policies together with the five-year capital programme and its financing including cash flow, financing forecasts and revenue implications. Each Authority was to indicate its priorities, as required under Section 24(6), and how these are reflected in the capital investment programme. Also required were details of the extent of consultation with local authorities and other interested parties in the formulation of the plan.

The fundamentals of the guidance notes have been followed. Water Authority annual plans prepared on this basis now provide an essential link with the Department of the Environment (Thames Water Authority 1979, North West Water Authority 1978a, Wessex Water Authority 1978a). However, this ambitious attempt at comprehensive planning has presented several problems, although these should not obscure the gains which have occurred since 1974 before which plans rarely included goal statements, objectives and options accessible for public scrutiny. First, the 20-year time horizon has not worked, certainly as far as the 'plan as to action' envisaged in the Water Act 1973 is concerned. Only the most general statement about standards of service and overall priorities has been possible for such a long period, given the budgetary uncertainties even on a year-to-year basis. This shift away from long-term planning is unfortunate, given the long time horizons needed for water planning, but it reflects the instability of the national economy and of demand patterns – even five-year projections are highly problematic.

The second major problem with these annual plans is that as currently conceived they need to be all things to all people. Through the plans, Water Authorities are making 'bids' to the Treasury via the Department of the Environment for permission to borrow and spend. But they are also setting out plans and options for public consultation, and expenditure programmes for their operating Divisions. In many respects these different aims are incompatible. A carefully prepared plan becomes less than helpful as an internal budgeting base-line if, as happened in 1979, substantial arbitrary cuts are imposed on the total budget or, as happened earlier in the 1970s, Water Authorities are told at short notice to spend more than they had planned: in practice, cuts in public expenditure passed to the Water Authorities are bound to have an arbitrary impact on actual schemes because insufficient time is available to repeat planning exercises to accommodate lower finance levels. Thus unavoidable delays and inefficiency may result. Bids for permission to finance specific schemes are also incompatible with a request to the public for advice on how an Authority should spend money.

Nevertheless these plans do represent a considerable advance, not least in facilitating greater Water Authority accountability if the public were wise enough to use the plans in this way. Foremost in developing the annual planning cycle has been the Thames Water Authority (1979), which has its own planning Directorate. One important change sought by Thames is to increase the amount of 'top-down' planning. Here the Authority as a whole decides policy, usually centred on indices for standards of service, and this is implemented with plans and schemes at Divisional levels. Currently much planning is 'bottom-up': schemes are initiated at Divisional level according to perceived need, ratified by the regional authority, and included in the budget bid to the Department of the Environment. With the 'bottom-up' approach standards of service can become inequitable, owing to different divisional perceptions of need. However, with the 'top-down' approach the measurement and equalisation of standards of service is far from easy. Water Authority planning is currently excessively 'bottom-up' in character, but only time will tell whether alternative initiatives will succeed.

The water supply function of the Water Companies. In the Water Act 1973 no change was made in the monopoly public supply of water by the former statutory water undertakings some of which continue as the Water Companies. However these companies act as agents of the Water Authorities which in turn are obliged to make water available for the companies to resell. There are 30 such companies (Fig. 2.2), 28 of which are active and these supply some 25% of the population of England and Wales with 22% of the total water supplied; there are no Water Companies in Scotland.

The Water Companies were established under their own Acts of Parliament, mainly in the nineteenth century (Rennison 1979), and are profit making but they are statutory rather than private companies as is often thought: the latter implies considerable freedom of action whereas the Water Companies are strictly controlled by the Water and Companies Acts, which limit the amount of capital employed and the rates of dividend paid to shareholders. The principles by which the Water Authorities fix their charges are adopted by the Water Companies and under agency arrangements the

Companies submit annual programmes to the Authorities showing the schemes proposed for the construction of source works, trunk mains, and water treatment plant.

The Water Companies are clearly a structural anomaly in the water industry and recognised as such by government (Department of the Environment *et al.* 1976). However, the Companies and the Water Authorities appear to be working well together. The 1974–79 Labour Government was committed to bringing these Companies into the Water Authorities (Department of the Environment *et al.* 1977) but since nationalisation is the issue the two main political parties disagree and this rationalisation may not materialise.

The sewerage function of District Councils.   Another anomaly in the water industry is the District Councils' role as agents for Water Authorities in the execution of their sewerage function. When the government proposed that the Water Authorities took over this function completely, local government and parliamentary opposition was such that this proposition was amended (Jordan, Richardson and Kimber 1977). It was feared in local government circles both that the removal of this function from their engineering departments would leave these no longer viable and that the essential coordination of sewerage provision with the District Council land use development control responsibility would suffer if sewerage was a regional responsibility. Therefore the government relented and under Section 15 of the Water Act 1973 District Councils are required to prepare and annually revise a programme for their sewerage function, carry out the programme approved by the Water Authority providing the necessary staff and facilities, and to conduct any necessary legal proceedings (Redknap and Scott 1976). In return the Water Authority reimburses the District for the expenses incurred.

There is no doubt that this agency arrangement is imperfect. The responsibility for identifying sewerage planning problems by the Districts is separated from the source of finance at Water Authority level. This imbalance, coupled with the large number of Districts liaising with each Authority and the duplication of professional staff in both Districts and Water Authorities creates diffficulties for the planning of capital works programmes. Water Authorities themselves have not been allowed to terminate these agency agreements, although this is subject to review (Department of the Environment *et al.* 1977). In some Districts it has not been possible to continue the sewerage function during a period of financial difficulty and this has passed to the Authority concerned.

Central government departments

Central government departments are very powerful elements within the water planning system. They have ultimate power over the financing of capital works programmes and, to a lesser extent, over revenue expenditure. Senior civil servants also have power to promote or block change within the system. For example, the under-secretary at the Department of the Environment played a central role in the late 1960s in promoting multi-functional regional authorities in England and Wales (Jordan, Richardson and Kimber 1977) and the chief engineer at the Scottish Development Department has a strong personal infuence over the organisation of the Regional Council water departments in Scotland (Coppock and Sewell 1978).

The Department of the Environment.   The role of the government departments at the pinnacle of the water planning system should be to set goals and determine general policy and to ensure that the other policy-making and executive agencies transform these into plans, schemes and action. Thus the Secretary of State for the Environment has the duty under Section 1 of the Water Act 1973 with the Minister of Agriculture, 'to promote jointly a national policy for water in England and Wales' and to 'secure the effective execution of so much of that policy as relates to:

- the conservation, augmentation, distribution and proper use of water resources, and the provision of water supplies;
- sewerage and treatment and disposal of sewage and other effluents;
- the restoration and maintenance of the wholesomeness of rivers and other inland water;
- the use of inland water for recreation;
- the enhancement and preservation of amenity in connection with inland water; and
- the use of inland water for navigation'.

Following from these statutory duties the Secretary of State agreed overall expenditure principles with Water Authorities for different water planning functions (Table 1.2). Such broad priority rankings are intended to be a framework within which individual authorities allocate expenditure. A further duty of the Secretary of State is 'to collate and publish information from which assessment can be made of the actual and prospective water resources in England and Wales'. This duty led to the creation of the Water Data Unit as part of the Department.

  The goal-setting function of the Department is not well defined in these statements of duties and priorities and thus must inhibit rational planning; they are not defined more closely partly because it is much easier for the civil servants and politicians concerned if the goal to be achieved is not detailed, only the general direction of movement specified. Therefore no standards are set for 'the wholesomeness of rivers', simply an intention is stated that it be restored and maintained. Consequently when there is marginal improvement in river pollution levels the government and the Department can claim that its duties are being carried out successfully, irrespective of the rate of improvements.

Related to the duty to promote a national policy for water the Department has the responsibility of overseeing through the National Water Council the corporate planning functions of the Water Authorities, and as such requires medium- and long-term plans from the Authorities as well as determining expenditure ceilings. Within the Department's Water Directorate, divisions 1 and 2 are concerned with the southern and northern English Water Authorities respectively. Their liaison work involves professional advice particularly on coastal protection, allocation of capital ceilings, application of cash limits to capital expenditure programmes and statutory work on Bills and Orders. Other divisions are responsible for financial policy, overall water pollution policies and problems, appeals on licencing applications, liaising with Water Companies and the British Waterways Board and links with the European Economic Community. In addition there is a separate Water Engineering Directorate with a Research and Development Division, a Chemical Division and Liaison Division each of which gives advice on technical aspects of water planning.

The Welsh Office has a small section concerned with water, but this is not concerned with setting policy as is the Department of the Environment. Its main role is that of overseeing the planning function of the Welsh Water Authority.

The Ministry of Agriculture, Fisheries and Food.   This Ministry has a more minor role in water planning than the Department of the Environment, being concerned only with land drainage. In Britain this embraces both urban flood protection and agricultural land drainage related to both inland rivers and coastal areas.

The reason for this somewhat anomalous separation from the Department of the Environment of one minor water planning function – over and above the Ministry's wider interest in fisheries – lies in the traditionally strong ties between the Ministry of Agriculture and agricultural field drainage, which is often inextricably linked with flood alleviation works in both urban and rural areas. Proposals prior to 1974 for the Department of the Environment to oversee the whole of the water industry were successfully resisted by the powerful farming lobby, supported by the Ministry of Agriculture civil servants, who feared that land drainage would be swallowed up by more pressing needs of the sewage and water supply sides of water planning (Richardson, Jordan and Kimber 1978). Therefore the Ministry of Agriculture, Fisheries and Food has the duty of 'securing the effective execution of so much of that policy (i.e. the national policy for water discussed above) as relates to land drainage, and to fisheries in inland and coastal waters' (Water Act 1973, Section 1). To this end there are two divisions within the Ministry, one concerned with land drainage and the other with fisheries, and also a Land Drainage Service as part of the Agricultural Development and Advisory Service, which gives advice to farmers on all aspects of farm management.

The Scottish Office. Unlike the Welsh Office the Scottish Office has for Scotland virtually all of the duties and functions of the Department of the Environment and the Ministry of Agriculture, Fisheries and Food in England and Wales. The Secretary of State for Scotland has the responsibility for approving and monitoring the expenditure of the water departments of the Regional Councils and also under the Water (Scotland) Act 1946 the duty to publish assessments of Scottish water resources.

The internal organisation of the Scottish Office includes two separate departments concerned with water which are virtually government ministries in themselves, with the Scottish Office serving as a figurehead. In theory these departments only have power to advise the Secretary of State but in practice they have considerable executive responsibilities. The Department of Agriculture and Fisheries in Scotland, as with its counterpart in England and Wales, has a minor role in water planning, principally to give grants for agricultural land drainage schemes and to administer the production of fresh water fisheries under the Salmon and Freshwater Fisheries (Scotland) Act 1976. The more important department, however, is the Scottish Development Department which was created in 1962 with an under-secretary responsible for water and a Chief Engineer coordinating technical advice to Regional Council staff supported by a small research budget. The Department has responsibility for overseeing the work of the Regional Councils and the River Purification Boards. Links with the Regional Councils are strong, with regular meetings between the civil servants and the Directors of Water and Sewerage from the Regional Councils. Links with the River Purification Boards are less strong, reflecting the lack of senior engineers in the Department in the field of river pollution. The Chief Engineer's traditional role has been in water supply (Coppock and Sewell 1978).

The British Waterways Board

The British Waterways Board, established under the Transport Act 1962, owns and is responsible for the management of about two-thirds of Britain's publicly owned navigable waters. These are mostly in England and Wales and consist of canal and river navigations together with their associated reservoirs, docks, freight and hire cruiser fleets, warehouses and some waterside land and buildings. Following a review of the future of waterways the Board was given under the Transport Act 1968 the power to provide services and facilities for amenity and recreational purposes (British Waterways Board 1965). However, the canals and feeder reservoirs are also used for water supply to industrial, commercial and agricultural users, for water transfer for water supply purposes and for land drainage and effluent disposal.

The British Waterways Board's internal organisation, with its Freight Services and Amenity Services divisions, reflects the two main functions of the inland waterways: commercial freight carrying and recreation and amenity. The Board is responsible to the Secretary of State for the

Environment, who appoints members of the Board of nine. Central government views the future of the canals as mainly concerning amenity and water-carrying rather than freight-carrying. This is despite the favourable record of profitability of the freight services and the Board's attempts to secure greater recognition for the waterways' commercial role.

Under the 1973 Water Bill proposals, the Board was to disappear with the waterways passing into the hands of the ten Water Authorities. However, these proposals were omitted from the Water Act 1973 following arguments that a strong single-purpose authority is in the best interests of the waterways which, of course, cut across river catchments. Again in 1977 the government proposed to abolish the Board and transfer its duties to a national navigation executive in a National Water Authority (Department of the Environment *et al.* 1977).

The inevitability of subsidy was accepted by the government following the review of the future of the waterways during the 1960s. The Board is currently financed by grants and loans from the Department of the Environment, by bank overdraft facilities from the Treasury and by revenue generated from its trading activities. It operates at an annual financial loss which in 1977 amounted to about £12·5millions out of a total expenditure of £15·8millions (Ch. 5).

Advisory and research organisations in the water planning system

Complementing the major executive agencies are the numerous advisory organisations and research units. These play an important part in collecting data, collating opinions, and formulating and evaluating alternative policies, plans and schemes. As such these organisations aim to improve decision making but not to make major planning decisions and in general they have no implementation roles.

At a national level these agencies include the National Water Council which coordinates the activity of the Water Authorities, the Water Space Amenity Commission which advises the English Water Authorities in the field of water recreation and the Water Data Unit which collects and collates data relevant to all types of water planning for the whole of Britain. In addition there is a large number of other research organisations including the Hydraulics Research Station, the Water Research Centre and the Institute of Hydrology, each with special skills and particular interests and each undertaking both basic and scheme-specific research. Also agencies like the Country-side Commissions and the Nature Conservancy Council advise Water Authorities on the impact of their projects on landscape and wildlife. Many of these diverse organisations service the policy-making and executive agencies in both Scotland and England and Wales and also contribute to the work of private consultants in the water planning field. Their strength lies in the expertise represented in the many different organisations. Their weakness is a direct corollary of this diversity, being the difficulty of coordination and the resulting overlapping roles.

Formal advisory agencies at a regional scale are mainly committees within the Water Authorities or Regional Council structure rather than separate agencies. For example, each Water Authority in England and Wales has a statutory responsibility to establish a Fisheries Advisory Committee. Such committees have the important function both of increasing local representation, thereby enlarging the democratic base of decision making, and of widening the range of expertise used to guide planning decisions in particular fields. Nevertheless one of the deficiencies identified by the government in its review of the water industry (Department of the Environment *et al*. 1976) was the weakness of the planning system at national level. This review led to the suggestion (Department of the Environment *et al*. 1977) for the conversion of the National Water Council into an executive National Water Authority, incorporating several advisory and research organisations such as the Central Water Planning Unit.

The Central Water Planning Unit was created in 1974 when the Water Resources Board was abolished but was itself abolished following the 1979 general election. The Unit was part of the Department of the Environment and employed many specialists previously in the Water Resources Board. Its role was to advise the Department on the national planning of water, including inter-regional transfer, and to undertake research to support this role, for example into water use and water demand prediction (Naughton 1974). Given the autonomy enjoyed by the English and Welsh Water Authorities relations with the Unit were often strained to the extent that proper planning was jeopardised through lack of cooperation over data. Transfer to a National Water Authority would have given the Unit a clearer central planning role but given the new Conservative government in 1979, and its general antipathy towards centralised planning, proposals for the Authority were shelved and the Unit was disbanded.

The National Water Council

The National Water Council is the primary advisory organisation in the British water industry and as such comes nearest to being a policy-making and executive agency. However the Council has no planning responsibilities and no executive powers. Its main functions are as a consultative and advisory focus for the industry as a whole and to provide common services to the industry. The Council's annual budget is small at just under £2millions (1978), derived almost entirely from the Water Authorities in proportion to their size. Education and training expenditure amounts to a further £2·3millions, levied from the Water Authorities, the Water Companies, the Scottish water undertakers and the Northern Ireland Water Service.

The advisory function is exemplified by the Council's role as a main line of communication between the Water Authorities in England and Wales and those government departments with water responsibilities and interests. For example, the Council has given advice to government in the field of financial and economic policies with a report reviewing water charging practices and the implication of equalisation of charges following the 1974 reorganisation (National Water Council 1976). Another responsibility was the evaluation for the government of the Water Resources Board's national water strategy (Ch. 3). Despite the undoubted influence of the Council the independence of the Water Authorities is absolute: they have direct access to Ministers and are not obliged to approach government through the Council. In addition to advising government the Council also coordinates activities of the Water Authorities in order 'to promote and assist the efficient performance by Water Authorities of their functions' (Water Act 1973, Section 9.5). To this end the Council both provides a forum for debate for the Water Authority chairmen, who all sit on the Council, and can be called in by two Water Authorities to act in matters of common interest. In this capacity as arbitrator the Council approaches having an executive function, although the use of these powers is likely to be very limited.

The Council's remit of providing means of liaison between Water Authorities is important bearing in mind the autonomy of the Authorities: an example is the collaborative project to enlarge the Craig Goch reservoir in mid-Wales to provide water for several Water Authorities. In the field of negotiation and consultation with interest groups the Council has regular meetings with the National Farmers' Union to discuss water charges, pollution problems, the use of fertilisers and the disposal of sewage plant waste products on agricultural land as a fertiliser.

An important aspect of the Council's role in technical and research fields is the work of standing Committees, including those on Effluent Treatment, Waste of Water, Sewers and Water Mains, Water Regulations and the Disposal of Sewage Sludge. Through these Committees the Council can disseminate the latest advice and technical knowledge from researchers, practitioners and government departments to those involved in scheme design. In attempting to promote the efficiency of the Water Authorities in this way the Council has links with the Water Data Unit and, while it existed, with the Central Water Planning Unit. Relationships between the Council and these Units have not always been easy in comparison to links with the independent Water Research Centre (Stott 1976), and this formed one of the areas for government attention in the review of the Council's future (Department of the Environment *et al*. 1977).

The Council's function as a provider of common services entails running training schemes and industrial relations services such as negotiations on salaries, conditions of employment and superannuation administration, all important central functions within a nationalised industry. In addition the Council has the responsibility for testing and approving water fittings. The Council is statutorily obliged to provide training facilities for the Scottish Water industry (and that in Northern Ireland) and the Scottish water authorities take part in the other common service arrangements, either with representatives on standing technical committees or through the Scottish Sub-Committee of the National Water Council.

The membership of the Council totals 21 and, including the chairmen of the ten English and Welsh Water Authorities, all members are nominated either by the Secretary of State for the Environment or the Minister of Agriculture. The membership represents many fields of interest in water matters such as farming, recreation and research 'ensuring that when some large topic of significance is referred to the Council, the view it gives is not only that of the Regional Water Authorities but a general view, a national view' (Ardill 1974). In 1975 a somewhat different perspective was expressed by Greenfield (1975):

> ❮ Among these 21 advisers and consulters there are three former Tory ministers (including the chairman Lord Nugent), a merchant banker, a farmer and a chartered surveyor, four company directors and a major landowner. Of the nineteen men, six went to Eton; three were in the Guards and one in the Hussars, two have been office holders in the Country Landowners' Association and one is a master of foxhounds. The Council's knowledge of water and its ways is not called into question but some might hesitate before endorsing its claim that it expresses a general, national view. ❯

The methods of the National Water Council are unusual within the British water industry in that meetings of the Council are closed to the public and minutes, sent to the Water Authorities, are confidential. The Council sponsors meetings between officers of all the Authorities including finance officers, directors of operations and public relations, but issues no information about the proceedings (Greenfield 1975). This element of secrecy is defended with reference to the openness of the Water Authorities which the Council seeks to influence, and the necessity for confidentiality of government departments.

The future role of the National Water Council is uncertain, although the concept of a National Water Authority has been abandoned. One of the problems with the Council's present consultative function is that since it has no executive powers it has no authority to commit Water Authorities to specific policies, only to advise them of what might be in the national interest. Herein lies a natural tension between the autonomous regional executive structure and the national consultative focus of the water industry. However, the major power and influence within the Council lies with the ten Water Authority chairmen and with the disbanding in 1979 of the Central Water Planning Unit the Council could agree, with the approval of the Secretary of State, to interpret its role to include a central planning function for the whole water industry. This would remove the anomaly created in 1974 whereby the main planning agency, the Central Water Planning Unit, was independent of the crucial responsibility for water planning at Water Authority level.

However such a role for the Council would perpetuate the lack of direct public accountability at the centre of the water planning system in England and Wales.

National advisory bodies in Scotland

There is no body in Scotland comparable to the National Water Council. Organisations exist to promote consultation between staff in the Regional Councils and River Purification Boards and to present a united approach to the Scottish Development Department. These organisations include those specific to the water field, including Scottish Association of Directors of Water and Sewerage Services and the Scottish River Purification Advisory Committee, and also the Convention of Scottish Local Authorities which has a broad role in promoting the interest of the Regional Councils. It is perhaps an advantage that interest and pressure groups in Scotland deal directly with the Scottish Development Department or the Regional Councils while on technical matters staff from the Scottish Regional Councils and Scottish Development Department sit on National Water Council Technical Committees.

The Water Data Unit, the Water Research Centre and other research agencies

Research is of central significance to water planning, since so many policies involve uncertainties about future demands for water services and so many plans and schemes involve technical and economic considerations which may be uncertain when applied to particular circumstances. Current research agencies service both the advisory and the policy-making and executive agencies in the water industry by undertaking research, collecting and collating data (White 1974). As yet all have had a short life. Each is a product of the 1974 reorganisation but each still reflects its prior history, in turn reflecting the long time scale necessary for research in the water field where it may take many years to collect the necessary data, complete a research project and feed the results into the planning process.

The Water Data Unit was created within the Department of the Environment in the 1974 reorganisation to provide information on a national basis for the Water Authorities and for government. The Unit has a professional staff of 20, chosen on a multi-disciplinary basis to reflect the multi-functional concept of the new Authorities. The principal functions of the Unit are to advise on the standardisation of water data collection, to collect and process water data required for planning new projects and monitoring existing schemes, and to provide a computer service for the water industry. In addition the Unit sponsors research in relevant subject areas but this centralisation of water data gathering is the important gain of the water industry reorganisation in this field and should provide a more accurate basis for future plans.

The Water Research Centre comprises what previously had been the Water

Research Association, the Water Pollution Research Laboratory, and the technology division of the Water Resources Board. Owing to this history, and particularly the emphasis on water pollution, the Centre's current activities are clearly centred on the technical aspects of water – for example on the toxicity of dyes and laundry effluent to fish, or mathematical modelling of the Humber estuary – and relate less strongly to research on long-term water strategy or social and economic aspects of water planning. The Centre has a staff of some 550 and is financed primarily by the Water Authorities paying a membership subscription in proportion to their revenue expenditure. Scottish water departments are also members, as indeed are consulting engineering firms, Northern Ireland Water Authorities, polytechnic and university departments and other research bodies. Two-thirds of the finance of the Centre comes from its members but substantial financial and other support comes from government through the Department of the Environment. However, the Centre is an independent organisation as befits one concerned with basic research and is managed by its members through an elected Council which ensures independence coupled with strong links with the Centre's customers to ensure pertinent research.

Water research is conducted in many other agencies and organisations, some of which like the Institute of Hydrology are directly funded by government agencies, in this case the Natural Environment Research Council, and others like the polytechnics and universities are less directly connected with government. A feature of the 1974 reorganisation was the development of research roles within the Water Authorities, particularly to support their statutory duty under Section 24 of the Water Act 1973 to prepare plans and assess the demands for their services in their areas. In addition much research relevant to water planning schemes is undertaken in the conservation field by County Naturalist Trusts which exist throughout England and Wales and who monitor wildlife numbers in and around water bodies. Most of this information is collated in the records of the Nature Conservancy Council with whom Water Authorities are required to consult in appropriate cases.

It is clear that water research is highly fragmented. This may not be detrimental to progress since much valuable work can be done on a small scale. However, much of the research undertaken is very conventional in its technical and scientific orientation. While this research is undoubtedly important to efficient water scheme design, there is very little research on the important social and economic aspects necessary for efficient water planning. In comparison, for example, with the housing field, there is very little research on 'alternative' non-technical means of achieving water planning goals such as water demand regulation (Ch. 3) or alternative approaches to flood damage reduction (Ch. 6). This conventional approach may well reflect the high proportion of government finance in water research in contrast again to the housing field where independent charitable trusts allow more innovative research projects.

The Water Space Amenity Commission

The Water Space Amenity Commission is the smallest national advisory and research body of the post-1974 British water industry, yet arguably it has the largest task. With a full-time staff of just five, and an annual budget of only £82 000 (1977) the Commission has the statutory duty under the Water Act 1973 (Section 23) 'to advise the Secretary of State for the Environment on the formulation, promotion and execution of the national policy for water so far as relating to recreation and amenity in England'. The Commission, which is financed through the National Water Council, is also responsible for advising, encouraging and assisting the water industry on all matters relating to recreation and amenity.

The Commission itself, as opposed to the full-time staff, is composed of 11 members – appointed by the Secretary of State – and the ten Water Authority chairmen. This advisory body therefore follows the general pattern in national advisory and research agencies of relatively sparse representation by local authority or other elected representatives. However, the members appointed by the Secretary of State show a wide range of interests and close albeit informal links with most organisations within both the water recreation field and other amenity areas. For example, members in 1977 also held positions on the Salmon and Trout Association, the Sports Council, the Standing Committee on National Parks, the Central Council for Physical Recreation and many other organisations (Water Space Amenity Commission 1977a).

The Commission is a new organisation and one of its first tasks was to set priorities for its advisory role (Water Space Amenity Commission 1977a). These published priorities show a focus at the national and regional level, as perhaps befits a small organisation, and the Commission clearly aims to act only in an advisory capacity rather than take a more active planning function. This role and the national and regional focus means, however, that research and planning for water recreation at a more local level is left to the Water Authorities whose staff have traditionally not seen recreation as within their sphere of interest. The national focus contrasts with the Sports Council which with its own regional structure and grant-aid facilities has a greater influence on recreation planning in its field. One major deficiency of the Commission is that it lacks the 'teeth' of grant-aiding water recreation and amenity schemes (Hanson 1975). Despite the Water Act 1973 clearly reflecting national priorities for the development of water recreation, this concern is not supported by national financial resources as is, for example, increased food production in the land drainage field. Therefore the burden of financing water recreation even for a truly national resource such as the Norfolk Broads falls on the regional community through the Anglian Water Authority rather than on the country as a whole.

As a consequence of its size and the lack of grant-aiding powers the Commission has turned out to be largely a public relations organisation. In the context of water recreation this may be satisfactory, in that Water Authorities have needed advice on developments within this field and the Commission, through its working parties, has produced useful reports suggesting ways of reconciling water planning practice with amenity and nature conservation interests (Water Space Amenity Commission 1978). However, within the context of recreation planning as a whole, with local authority experience going back to at least the Countryside Act 1968, the Commission introduces yet another agency into an already fragmented structure (Ch. 5).

Advisory Committees within Water Authorities

Complementing the national advisory and research agencies a consultation machinery is built into the Water Authorities themselves, in the form of Advisory Committees. Some of these are statutory bodies required under the Water Act 1973 while others have been established by the Authorities voluntarily. All attempt to allow the public and sectional interests to have a greater say in water planning at the regional scale, in contrast to the lack of public participation in the national advisory and research agencies.

Under the Water Act 1973 each Water Authority must establish and consult a fisheries advisory committee. Typically, there is one regional and several area or local committees for each Authority and they are chaired by Water Authority officials and have representatives of trout fishermen, the coarse fishermen, the National Farmers' Union, the Country Landowners' Association and the Sports Councils and other 'persons who appear to them to be interested in any such fisheries in that area' (Water Act 1973, Section 19a). The statutory advisory committees should not be confused with the Recreation Fisheries and Amenity Committees of the Water Authorities which consist of Authority officials and members with special interest in recreation. These committees serve as forums for determining policy and resolving potential and actual conflict between recreational and fishing interests and therefore are properly part of the executive machinery.

The use of advisory panels or committees in other areas of water planning is not a statutory duty although other committees have been established in all Authorities. The Wessex Water Authority, for example, has three local Water Advisory Committees including representatives of the District Councils, which are relatively poorly represented on the main Authority, and of the Country Landowners' Association, the National Farmers' Union and the Confederation of British Industry. The statutory fisheries advisory committee is also represented, showing how committees interlock so that, in theory, everyone knows what everyone else is doing.

The professional composition of the water planning institutions

There is no doubt that the professional composition both of the policy-making and executive institutions and of most of the advisory and research agencies is unbalanced in favour of those with engineering backgrounds.

Whilst specialisation and professionalisation breeds expertise and high standards, it can also lead to a narrowness of approach and adherence to established practices even when these do not provide the best solution to specific problems. Specialists tend quite naturally to perceive a given problem strictly in terms of their training. Therefore both the perception or identification of problems, social goals, priorities or needs and the solutions adopted to meet these stages in the planning process reflect these professional interpretations. There is evidence that the engineering profession is no exception to these rules: although generalisations are dangerous the profession tends to be intensely technical in its approach to problems and rather reluctant to involve others in problem-solving. There tends to be a strong allegiance to the established agency's goals and few major changes are suggested to establish policies and practices (Sewell 1971).

In England and Wales the Water Authorities, government departments with water planning responsibilities and other policy-making agencies are dominated by engineers. A highly significant feature of successive water industry reorganisations since 1945 has been the tendency for engineers to continue in senior executive posts from one administration to the next. Past dependence upon water engineers to solve the country's water supply problems led naturally to the chief executives of new water agencies being mainly engineers, or exceptionally lawyers and accountants. These chief executives were supported by specialists trained in engineering techniques who also relied to an extent upon engineering consultants. The River Boards and River Authorities were led mainly by engineers and during the 1974 reorganisation the continuation of engineering dominance was ensured by the application of two recruitment principles, 'passing on the torch' and the 'ring fence' (Sewell and Barr 1978). A deliberate policy of recruiting internally was adopted, as a result of pressure from professional Institutions and Trade Unions, and as many employees as possible from the River Authorities were employed in the Water Authorities ('passing on the torch'). Restrictions were placed on recruitment from outside so that few previously employed outside the water supply and sewage disposal authorities were employed by the Water Authorities (the 'ring fence'). Even with the coming of corporate management, and therefore the need for other specialists such as economists and planners, many senior posts were still filled by engineers who are expected to develop a broader perspective.

Engineers also dominate the Scottish water industry and the national water policy in Scotland is the responsibility of a Chief Engineer in the Scottish Development Department. The heyday of the engineers in Scotland followed the Water (Scotland) Act 1967 when, in the single-purpose Regional Water Boards, water supply functions did not have to compete directly with other planning areas for funds and the engineer was master of his own house. Now that water is the responsibility simply of departments within the Regional

Councils the influence of the water engineer is reduced but nevertheless engineers still dominate the water planning process after the budgets have been agreed.

The dominance of engineers is also found in many of the advisory and research organisations. The advisory committees within Water Authorities are generally broadly based, and of course the elected members to the Scottish Regional Councils are likely to have a wide range of experience. However the professional staffs of national advisory agencies in Britain are certainly dominated by engineers and scientists. This emphasis on engineering and science is appropriate where technical advice is required, as from the Hydraulics Research Station, but the main deficiency is that this emphasis on engineering is not complemented by any research units or agencies specialising in the social and economic aspects of water planning and incorporating the appropriate professionals.

Interest and pressure groups and water planning

The water industry, certainly in England and Wales, has set itself against using its charges to redistribute wealth from one section of society to another (National Water Council 1976). This does not prevent very many groups from pressurising the industry to arrange its policies, plans and schemes to promote their interests, financial or otherwise. Interest and pressure groups, however, are by their very nature fragmented and therefore often are weak, each tackling a particular problem as best it can. Nevertheless these organisations do influence the path of water planning and in certain circumstances they can exert the decisive influence.

Types of interest and pressure groups

Except where there is statutory provision for consultation between Water Authorities and fishery interests there is no formal structure of linkages either between the interest and pressure groups themselves or between these organisations and the formally constituted executive agencies; interest groups may indeed be working in opposition to one another and the pressure groups are often not focussed on the same goals. Therefore these groups can best be examined within three broad and necessarily overlapping categories based on the aims of the different groups rather than their role in the decision-making process which, in any case, is highly variable (Wootton 1970, Lowe 1977). There are, first, the professional and employee associations, secondly those groups with a direct financial or business interest in water policies and plans and finally, there is the very large number of recreation interest groups, amenity societies and similar organisations. In addition, there are other groups such as local amenity societies or political parties like Plaid Cymru which on occasion may attempt to influence the water planning system on particular policies or local plans and schemes but at other times are latent.

The professional bodies exert a strong influence on overall water policy and this influence is probably most felt at government level during periods of water industry reorganisation and review (Okun 1977, Institution of Water Engineers 1972, Jordan, Richardson and Kimber 1977). The water industry is professionally divided in two ways. First, there are several engineering professional bodies with members within the water industry, such as the Institution of Water Engineers and Scientists, the Institution of Public Health Engineers, the Institution of Civil Engineers and more peripheral bodies such as the Institution of Mechanical Engineers. Secondly, the finance and legal sides of the water industry have their own professional bodies, such as the Association of Public Service Finance Officers, with members in Water Authorities, Regional Councils and the advisory and research organisations. The interest of all these associations is in the standards of behaviour, professional ethics and the rewards of their members, including the water planners themselves.

Those groups with a direct financial or business interest in water planning are similarly fragmented but include some of the most powerful agencies and companies in the country. For example, Imperial Chemical Industries are very dependent on water for their efficient operation and the costs of this water and charges for waste water treatment can critically affect their profitability. Companies such as ICI attempt to influence the work of Water Authorities directly (Gregory 1975, see Ch. 3) but also indirectly through the Confederation of British Industry which approaches the water planning system both at government and at local level as the representative of all private industry (Dart 1977a). In the same way the National Farmers' Union operates on both the Regional Land Drainage Committees and the Ministry of Agriculture, Fisheries and Food. In all cases the groups attempt to promote or to mould water policies, plans and schemes to further their own interests, which in essence means their own prosperity or that of their members, or to prevent implementation of plans which pose a threat to those interests.

Recreational groups generally promote the provision of relevant facilities and the maintenance of environmental quality. The many amenity groups, itself an umbrella term covering many widely different organisations, often aim to prevent the policy-making and executive agencies implementing their plans, for fear of environmental deterioration, rather than promoting new developments. For example, the Royal Society for the Protection of Birds together with many other amenity and scientific societies had a major role in forcing a compromise in the case where the Southern Water Authority was proposing to drain the Amberley Wild Brooks in Sussex (Ch. 6). Many amenity groups are simply local organisations like the Women's Institute who may oppose the siting of sewage treatment works, water supply installations or recreation development and each has a part to play in the planning process. Some groups are created specifically to oppose or promote schemes.

Others take on issues as they arise. This reduces the efficiency of their influence on the planning system but such an incremental or *ad hoc* approach to opposing planning decisions is forced on groups if, as is often the case, the plans themselves are not part of an overall strategy.

Methods of participation of interest and pressure groups

There are three basic ways in which the groups influence the decision-making process. First, they may be actively involved within Water Authorities, Regional Councils or central government as allies of senior civil servants or engineers against other interests (Richardson, Jordan and Kimber 1978) or as participants in the policy-making and executive system. Therefore, for example, members of the National Farmers' Union sit on the Regional Land Drainage Committees, and the Royal Society for the Protection of Birds and the National Anglers' Council are both represented on the Water Space Amenity Commission. These groups are generally not represented as such on these bodies but when the Water Authority or the Department of the Environment appoint people to the many Boards, Committees or other consultative positions within the water planning system it is often easier to appoint someone from an established interest or pressure group than to select some ordinary member of the public who happens to be interested in birds or angling. Furthermore, appointment of people from established groups serves to indicate to these organisations that they are represented in the planning system and that they should use these formal channels to communicate their views on particular water planning matters rather than excite public debate.

The second method by which interest and pressure groups participate within the planning system is by offering advice to government, Water Authorities or Regional Councils at the consultation stage of planning when the policy-making agency is reviewing alternative strategies prior to setting objectives and designating schemes. Thus, for example, the Council for the Protection of Rural England gave evidence to the Parliamentary Select Committee on Nationalised Industries concerning the accountability of the water industry to Parliament and the public at large. To be effective, interest and pressure groups seeking to influence the planning system in this way need close contacts with relevant senior civil servants and regional water authority engineers. They also require considerable expertise within their organisations, since they cannot rely on assistance from the professionals within the policy-making institutions as can those groups with formal roles within the Water Authority or Regional Council planning systems.

The third way in which interest and pressure groups can influence water planning is simply by responding to proposals by the policy-making and executive agencies, and the second and third of these categories may often merge. Perhaps a group initially offers advice to an agency and subsequently the same group opposes a plan or scheme by more direct means. One such means is to give evidence at a public inquiry, although few proposals arrive at this stage of possible confrontation, but on many occasions a scheme or plan is opposed with a vigorous campaign by local or national pressure groups using the press or lobbying Members of Parliament, local Councils or their elected representatives within the water planning institution in an attempt to modify or prevent the offending development. Equally, many decisions occur whereby the executive agency puts forward suggestions upon which interest groups comment and a compromise is reached.

These processes of consultation, bargaining and compromise between interest groups and executive agencies is central to the concept of fair decision making within a democratic society. In theory each point of view should have equal access to decision makers – whether they come from small local groups or large national agencies. Furthermore, conflicts between goals and priorities should be resolved publicly – such as where the Ramblers' Association promote access to reservoirs whereas ornithologists face deterioration of their study sites. In practice certain key groups have much greater power and ease of access to decision making and conflict is often either unresolved or settled privately in favour of the more powerful interests involved in a particular policy, plan or scheme (Richardson and Jordan 1979).

The wider planning system: local, national and European

Water and local authority planning

The success of water planning – whether social needs are met – is fundamentally related to the integration of water planning with local authority responsibilities for land use planning including the planning of housing, hospitals, roads and recreation.

The potential for close integration of land use and water planning is greater in Scotland than in England and Wales, where problems abound not just owing to the separation of water services into independent and autonomous Water Authorities but also because the local authority planning function is itself split between Districts with local control and Counties with a strategic function (Williams, A. 1977). The most basic point of integration is at the local authority structure planning stage – although local authorities also have a central role in emergency and disaster planning – where the County Council is sketching the future of its area, into which local District plans will then fit and on which will be based all subsequent land use development control decisions.

When preparing plans for water supply extension, sewerage replacement and recreation developments, Water Authorities must, in theory, consult and 'have regard to' the structure plan of the relevant area (Water Act 1973, Section 24(8)). In practice few Counties had completed their structure plans, required under the Town and Country Planning Act 1971, by the time Section 24 planning commenced in 1975 so that basic information for the water planning exercise, such as population projections, was not available. This involved separate investigations by the Authorities, thus duplicating research (Payne 1978).

There is undoubtedly conflict between the requirement for Water Authorities to be financially self-sufficient and their duty to provide water services such as water supply and sewerage (Simkins 1974). The danger of poor integration in these circumstances is that the Water Authority, in deciding priorities for water services based on financial considerations, will prejudice land use planning decisions made by both Counties and Districts based on wider social considerations. However, these latter institutions in theory have absolute power over land use and in practice have direct democratic responsibilities to their electorates (Cordle and Willetts 1976). Nevertheless, many District Councils have little expertise in water fields but Water Authority attempts to curtail their expenditure within the agency arrangements for sewerage in the interests of budgetary control have aroused opposition for fear of undermining the democratic autonomy of the elected Councils (Smith and Simkins 1975).

The essential ingredient for smooth operation is liaison and coordination. Water Authorities require basic information on housing priority areas, industrial developments requiring pollution treatment capacity and recreation development plans, all of which only District or County Councils can provide. There is no statutory duty to establish coordination committees between Water Authorities and local authorities, as there is between regional health authorities and local government, and Water Authorities have been reluctant to formalise liaison in this way (Simkins 1974). Informal liaison, however, is hampered by the differences in boundaries between Water Authorities and Counties and Districts and by the need for communication at both levels of local government and at both headquarters and divisional Water Authority levels (Capner 1979). The role of the local authority nominees to Water Authorities should be crucial to liaison yet these members appear to have relatively little influence on Water Authority decisions (Payne 1978) and indeed are encouraged not to see their role as representatives of their constituent Councils but members of the corporate Water Authority (Okun 1977). Given the size and financial power of the Water Authorities, and their problematic role as suppliers of services on a cost-effective basis, it is not surprising that there are continuing problems of integrating local authority planning and Water Authority planning (Williams, A. 1977) despite the Water Authorities initiating elaborate liaison systems, with specialist planning staff, to counterbalance their engineering dominance (North West Water Authority 1976a).

Water in national economic planning

Financial allocations to the water industry and hence to water planning involve political decisions of the highest importance since they affect the level of government expenditure which is an area of fierce public debate. All such expenditure must be authorised by parliamentary resolution and although Parliament does not directly approve either the total or the composition of local authority expenditure, government influence on such expenditure is powerful.

In theory decisions on public expenditure are part of a national annual review of total future public expenditure based on comprehensive surveys of existing plans and the need for changes, covering both the year immediately ahead and the three succeeding years; plans for years farthest ahead are the least firm. In the first stage, civil servants analyse all existing expenditure and possible changes, coordinated by the interdepartmental Public Expenditure Survey Committee of civil servants chaired by the Treasury. The analysis provides ministers with information on the state of existing plans, the amendments proposed by government departments and their rationale, and possible economies should the necessity arise. The financial plans of the nationalised industries, including the water industry in England and Wales, are reviewed in parallel to the evaluation of direct government expenditure.

In the second stage of the review ministers reach collective decisions on both total future expenditure and the allocation to the various departmental programmes, given the prospects for the national economy over the period covered. Ministers have to weigh priorities between programmes, perhaps between water and hospitals, taking into account the annual consultations with local authorities and nationalised industries. In the third stage a White Paper is published detailing the government expenditure plans and the government informs its departments, the nationalised industries and the Water Authorities of the approved level of their investment programmes for the coming years.

In practice the government expenditure review procedure is much more haphazard because fluctuations in the national economy can necessitate sudden alteration of expenditure patterns. This can be in the form of cuts or accelerated investment and naturally these make long-term water planning extremely difficult.

Central government controls directly only the capital expenditure of local government, and hence the Regional and Island Councils' expenditure on water, mainly through control over borrowing. Local authorities' power to raise rates gives them some independence from government financing but in practice local authorities both take account of government guidance through a continuous process of consultation, for example with the Convention of Scottish Local Authorities, and also their revenue expenditure is profoundly influenced by the annually determined level of the rate support grant.

Complementing the annual budgeting, which is necessarily concerned with changes at the margin of expenditure, further reviews examine the overall priorities of government. In addition each government department is responsible for evaluating the value-for-money of its expenditure. A further process involves the control of approved expenditure using strict expenditure cash limits, a finite contingency fund for over-expenditure, and close computer-based monitoring of central government, local authority and nationalised industry expenditure against forecast 'profiles' for each quarter of the year.

Therefore the expenditure of both the Scottish Local Authorities and the English and Welsh Water Authorities is very tightly controlled by government and Parliament via the Scottish Office, the Department of the Environment and the Ministry of Agriculture, Fisheries and Food. The process of evaluation appears systematic but arbitrary expenditure level changes are not uncommon and wholesale re-evaluation is rare. Nevertheless the Public Accounts and the Expenditure Committees of the House of Commons have key roles in scrutinising public expenditure and examining ministers, civil servants and others as to their expenditure plans and priorities, thereby maintaining some democratic control other than ministerial control over how much is spent on water and other public services in Britain.

The developing role of the European Economic Community

As the Community and Britain's relations with her fellow members mature so the role of the Community in the water planning field increases (National Water Council 1978a). The Community, firstly, can give grants from its budget to promote schemes meeting Community objectives. Secondly, directives are issued to member countries with which they are obliged to comply and these currently concern the quality of drinking water, certain forms of river pollution and the quality of bathing beaches. These directives set standards, and in this respect run contrary to British water industry tradition (Chs 3 and 4) but, among other motives, the Community is concerned lest certain countries allow low environmental standards and thereby attract industrial development and growth in unfair competition from those forced or hoping to set higher standards.

Evaluation

A proper evaluation of the effectiveness of the water planning system in Britain can only follow a detailed examination of the different functional areas in the water field in the subsequent Chapters. However some institutional problems have been identified in this Chapter, concerning both the patterns of responsibilities and the areal units used in the water planning system, which will focus our thoughts when reviewing subsequent material.

First, we must question whether the water planning system is sufficiently accountable to its public, especially in England and Wales where the regional structure of large multifunctional agencies includes neither direct local nor direct parliamentary accountability. Secondly, the research and advisory agencies at a national level appear to be insufficiently coordinated and, despite the large number of national agencies, there is no national water policy of any substance. Thirdly, the interest and pressure groups are themselves inherently poorly coordinated, and coalitions between groups to increase their power and influence are rare. As a result many of these organisations lack precision and force in their attacks on the policy-making and executive agencies within the water planning system. Finally, the integration of the water planning system with the wider planning system appears to be imperfect. This concerns particularly the land use planning work at local authority level where conflict can arise, partly owing to the mis-match of administrative areas, which highlights the potential structural advantages in the Scottish system. Also the annual government budgeting system appears to provide a major source of inefficiency and weakness in the water planning process which requires long time horizons to be truly effective.

Selected further reading (for full bibliography see pp. 254-66)

For events leading to the Water Act 1973 see:

Okun, D.A. 1977. *Regionalization of water management*. London: Applied Science Publishers.
Jordan, A. G., J. J. Richardson and R. H. Kimber 1977. 'The origins of the Water Act 1973'. *Public Administration* **55**, 317–34.

Deficiencies in water planning in England and Wales as seen by the government are described in:

Department of the Environment, Welsh Office, Ministry of Agriculture, Fisheries and Food 1977. *The water industry in England and Wales: the next steps*. London: HMSO.

The above three items should be studied in conjunction with the relevant Acts of Parliament:

Water Act 1973.
Local Government (Scotland) Act 1974.

These and other Acts are most readily found in *Current Law Statutes* (London: Sweet and Maxwell) for the appropriate year.
    The present water industry is well described in the first of the following, while the second was instrumental in recommending the present structure. The third is a critical independent analysis.

National Water Council 1978a. *Water industry review 1978*. London: NWC.
Department of the Environment 1973. *The new water industry: management and structures*. London: HMSO (The 'Ogden Report').
Sewell, W. R. D., and L. R. Barr 1978. 'Water administration in England and Wales: impacts of reorganisation'. *Water Resources Bulletin* **14**(2), 337–48.

For a useful analysis of the role of pressure groups in water planning and other environmental fields see:

Richardson, J. J., and A. G. Jordan 1979. *Governing under pressure. The policy process in a post-parliamentary democracy*. Oxford: Martin Robertson.

A critical analysis of the relationship between the water industry, local government and town and county planning can be found in:

Payne, B. J. 1978. *Water authorities and planning authorities: a study of developing relationships.* Department of Town and Country Planning Occasional Paper No. 1. Manchester: University of Manchester.
Drudy, P. J. (ed.) 1977. *Water planning and the regions.* Regional Studies Association Discussion paper 9. London: RSA.

3 Planning water supplies

Britain has one of the most advanced and highly developed public water supply systems in the world which serves about 99% of dwellings in England and Wales and only slightly less in Scotland. These proportions are similar to the Netherlands but much higher, for example, than the United States where 75% are served by public supplies. Britain's public supplies are generally reliable and of a high quality and most of industry is serviced by the system although many firms also have their own private water supplies.

Despite these successes there are still considerable problems. Protecting the quality of water supplies, and thereby public health, is traditionally regarded as the top priority of the British water supply industry. Yet despite the mid-nineteenth-century public health revolution and the more recent refinement of methods of protecting and treating water supplies, improving drinking water quality standards enormously, public health risks cannot be completely eradicated. Clean water is becoming more scarce in places where it is needed most and it is increasingly difficult to ensure that the quality of drinking water is adequately safeguarded.

Water has become more expensive in real terms and water supplies are a large item of national expenditure. Because of its age much of Britain's water distribution network requires expensive renewal. The economic and social costs of major water supply developments are also high, focussing attention on our society's profligate use of water. Thus the need for greater economy in water use is leading to a search for more efficient water using equipment in homes and factories and for financial incentives to use water sparingly. With the increasing real costs of water supplies and the growth in conflicts about the use of water and associated land, the social and political acceptability of establish water supply practices is changing, placing new stresses upon the water supply planning system.

Rainfall deficiencies periodically cause water supply emergencies causing serious though rarely lasting disruption. Whilst some areas of Britain are more vulnerable to drought than others, the 1975–76 drought showed that water supplies can be maintained without undue hardship even in extreme conditions. However, droughts raise difficult questions about standards of reliability of water supplies and how much society is willing to pay for security of supplies.

Britain's water resources are basically adequate, especially in Scotland. However, availability problems arise largely because of the inverse distribution of resources and population and because of the growing shortage of cheap, accessible, clean water sources. Overcoming these difficulties not only raises technical problems but also legal, social, financial and political issues concerning how water supply services are best organised, administered and financed. In the water supply field, as in the water field as a whole, these issues include whether or not the water supply industry requires predominantly central or regional control, and whether or not the financial resources allocated to it are used properly to achieve the correct objectives. Definition of what is correct varies from time to time, but it usually involves the priorities to be given to social, economic and political planning objectives such as economic efficiency, profitability or equity.

Ultimately society is responsible for articulating its needs and for providing guidance upon how much should be spent upon our water supplies. The Water Authorities spend about 40% of their total annual budget directly on the maintenance, improvement and extension of water supplies and the development of new sources. Taking expenditure on the revenue and capital accounts together, this amounted to about £670millions in 1977–78. To this must be added an annual expenditure of about £160millions by the independent Water Companies and about £40millions by the Scottish regional water authorities. Because effluent disposal, pollution control and water supply are increasingly interdependent services, the total costs of providing clean water supplies are even higher than these figures suggest.

Britain's water resources

The basic problem of water supply planning is to provide water, of an acceptable quality, in the right place at the right time, as economically as possible. Society requires a continuous supply of water but water resources are derived from rain which varies as to when and where it falls. Concentrations of urban population frequently produce demands well in excess of local resources, and demands during a dry spell commonly exceed supplies. Furthermore, the availability of clean water for supply close to cities is reduced because some of this water is needed for effluent dilution and disposal.

Regional availability and need

There is no intrinsic shortage of fresh water in Britain. Assessments of the balance between total rainfall and runoff and total water abstraction or consumption show that, for the foreseeable future, total rainfall and runoff are likely to be adequate to meet demands (Water Resources Board 1973). However, the gross yield of Britain's water resources presents an over-optimistic estimate of available resources, while total water demands present an equally misleading pessimistic view of the need for extra resources.

About half of the rain falling over England and Wales is lost to the

Table 3.1 Regional water availability and need.

1 region	2 average annual rainfall mm	3 average runoff (Net resources)	4 population 000s	5 total abstraction 1974 Ml/d	6 ratio of col. 3 to col. 5	7 total abstraction minus thermal electricity generating abstractions 1974 Ml/d	8 ratio of col. 3 to col. 7
North West	1 243	33 200	7 052	6 107	5·4	4 959	6·7
Northumbrian	885	12 800	2 672	1 058	12·1	1 058	12·1
Severn Trent	767	19 000	8 189	8 427	2·2	4 128	4·6
Yorkshire	836	17 700	4 534	5 408	3·3	1 994	8·9
Anglian	613	9 200	4 636	2 200	4·2	1 762	5·2
Thames	705	8 300	11 775	4 090	2·1	3 665	2·3
Southern	778	9 300	3 760	1 482	6·3	1 441	6·5
Wessex	866	10 800	2 230	882	12·2	879	12·2
South West	1 180	21 500	1 347	693	31·0	531	40·4
Welsh	1 307	49 600	3 000	8 419	5·9	3 362	14·8
Average	905	19 000	4 919	3 877	4·9	2 378	7·9
Total	–	190 000	49 195	38 766	–	23 779	–
Scotland	1 419	200 000	5 217	4 236*	47·2	3 535*	56·6

Sources: Water Resources Board 1973, Department of the Environment, Water Data Unit 1976, 1977, Scottish Development Department 1973, Scottish Information Office, Undated.

Note: Data in Cols 1 and 2 are for regions with boundaries as originally proposed in 1971 and on which WRB data are based. The eventual boundaries, for which data in the remaining columns represent, were only slightly different.

* = 1973 figure.

Ml/d = Megalitres per day.

atmosphere through evaporation but the remainder still yields an average annual runoff of 190 000 megalitres per day (Ml/d) (Table 3.1). Only about 25% of rain falling over Scotland is evaporated resulting in Scotland's total average annual runoff slightly exceeding that for England and Wales, despite having only half the land area and less than one ninth of the population of England and Wales/ Although there are regional variations in England and Wales public water supplies are derived in roughly equal proportions from rivers (32%), upland reservoirs (35%) and groundwater sources (33%), with private abstractions being mainly from surface and groundwater sources (National Water Council 1978a). Scottish public supplies are taken almost exclusively (96%) from natural lochs, reservoirs and rivers. In 1974 total water abstractions in England and Wales were 38 766 Ml/d or about 20% of average runoff. Water abstractions include water which is re-used and the amount of water actually consumed is considerably less. About half the water used by industry is for cooling purposes only and, like most of the water used by the electricity generating sector, it is passed back to rivers enabling re-use further downstream. In 1973 Scotland's total water abstractions only amounted to about 2% of its average runoff, making Scotland rich in water compared with England and Wales. However, water transfer between Scotland and England and Wales would be prohibitively expensive.

Spatial and temporal inequalities

The comparison of total water availability and water use presents a picture which, in terms of the actual margin between water supplies and water demand, is more apparent than real for many British regions. When spatial and temporal inequalities in water availability and use, and the actual levels of regional development of water resources for supplies are allowed for, the picture is less optimistic.

Complications arise because of the uneven areal distribution of rainfall and runoff on the one hand, and water abstraction and consumption on the other (Table 3.1). In the drier parts of the Anglian region residual rainfall is about twenty times less than in the North West and Wales. Not surprisingly, even when variations in the size of regions are allowed for, average annual runoff is higher in the uplands of the north and west and lower in the lowlands of the south and east (Smith 1972). Regional variations in water abstraction and consumption are related to population distribution and to the distribution of electricity generating industry abstractions.

Water availability in terms of average annual runoff can be expressed as a ratio of water abstraction (Table 3.1). The regional ratios show that the eastern and central regions including the Thames, Anglian, Yorkshire and Severn Trent regions, are 'water-scarce', whilst the remainder are comparatively 'water-rich'. However, the large re-usable abstractions of the electricity generating industry do not represent an absolute call on water resources. If they are deducted from the total abstraction figures of each region (Table 3.1, col. 8) a more realistic ratio of water availability to water consumption can be calculated, making Yorkshire a comparatively 'water-rich' region whilst the North West and Southern regions become 'water-scarce'.

Variations in rainfall and runoff over time, and the occurrence of dry spells, further narrow the gap between water availability and use. The minimum runoff which can be expected during dry weather is much less than the average on which Table 3.1 is based. Runoff in a really dry month can, for example, be between only 6% and 20% of the average for that month depending on the region. Because the lowest runoff per km² occurs in the 'water-scarce' regions this further exacerbates their position. Water consumption, too, is variable over time, particularly from season to season. For example, the population of the Welsh region can temporarily increase by 25% through the influx of holiday-makers.

Levels of water resource development

At existing levels of water resource development only a small percentage of total available runoff is harnessed to our needs, and for economic reasons by no means all of the average runoff could be made available for water supplies. Without manmade water storage the only flow which could be relied upon for water supplies would be the minimum flow which occurs naturally after a long dry spell. By itself this cannot sustain more than a fraction of existing water use, and so the minimum flow has been increased by storing water from high natural flows and drawing upon it when flows are low. Water storage developed up until 1971 in England and Wales represented 19% of average runoff. Storage varies between 36% in the dry, populated Thames region, to only 12% in the South West. Dry weather flows can be built up by providing even more storage. However, whereas the lowest flows persist for only a short time and can be greatly increased by using a small volume of storage, successive additions to natural dry weather flows have to be supported by storage releases over successively longer periods and so require relatively greater volumes of storage to sustain them. Ultimately it becomes uneconomic or impracticable to control flow further in this way.

The margin between water availability and use in Britain is, therefore, surprisingly narrow and demands on some rivers are equal to, and some cases above, their natural dry weather flows. Water re-use is important because it eases the water supply position. Greater use is being made in Britain of lowland river abstractions and in this way effluents from sewage and industrial treatments plants may be re-used downstream after natural dilution, river self-purification and further water treatment. However, these practices raise new water quality problems.

Water quality and its public health significance

Water quality variations have both natural and human causes. In natural water, for example, calcium content varies with rock source giving different degrees of water softness and naturally occurring chemicals give water colour and taste. Water may be polluted by industrial or agricultural waste and, for example, many of Britain's lowland rivers are affected by human contamination (Fig. 4.1). Even water supply reservoirs may occasionally be affected by accidental pollution (North West Water Authority 1975). The public health significance of water quality has been recognised since the cholera outbreaks in the mid-nineteenth century were associated with sewage contaminating water supplies.

Water treatment.   The effectiveness of water treatment for the removal of pathogenic bacteria was recognised at the turn of the century. The concept of 'lines of defence' against contamination of water sources prior to public use was accepted in the 1940s. The first line of defence is to eliminate potential sources of contamination, followed by a second line which is long storage. Protection of water sources from the public to minimise contamination risks was widespread in the first half of the twentieth century, but increased public mobility and recreational activity now makes widespread public exclusion from gathering grounds problematic (see p. 176). Some bacteria are eliminated by storing water for up to 30 days and suspended solids, hardness and colour levels also all tend to fall. Clarification and filtration in which suspended material, including many pathogenic bacteria, are removed by filtering through sand, is a third line of defence. This is commonly followed by disinfection by chlorination or ozonisation. Other forms of treatment have been devised for particular types of water, for example water softness can be enhanced or reduced (Fish 1973). Scotland is fortunate in having many remote clean water sources requiring minimum treatment before public use but elsewhere water treatment requirements are commonly more burdensome and the number of lines of defence used varies according to the pollution risk and to the age of treatment plants.

Water treatment is becoming more elaborate and the associated water quality and treatment research effort undertaken, notably by the Water Research Centre, is now considerable. Such research is necessary because of the likely growth in dependence on polluted lowland river sources for public supplies, as demands grow and upland sources become more difficult to develop. Already river water commonly containing domestic and industrial effluents provides nearly one third of the total abstractions for potable water supplies in England and Wales and London's potable water supplies are derived largely from the polluted rivers Thames and Lee.

Health risks.   There is also growing concern in the water industry about new public health risks (Bell 1978). These are of two types: those which are now recognised through advances in medical and water quality knowledge, and those which have been created by the post-1945 chemical industry revolution.

Research in Britain and abroad reveals that death from cardiovascular disease is associated with water softness. Recent research in British towns shows that there is a significantly greater number of deaths from the disease in towns supplied with soft water compared with towns using hard water, although there is certainly no suggestion that this is a major cause of the disease (National Water Council 1978a).

Concern is growing in the water industry about hundreds of new organic chemical compounds, many of them synthetic, which are manufactured and introduced into the environment annually, producing a possible new threat to drinking water quality (Central Water Planning Unit 1976a). Concern is greatest for highly urbanised and industrialised catchments, such as the Thames, where polluted rivers are used for public supplies. Organic compounds of both natural and synthetic origin may enter rivers in countless different ways. Rainfall conveys organic substances in the atmosphere to receiving rivers and sewage effluent is a major source of organic pollutants. Other sources include runoff from land treated with pesticides and weed-killing sprays and from vehicle oil washed off motorways. It is not yet possible to evaluate accurately the health risks associated with organic substances in water. Sewage and industrial treatment and water supply treatment are not designed to remove such chemicals: indeed treatment chemicals such as chlorine themselves react with some natural organic substances to produce potentially hazardous substances. Effective methods for monitoring organic pollutants in water are not yet available.

Many organic compounds have been shown to be carcinogenic and there is some evidence that long-term exposure to low concentrations of some of them is an important factor in some chronic diseases (Fielding and Packham 1977). Until the levels of concentration of organic compounds in British rivers can be determined, and the significance of long-term ingestion of low levels of each compound and their combinations can be found, clear conclusions are not possible. Therefore, it is now difficult to demonstrate that water supplies taken from a river in a highly developed catchment are safe for long-term consumption (Okun 1977). The Thames Water Authority is seeking comprehensive information on the composition of wastes from industries in order to evaluate problems in its area.

Significant increases in nitrate concentrations in many groundwater and river water sources used for public supplies in Britain have been detected. Evidence points firmly to farmland as a major source but natural nitrate production by mineralisation and atmospheric fixation and through rain-water leaching may be as important as fertilisers (Hollis 1979). There is little firm evidence on which to quantify health hazards. The main risk is of methaemoglobinaemia in bottle-fed infants, of which there have been about ten cases in this country since 1950, and there is also a possibility of increased cancer incidence. Experimental nitrate-removal plants have been installed in the Anglian region and whilst a 40% reduction has been achieved, this form of water treatment, like all others, adds to the cost of providing wholesome supplies.

The social context of water supply planning

Public health requirements are likely to continue to be a crucial influence on water supply planning. Fortunately Britain no longer faces the water-related disease problems it once had but the maintenance and improvement of standards of potable water quality and supply reliability remain a considerable challenge. This is so because of the continually changing health context, high public expectations and the pursuit of higher standards at a time when clean water supplies are increasingly costly.

As well as maintaining and improving quality and reliability to meet its legal 'sufficiency' and 'wholesomeness' water supply obligations (Water Act 1973, Section 11), the water supply industry also has to cope with rising levels of water consumption by existing consumers and is legally required to provide supplies for new consumers. The pressure of demand on existing supplies varies considerably with pauses and surges in population and industrial growth and patterns of demand also change with regional shifts in population, the diffusion of water-using innovations and changes in standards of living.

Society's evolving attitudes towards public involvement in the water supply field are demonstrated by the historical development of legislation and public water supplies. An historical view helps to explain current attitudes and policies and directions of rationalisation in the water supply industry.

Legislation and the development of public water supplies

Water supplies in Britain have been developed both through the efforts of private riparian owners and entrepreneurs and through organised public effort. The present public water supply planning system has grown through legislative change which promoted the replacement of private by public enterprise and through rationalisation and reorganisation.

The nineteenth century: public health and public intervention. Advances in public health care and the growth of local authority water supply functions were the main developments of the nineteenth century (Dracup 1973, Mukhopadhyay 1975). The concentration of population and industry during the century caused pollution of local drinking water sources resulting in widespread cholera epidemics. Edwin Chadwick's survey of 1842 exposed appalling sanitary conditions in British towns (Smith 1972). The 'Great Sanitary Awakening' led to the Waterworks Clauses Act 1847 and the first Public Health Act in 1848. The former Act included provisions for protecting drinking water and was the main water supply legislation in England and Wales until 1945. The Public Health Act 1848 allowed the creation of local health boards in towns to control and provide water supplies. Local authorities were encouraged to extend their water supply function by the Public

Health Acts 1875 and 1878. During the 1830s 11 municipal water supply undertakings existed but by 1878 there were 78 and these grew in number to over 780 by 1914. Local authority undertakings succeeded where private companies failed to provide a wholesome supply for the poor.

Progress in the towns was not matched in rural areas where, because of low population densities, the cost per head of piped supplies was high. The 1878 Act, which included piped water to rural areas, proved to be largely unsuccessful because local parishes were unable to shoulder the financial burden. Whereas by 1914 nearly all towns had piped supplies, only 4784 out of 12 869 rural parishes were in a similar position.

Nineteenth-century developments in Scotland paralleled those in England and Wales. Legislation empowering local authorities to supply water appeared first in various Police Acts and the first Scottish Public Health Act in 1867. Private companies failed because they supplied polluted water and because of lack of finance, and nearly all were replaced by 1900.

During the nineteenth century clean water sources became hard to find and towns like Manchester, Birmingham and Glasgow turned to more distant high quality upland sources in the Pennines, Wales, Lake District and the Scottish uplands. One effect was to reduce reliance upon urban river sources so removing incentives for pollution prevention. However, undeveloped sources soon became scarce and competition for them grew.

1900–1945: the scramble for water rights.   Prior to 1945, public water supplies were developed by towns buying land, and thereby water rights, under or adjacent to rivers or lakes and over aquifers. However, parochial attitudes and the common law combined to produce increased competition as water sources grew more scarce and the towns, each acting independently, scrambled to develop them. An inefficient and unfair pattern of water supply resulted. Towns claimed sources but failed to use them to full capacity whilst other, smaller localities, were often without water supplies. The need for coordinated efforts became clear (Dracup 1973).

Development of water sources and abstractions by water suppliers also began to conflict with the interests of industrial water users and riparian owners. In 1910 a private parliamentary Bill was promoted to restrict water suppliers' powers to protect private interests, again underlining the need for a central water management authority representing all interests. Government plans to introduce new legislation were curtailed by the 1914–18 war and despite recommendations of successive Advisory Water Committees emphasising that the common law impeded public water supply development, the government delayed new legislation until 1939 when its passage was again interrupted by war.

Legislation in Scotland also did not provide adequate powers for the public acquisition of water rights and local authorities resorted to private legislation to develop water supplies. In Scotland particularly, many rural areas were not connected to a public supply. However, during the period rural water supplies eventually received special government attention, especially after the 1934 drought.

1945 onwards: rationalisation, river basin management and regionalisation.
The post-1945 era was one of coordination and planning (Dracup 1973). The Water Act 1945, concerning England and Wales only, finally recognised the need for a national water policy and a coordinated approach to water management (Mitchell 1971, Craine 1969). The multiplicity of water under-takings led to failure to reap economies of scale, to conflicts of interest and to general confusion. The Act empowered the Minister of Health to order amal-gamation of water supply undertakings which by 1945 numbered 1186. Initially regrouping was attempted by persuasion but this largely failed still leaving 1030 water supply undertakings by 1963. However, under more aggressive policies numbers declined to 172 by 1972 (Okun 1977). The Water (Scotland) Act 1946 gave similar powers to the Secretary of State for Scotland and provided a framework for water management in Scotland until 1968 although progress towards amalgamation was slow. In 1944 there were 210 water undertakings in Scotland. Although in Scotland private water companies disappeared in 1946, by 1968 there were still 199 water supply undertakings. Advisory Water Committees were established in both Scotland and England and Wales after these Acts but, like their predecessors, they lacked executive power.

Following suggestions made as early as 1867, the River Boards Act 1948 formed 32 River Boards for the management of rivers in England and Wales, from source to mouth. Although Catchment Boards had been established in 1930 for land drainage purposes, the 1948 Act was a major advance because it recognised the sense of using river basins as management units. By placing entire catchment areas under one authority, thereby recognising the impor-tance of hydrological boundaries as natural administrative units for water and by reducing the number of authorities involved, the Act enhanced oppor-tunities for coordinated management of land drainage, pollution, fisheries and navigation interests. However, the 1948 Act still suffered from common law barriers to effective water supply planning. Water supply development was excluded from River Board duties because it was believed that this would conflict with the rights of riparian owners.

Common law water rights were modified under the Water Act 1945 and abstraction from aquifers was licensed and controlled. However, it was not until the Water Resources Act 1963 in England and Wales that riparian water supply rights were removed completely by the establishment of a licensing system for all water taken from surface and underground sources (Rees 1978). The 1963 Act replaced the River Boards with 27 River Authorities based on similar river basin boundaries. The legislation was concerned primarily with the urgent problem of making sufficient quantities of water available and River Authorities were allowed to develop water supplies for water undertakings. Anticipating the legal and practical problems which the shift of water rights in favour of the public interest might cause, the Act also required River Authorities to determine minimum acceptable flows on rivers to safeguard riparian interests. The 1963 Act also created the Water Resources Board as successor to the Central Advisory Water Committee. The Board had no executive powers and was responsible for advising on and coordinating regional and national water supply policy. The terms of reference of the Water Resources Board also excluded pollution prevention, thereby reducing the value of its national water strategy produced just before its abolition (Okun 1977). The lack of regard for water quality proved to be a major weakness of the 1963 Act and the recognition of the inseparable nature of the management of water supply and river pollution control formed the rationale for the Water Act 1973.

The Water (Scotland) Act 1967 recognised the failure of water supply undertakings regrouping policy in Scotland. Thirteen Regional Water Boards and a Central Scotland Water Development Board were established in 1968, the latter to provide bulk water supplies to the populous central lowlands. The new Boards were organised according to river basin boundaries and the reorganisation resulted in improvements in Scottish water services. However, the Regional Water Boards were replaced in 1975, following the Local Government (Scotland) Act 1974, when water supply as well as sewerage and sewage disposal functions were given to the new Regional and Island Councils.

Current social attitudes towards water supplies

British society has a high degree of confidence in its tap water. This confidence, however, breeds indifference and a remarkable lack of sophistication in public knowledge about and regard for water. The community is accustomed to ubiquitous, abundant and pure water supplies and experience has led most of us to expect them to be reliable and cheap. Ironically, whilst the public image of water supplies reflects favourably upon the work of water engineers and scientists, it has also led to water supplies to be largely taken for granted.

Public awareness of, and debate about, water as a limited resource is rarely sustained for more than a few weeks after droughts. Discoloration or abnormal taste or odour, which occasionally occurs in some areas, is one of the few events which make customers aware of their water supplies. Life-styles are geared to almost limitless water supplies and only in high water consumption, cost-sensitive industries does sustained economising occur. Rising standards of living have led to present levels of per capita consumption being viewed as a basic necessity even though consumption is substantially above the levels necessary to maintain public health.

British society's generally low regard for water is partly explained by its traditional cheapness – under 20p per tonne. Prior to 1974 the cost of water to the consumer was kept low through government rate support grant subsidies and outdated accounting systems which failed to provide adequately for renewal of treatment and distribution systems. Subsidies were removed in 1974, causing the cost of water to the consumer to increase dramatically. This caused great public concern and even anger in Wales where price rises were steepest. In addition, public concern about water shortages is rarely tempered with a proper appreciation of the opportunity-costs of insuring against extreme drought, say in terms of forgoing new hospitals.

Water has an exaggerated reputation for purity, both at the points where it is gathered and at the tap. It is taken for granted that water supplies are bacteriologically and chemically pure as well as wholesome. Few recognise the growing range of potential health hazards which may threaten drinking water quality. Fluoridation is one of the few cases where public awareness of drinking water quality has been raised. In some areas, fluoride is added to public supplies to protect children's teeth but this practice has become intensely controversial. Some believe that fluoride increases cancer incidence and so the legal authority of the water supply industry to add fluoride is challenged. Despite continuing public disquiet there is, however, no firm evidence that fluoride does increase cancer incidence (Bell 1978).

Until recently in Britain there have been no formal drinking water quality standards, nor has there been significant public pressure to adopt them. Although 'wholesomeness' is generally interpreted as water which is clear, palatable and safe, beyond this the term remains largely undefined allowing administrative discretion and perhaps greater sensitivity in matching treatment standards to risks. Since 1970, however, water supply authorities have adopted British government and World Health Organisation drinking water quality standards, and there is increasing pressure from the European Economic Community to formalise public water supply quality standards.

Public opposition to reservoir proposals.   Water supply reservoir proposals have attracted considerable public opposition especially since the late 1950s. Such proposals have provoked passionate local environmental disputes, especially where farm land or remote but attractive valleys might be flooded. In England in the late 1960s the eventually successful proposal to build Cow Green reservoir in Upper Teesdale and the rejected proposal to build a dam at Swincombe on Dartmoor generated bitter disputes. Now plans for a reservoir at Roadford, an alternative to Swincombe, are being vigorously opposed by preservationists and similar opposition has developed to the Broad Oak reservoir proposals in Kent. However, the greatest ferocity was created by proposals to build, in Wales, reservoirs to supply English cities. Liverpool Corporation's Tryweryn scheme went ahead although sabotage attempts were made in 1962 and 1963. Plaid Cymru, the Welsh nationalist party, tried to prevent the building of Clywedog Dam in the 1960s by buying up land and explosions occurred at the dam site (Broady 1977). Bitter reactions, fuelled by the political nature of the controversy, were also experienced in the Dulas and Senni valleys in the early 1970s, and more recently over plans to raise the height of the Craig Goch dam in mid-Wales (Plaid Cymru 1976). Apart from political motivations, public opposition to new water schemes appears to have grown because of increased environmental awareness and a growing interest in preserving land under the threat of development.

The demand for water supply services

Demands for investment in water supply services arise in several ways. Investment is needed to extend water supplies to new housing estates and factories and on average the cost of providing water mains and sewers for a new house is about £1000 (National Water Council 1978a). Providing 'first-time' public water supplies to the small proportion of unconnected houses in the country is more costly, although the number of such schemes is small. Investment may also be required to cope with increases in per capita water consumption or to increase reliability of supplies, perhaps by developing links between water sources in a region, and for additional water treatment works. Finally renewal is necessary as the water supply system ages.

The demand for water supplies in Britain is met mainly by piped public supplies of potable water or by licensed abstraction direct from water sources. Some industry also receives a small amount of piped public non-potable water. Public supplies are either unmetered or metered. Unmetered consumption is charged for according to the rateable value of properties and not directly according to the quantity consumed, as is metered consumption (Fig. 3.1). Unmetered potable public supplies are used by households and often by commercial premises such as shops and offices. However, practice varies according to the policies adopted by former water supply undertakings and in some areas commercial premises may be metered. Industry consumes metered potable public supplies in canteens and lavatories as well as in manufacturing products like food where high quality water is essential. However, industry abstracts much of its water directly from source, often treating it before use.

Water abstractions.   In Scotland, except for powers derived from the Spray Irrigation (Scotland) Act 1964, there is no general abstraction legislation and therefore no accurate data on abstractions. However, for England and Wales estimates of quantities of inland water abstracted under licence are available although not in a consistent form before 1971 (Table 3.2). These data indicate that total abstractions actually declined between 1971 and 1975.

The fall in total abstractions is mainly due to a marked decline in power station abstraction. This is because of changes in the location of power stations which are being transferred to coastal sites and to increased water recycling as a consequence of changes in water cooling technology. Abstractions to public supplies have increased fairly steadily since at least 1961 (Central Water Planning Unit 1976b, 1977). However, during the 1975–76 drought supplies were restricted and abstraction declined. Direct industrial

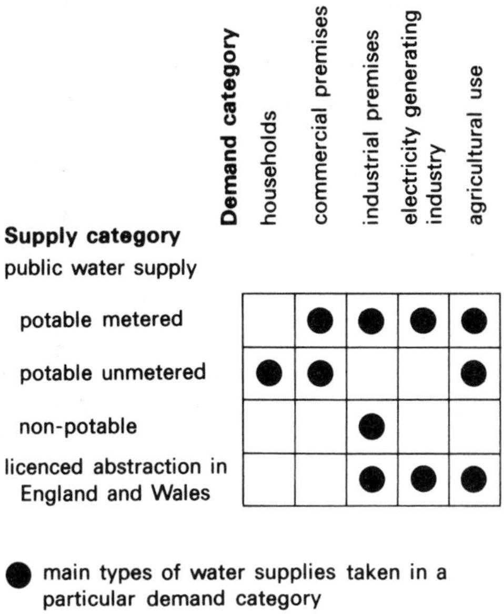

Demand category

Supply category	households	commercial premises	industrial premises	electricity generating industry	agricultural use
public water supply					
potable metered		●	●	●	●
potable unmetered	●	●			●
non-potable			●		
licenced abstraction in England and Wales			●	●	●

● main types of water supplies taken in a particular demand category

Figure 3.1 Major categories of water supply and demand.

Table 3.2 Abstractions of water in England and Wales 1971–76.

Year	Public water supplies Ml/d	Power stations Ml/d	Other industry Ml/d	Agriculture Ml/d	Total Ml/d
1971	14 400	19 200	7 800	200	41 600
1972	14 900	18 200	7 600	200	40 900
1973	15 200	17 800	7 400	200	40 600
1974	15 200	15 000	7 000	200	37 400
1975	15 400	13 700	6 600	300	36 000
1976	15 000	13 200	6 600	300	35 100

Source: National Water Council 1978a.
Ml/d = Megalitres per day.

abstractions also show a clear recent downward trend. This is owing mainly to changes in industrial processes, sluggish economic growth, increased effluent controls, increased efficiency and water economy stimulated by the introduction of licences in 1969, to higher charges and to water shortages.

Abstractions for agriculture have grown and are important because they tend to be seasonally and spatially concentrated. The increase in land area under spray irrigation in the 1950s began to upset the balance of water supply and demand, especially in the south and east. However, the Water Resources

Act 1963, which established abstraction licences and charges, caused a decline in the total area irrigated from 1965 onwards (Porter 1978).

The demand for public water supplies.   Apart from the temporary impact of the 1975–76 drought on water consumption there has been a fairly steady growth in unmetered public water supplies in England and Wales since 1955.

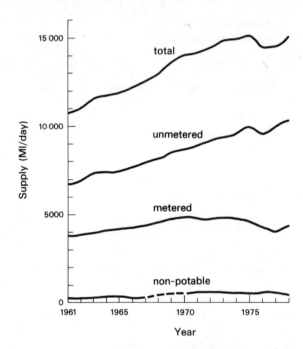

Figure 3.2   Public water supplies in England and Wales 1961 to 1978. (Full records were not compiled for non-potable water in 1968 and 1969.)

Consumption of metered water supplies has, however, been more irregular since 1970 falling to levels first reached in the mid-1960s (Fig. 3.2). Data for 1978 show, however, that the decline in consumption of metered water supplies begun in the 1970s may have ceased. Public water supply data for Scotland show similar trends with a growth in consumption between 1969 and 1975 but with the metered consumption component declining marginally after 1973 (Department of the Environment, Water Data Unit 1977). The irregular pattern of metered consumption in Britain may well be due to slower growth in industrial consumption since 1970 and to the same factors which may explain industrial water abstraction trends.

Demand for unmetered supplies is related to population growth and living standards. In both Scotland and England and Wales per capita demand for unmetered water has grown steadily reflecting both population increase and higher living standards. Now, however, national population growth has declined to replacement level. In Scotland per capita unmetered consumption is substantially higher than in England and Wales: 274 and 201 litres per head per day (l/h/d) respectively in 1975. This is not due to higher standards of living in Scotland but may well be related to higher levels of leakage from the water distribution systems.

Consumption of unmetered public water supplies is divided amongst four main categories, including household and commercial consumption, water which cannot be accounted for and water used for miscellaneous purposes. Of the 201 l/h/d of unmetered potable supplies consumed in England and Wales, it is estimated that between 100 and 120 l/h/d are consumed by households, although there is evidence of large variations in consumption between households (Central Water Planning Unit 1975). Recent research shows that lavatory flushing accounts for about 37% of average household consumption in Britain and a further 34% is consumed in baths, showers and wash-basins. Consumption of water by dishwashers, automatic washing machines and garden sprinklers, some of which may be considered luxury water uses, is relatively small on average for most households although it is significant at the aggregate regional and national levels (Central Water Planning Unit 1977).

A further 20 l/h/d of unmetered potable supplies are consumed by commercial premises, and about one l/h/d is consumed in fire-fighting and street cleansing. Water which cannot be accounted for is estimated to be between 60 and 90 l/h/d. Much of this water is lost through leakage in water mains, either through faulty joints or through bursts, and about 25% of public supplies are lost to the consumer in this way. In older residential areas, where mains have aged and bursts are frequent, leakage may be as high as 50–60% of the total water put into the public supplies (Rees 1977b). Methods of leak detection and repair are not new, yet expenditure in this area should be increased until the costs of saving additional water units equal the costs of creating extra water supplies. For economic as well as technical reasons some leakage will always occur but Water Authorities can hardly expect to encourage consumers to save water when their own leakage rates are unacceptably high.

Investigations of metered water use by industry have been either for a range of industries in one region or for one industry across the country. Water for cooling purposes accounted for about two-thirds of all water used by industry in southeast England in 1966, and inter-industry variations in water use are wide (Rees 1969, Herrington 1973). Of 158 food industry factories in England and Wales 149 had a mains supply, accounting for between 1 and 2% of public water supplies in 1975, with 70 abstracting water privately (Central Water Planning Unit 1976c).

Using extrapolation methods and estimates based upon the mid-points of ranges of alternative forecasts of the future, the Water Authorities now expect the demand for public water supplies to increase by about 42%

between 1975 and 2001. This is equivalent to an average annual growth rate of 1·3%, substantially lower than the 2·5% growth rate which occurred between 1961 and 1975 (National Water Council 1978a).

The hidden problem: ageing water mains.   An estimate of the total replacement cost of the water distribution system in England and Wales has totalled £8000millions (National Water Council 1978a). The problem of ageing water mains is not as serious as that for sewers which have suffered greater neglect, but thousands of miles of buried water mains are old, sometimes over 100 years old, and substandard. Already annual replacement costs are high and they are growing. The problems are worst in the conurbations such as the former Lancashire coalfield which was developed in the nineteenth century, and are often shown up by increases in bursts, heavy leakage and water discoloration. The renewal problem has crept up upon the water supply industry insidiously over the last century while the doubling of population and increase in standards of service led to continuous investment in new systems and neglect of existing ones.

The economic and financial climate

During the 1970s water supply planning faced an increasingly harsh economic and financial climate. The 1974 reorganisation philosophy had emphasised economic criteria and Water Authority self-financing and as the economic recession deepened government-imposed expenditure cuts began to take effect (see p. 31). Although reorganised differently, Scotland's water supply industry also felt pressures created by the recession and particularly the need to minimise rate increases.

In 1972 and 1973 anti-inflation measures resulted in a freeze on water supply charges and water supply expenditure soon became out of balance with income. At the same time it was clear that not only was water underpriced but that the cost of supply was increasing in real terms. The publication of the Water Resources Board's national water strategy in 1973 demonstrated the high cost of inter-regional water supply schemes which were then believed necessary for the future. The proposals were estimated to cost £1400 to £1500millions at 1972 prices, excluding the annual cost of operating systems and the cost of local schemes (Water Resources Board 1973, Rees 1977b).

Following the freeze on water supply charges and the sudden withdrawal of the rate support grant on reorganisation, water supply charges increased by 40% in 1974—75 making consumers aware of the true costs of water services. Unfortunately, reorganisation coincided with high rates of inflation and largely because of the recession, and extraordinarily high interest rates which adversely affected the capital-intensive water supply industry, 1975—76 saw a further swingeing 40% increase in water supply charges to keep the water industry solvent. Charges continued to increase during the 1970s and overall between 1974 and 1979 in England and Wales the average household bill for all water services increased from 37p to 73p per week (National Water Council 1978a).

The water supply planning system

To understand the water planning process and resulting policies, plans and schemes it is necessary to examine technical-engineering approaches to water supply planning and water demand forecasting. Until recently the incentive for water supply planners to question the wisdom of conventional approaches has not been strong, although the increasing scarcity of clean water sources, the tougher financial climate and the arguments of interest and pressure groups are proving to be powerful forces for change. The efficiency of institutional arrangements for water supply planning was considerably enhanced by the 1974 reorganisation in England and Wales, although apparently less so by the 1975 Scottish reorganisation. However, several features warrant further attention, including the continued existence of water companies, the problems of co-ordination of regional water supply strategies and the links between regional water authorities and other planning bodies.

The decision-making process and water supply investment

Regional water authorities in Britain are dominated by engineers trained largely to solve water supply problems by constructing new facilities rather than by minimising the need for them. Extending water supply capacity by engineering methods is the traditional approach and in the past certain factors encouraged extension of supplies. These included the abundance of pure water sources and their relatively low costs; traditionally this led to assumptions that water is a basic necessity which should not be limited. Consequently it became essential to satisfy all water requirements − a belief reinforced by public concern over water shortages.

The 'supply or requirements fix' of the water industry is suspect because it is based upon an unsystematic decision-making process and makes economic and social assumptions which are difficult to justify today (Rees 1976, Herrington 1976). An alternative rational economic approach has been advanced which emphasises efficiency in the use of existing water supplies and regional water authorities are now increasingly adopting mixed engineering-economic water supply policies, plans and schemes. This change is related to criticism and the impact of the 1975−76 drought which has helped force a rethinking of conventional approaches.

The supply−fix approach

The supply−fix approach is based upon deciding whether or not water consumption will exceed supply capacity at some point in the future, rather than upon a decision about whether or not the benefits of supply extension are likely to exceed the costs (Herrington 1976). A typical form of reasoning is as follows: forecasts show that a critical water shortage will occur in the next ten years because growing water consumption will outstrip the capacity of the existing supply system, therefore capacity must be extended to meet future requirements. The aim is to ensure future requirements are met and supply capacity is automatically extended: supply being led by demand. In Britain the most common form of recent supply extensions has been reservoir construction.

In the supply–fix approach the social value of extra water supplies – that is the benefits of supply extension – are assumed axiomatically to exceed the costs involved. Such an assumption may well have been justifiable during the nineteenth and first half of the twentieth centuries on public health and other social grounds. It may also be perfectly valid today where extra supplies are needed to support population and industrial growth. However, it becomes much more questionable when supply extension is proposed to cope with increased per capita consumption above already high levels: a frequent reason for many recent supply extension schemes in Britain. As with most commodities, the value per unit of water can be expected to decline as consumption increases (Rees 1978).

Typically, once a decision to extend supplies is made, costs enter the decision-making process for the first time. This is usually to enable alternative schemes to be compared and the scheme which minimises development costs per unit of capacity is usually selected. However, because costs and benefits should be examined earlier in the process to appraise a range of schemes of differing capacities, this decision-making procedure is rather unsystematic. Unfortunately, no attempts have been made in Britain to compare the benefits consumers derive from extra water with the costs of new capacity and unfortunately little is known about the social value of increased per capita water consumption above existing levels or how it might be measured.

Conventional reasoning was used in the Water Resources Board's national water strategy (Water Resources Board 1973). Water shortages were projected in 1981 and 2001 and a range of possible supply extension schemes were proposed. The costs of the options were then compared but the amount of extra capacity that was socially and economically justifiable was not properly questioned.

The supply–fix approach is not only associated with overemphasis upon supply extension, but also with premature capacity extension. In the past forecasts were often based upon scant knowledge of water demand and upon forecasting methods which now look highly questionable. Forecasts often tended to be rather generous and capacity was extended ahead of requirements. Not surprisingly large-scale engineering works were also favoured because they produced lower costs per unit capacity (Rees 1978).

The demand—supply approach

The alternative demand—supply approach, based upon the principle that water consumption is a function of the price per unit of water used to the consumer, leads to a more rational decision-making procedure. It is also likely to encourage consideration of a broader range of policy options. However, there are considerable practical difficulties in the approach. The feasibility of manipulating water consumption using the price mechanism depends upon the level of public dissatisfaction with existing flat rate water charges and the political acceptability of manipulating price in such a way as to influence water demand significantly. Pricing domestic water consumption according to volume used presupposes the introduction of water meters, the economic and political desirability of which remains controversial (see pp. 90-1).

Pricing policies could lead to sharp increases in the price of water which might be publicly unacceptable. For example, if standards of living rise sharply then water consumption might rise rapidly, so tending to outstrip supply capacity. But major water supply extension typically takes 10 to 15 years to complete. Given such a tendency towards imbalance between supply and demand the price of water would have to be raised substantially to contain demand. Expenditure on waste control would have to increase in parallel, yet the ability to predict changes in the willingness of consumers to pay for water supplies is poorly developed.

The disadvantage of the supply—fix approach is that it encourages inefficient water use because the cost of providing extra water may in some cases exceed the social utility of the extra supplies. By using price as a mechanism for allocating water, instead of using it only as a revenue-collecting device, the proponents of the demand—supply approach argue that water demand may be managed. Planners can determine what price consumers are willing to pay for varying amounts of water by finding the relationship between water consumption and water price. This relationship is a measure of the benefit that society gains from water supply capacity and enough additional water is provided when the consumers' willingness to pay just equals the cost of the extra capacity.

Water demand forecasting techniques

Until recently comparatively little was known in Britain about water demand. However, as part of a general programme to improve water demand forecasts, the water industry has actively pursued research in this area. With its abolition in 1979 the Central Water Planning Unit's water demand research was halted (Central Water Planning Unit 1975). However, as their research capability developed during the 1970s Water Authorities began their own detailed water demand research. Although this research has already yielded valuable results, full success also depends upon the ability of Water

Authorities to share research results to yield a better understanding of water demand and forecasting techniques.

There are two principal water demand and forecasting techniques. The first is trend-based or extrapolative forecasting whereby projections of future water consumption are based upon a trend-line derived from data on past consumption. The main shortcoming of this technique is the assumption that the factors influencing demand in the past will remain the same in the future. Trend-based techniques are also intellectually constraining because they make no attempt to understand why water consumption fluctuates.

For these reasons a second forecasting technique – the component or analytical technique – which analyses why water demand fluctuates, has been developed to enable more reliable prediction. First, water consumption is disaggregated into major components, such as domestic use, unmetered consumption and leakage. Secondly, variables which are likely to influence each component are identified and their likely impact on future water use estimated. For example, waste control policies may be expected to reduce leakage while the diffusion of water saving or water using domestic appliances may be expected to either reduce or increase future consumption. Changes in each component are predicted separately and then aggregated.

Trend-based forecasting has been criticised for generating high water demand forecasts largely because changes in variables affecting future demand have received inadequate attention. A major problem with recent water demand forecasts – and one which afflicts trend-based and component techniques alike – is the recent dramatic downward revisions of the Registrar General's official national population forecasts upon which Water Authorities base their demand forecasts. Rates of population growth have persistently fallen below expected levels, leading to overestimates of future water requirements (Rees and Rees 1972).

Most Water Authorities have used both analytical and trend-based forecasting techniques. The Severn Trent, North West and South West Water Authorities now rely almost exclusively upon analytical techniques. However, the Southern Water Authority was criticised at the Broad Oak reservoir public inquiry in 1979 for relying exclusively on what the Authority itself describes in its 1979 annual plan as 'naïve' trend-based forecasting techniques (Herrington 1979). Evidence given jointly for the Council for the Protection of Rural England and local organisations criticised the Authority's apparent failure to use recent research on unmetered water use. Further criticism was aimed at the Authority's use of exponential trend-based increases in per capita unmetered consumption for 1981 and 2001 at a time when other Authorities favoured more conservative linear trend-based increases considered to be more in line with future population changes.

Whether analytical techniques prove to be more reliable than trend-based ones is uncertain, but the trend towards more sophisticated forecasting is clear. Currently, the consequence of the move towards analytical techniques is lower water demand forecasts (Herrington 1979).

Interest and pressure groups

Interest and pressure groups have over recent years raised public conscious-ness of the wider social, economic and environmental implications of water supply schemes and have been successful in helping to change the climate of public opinion especially to reservoir proposals. This has been more apparent in England and Wales than in Scotland where schemes in low population density areas and where single land ownership simplifies negotiations, as with Lothian Region's Meggett scheme, often result in less controversy. The increasingly widespread opposition to reservoir proposals since the 1950s, and the growing effectiveness of the anti-reservoir lobby backed by academics and others, forced the water industry to recognise that the future supply of suitable reservoir sites could no longer be taken for granted. Indeed the difficulty of implementing new water supply schemes became a contributory reason for the 1974 reorganisation (Twort, Hoather and Law 1974).

The Council for the Protection of Rural England, the Ramblers' Associa-tion and the Conservation Society are examples of important pressure groups which commonly oppose reservoir proposals. The Council has employed a leading academic critic of the supply–fix approach as a consultant and its case for greater water use economy and fewer environmentally intrusive new schemes is well developed (Council for the Protection of Rural England 1974, 1977). The Council lobbies Ministers by submitting comments on consultative documents, white papers and water supply strategies. Pressure groups such as the Dartmoor Preservation Society, which has successfully opposed reservoir proposals on Dartmoor, are also important at the regional level. Many other groups seek to influence decisions. For example, the influential National Farmers' Union is concerned to see the loss of agricultural land by permanent flooding reduced to a minimum, although this does not necessarily mean that the Union opposes all reservoir schemes.

Interest and pressure groups are by no means only concerned about reser-voirs. Some pressure groups, including the Country Landowners' Associa-tion, consider that the Water Authorities' discretion in fixing charges is too wide particularly since the Water Act 1973 removed the right of abstractors to appeal against charges leaving the question of representation on charges unclear. The Confederation of British Industry has established a regular system of liaison with Water Authorities and is particularly interested in ensuring sufficient quantity and quality of supplies to industry and in water supply and effluent disposal charges.

Water supply policies, plans and schemes are influenced by interests which support and oppose options. An example of how non-water social goals can influence water supply plans through the influence of interest groups is the case of Cow Green reservoir in Upper Teesdale. Against a history of severe unemployment and assisted area policy in the North East, the expansion of Imperial Chemical Industries' operations on Teesside in the 1960s creating increased employment prospects produced demands for more water. These demands were translated into a proposal for a large regulating reservoir at Cow Green. Although tenaciously opposed by conservationists, the proposal gained the support of Teesdale Members of Parliament, trade unions and industrialists. This support proved influential in determining the government's reaction to the proposals and objections and the eventual building of the reservoir (Gregory 1975).

With the increased visibility and influence of preservation groups the main interests in water supply planning are now well recognised by Water Authorities. However, conflict over water supply strategies and particularly reservoir proposals continues to be intense. Similar fundamental arguments underlie major proposals and consequently these arguments are repeatedly made at public inquiries.

The public inquiry process and pressure group policies have influenced the development of each other over time. Public inquiries have become one of the main vehicles for expressing pressure group policies and they act as a catalyst for pressure groups to refine and develop their views. These views are then fed back into the inquiry process. For example, through public inquiries, such as the Carsington case discussed later in this Chapter, it has become increasingly clear that the scope of such inquiries should change to allow interest and pressure groups the right to question national policy.

Efficiency of institutional arrangements

An advantage of the 1975 reorganisation in Scotland was the reunification of sewerage and sewage disposal with water supply services which draw substantially upon the same expertise. However, the reorganisation which some engineers believe to have been a retrograde step, also created problems. The boundaries of the Regional Councils are based upon political rather than hydrological criteria and are less practical for water supply than the previous Regional Water Board catchment areas. Thus 'added areas' have been created in some cases within one Regional Council where water supplies are derived from an adjacent Region.

The regionalisation of water management in England and Wales in 1974 created an institutional framework which encourages efficiency in water supply operations. The large regional Water Authorities can integrate local distribution networks, reduce duplication, reduce risks of water shortages by increasing the flexibility of existing resources and reap economies of scale. In addition, in contrast to their Scottish counterparts the Water Authorities have boundaries which coincide with major river basins. This enhances the scope for managing resource interdependencies making possible comprehensive management of the whole water cycle. In theory the joint planning of water supplies, pollution prevention and waste disposal, allows optimum efficiency to be achieved in the use of water sources. In practice at the regional level, therefore, institutional arrangements appear to be close to the optimum, although the continued existence of independent Water Companies remains an anomaly.

The Water Companies' Association, the Water Companies' interest group, has campaigned vigorously against the proposal made in the 1977 government white paper on the water industry for Water Authority takeover of the companies. Although the public ownership issue is an intensely party-political one, arguments for and against have been advanced on efficiency grounds. The Water Companies argue that they are viable and that they bring efficiency of private enterprise to the water supply industry and, by being small, avoid the inefficiencies of large nationalised industry. They also point out that the proposals might cost £300millions in compensation. However, their opponents argue that continued independence may well produce inefficiencies by complicating the coordination of water supply and sewage disposal services and hindering the integration of supply networks. It appears that the Water Companies have remained mainly where they are efficient and where water supply is profitable.

In England and Wales, at the national level institutional inefficiencies still exist with responsibility for water supply planning being divided between Ministries and advisory and research agencies. The lack of an executive national authority means that the combination of regional water strategies could be less than efficient in national terms, although the National Water Council might take on an influential strategic water planning role in the future. National coordination is particularly important for the long term. At present regional rainfall in England and Wales broadly allows regional self-sufficiency. However, there are already substantial connections across regional boundaries and these are likely to become more important with time emphasising the need for coordination.

Links with other areas of planning

The planning and development of water supply and water distribution systems and the location of housing and industry have important implications for each other. Decisions made about one can prejudice development of the other and therefore coordination is essential. There are statutory requirements for Water Authorities to prepare medium-term (five-year) plans which are updated annually, but progress with forming plans is not aided by the absence of a firm national water policy. County planning authorities must prepare structure plans (10- to 15-year plans). In theory coordination of planning is possible, but in practice each authority knows relatively little of the others' long-term plans. Structure plans in many cases offer only hopes and aspirations and it is difficult to identify their implications for water supply development. Shorter-term planning is less problematic, particularly between Water Authority divisions and District Councils many of which have strong links with each other because of sewerage agency agreements (Payne

1978). Although consultation between authorities appears to be developing satisfactorily, without proper coordination Water Authorities can become *de facto* planning authorities and in turn planning authorities could determine water supply developments.

Problems of pre-empting water supply decisions exist in Scotland where the multipurpose arrangements do not necessarily ensure coordination. For example, in the Highland region difficulties have been experienced by the Regional Council water department because housing developments have been approved by the Scottish Development Department apparently without taking into account the subsequent need for new water services and the effect this has upon the water department's programme of expenditure (Highland Regional Council 1978).

Water supply policies, plans and schemes

Water supply policy making involves setting investment priorities and determining charging structures. The Water Act 1973 and the economic and financial pressures of the 1970s emphasised the need for a more explicit policy framework than previously. Consequently, Water Authorities now make explicit public statements about their priorities in annual and medium-term plans. In England and Wales changes in the methods of charging for water supplies have been necessary for the water industry to meet its statutory requirements. Because of the recent impact of inflation on charges and the implications of changing charging principles for particular groups of consumers, water supply charging is an especially sensitive area. The complexity of charging principles and proposals has caused considerable debate within the water industry and a continuing dialogue between the industry and water consumers.

Investment priorities

The Water Act 1973 and ministerial statements on investment priorities (Table 1.2) form a framework of guidelines for investment planning by the Water Authorities and similar guidelines exist in Scotland. Within these guidelines the regional water authorities set their own priorities in accordance with the particular needs of their regions. Priority setting often involves deciding how to allocate investment between resource developments to meet forecasted water shortages, regional interconnections of water distribution systems to improve water supply reliability and schemes to extend water supplies to new homes. For example, after meeting public health requirements the Wessex Water Authority places maintenance of existing systems, including water supply, as its second priority. Needs of housing and industry come next, but a slightly lower priority is given to meeting increased per capita consumption by existing consumers (Wessex Water Authority 1978a).

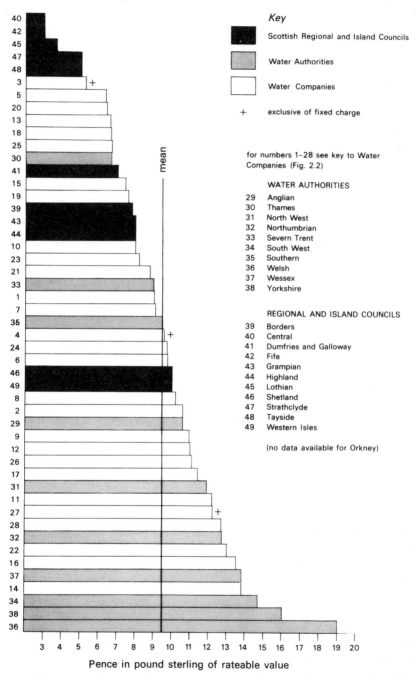

Figure 3.3 Domestic water charges in Britain 1978–9. Charges in England and Wales include the effect of equalisation levies and receipts.

Tayside in Scotland has inadequate water distribution facilities which severely restrict housing and industrial development. Water supplies are restricted and intermittent. The Regional Council therefore places the improvement of existing water supply services and the provision of supplies for housing and industrial development high in its priorities (Tayside Regional Council 1978).

Water supply charges: policies and principles

Charges for water supplies are much lower in Scotland than in England and Wales reflecting the relative abundance of accessible clean water in Scotland. There are also quite considerable variations in water supply charges between individual regional water authorities and water companies (Chartered Institute of Public Finance and Accountancy 1978) (Fig. 3.3). In 1978–79 the average domestic water rate was 6·4p in the £ of rateable value in Scotland compared with 12·4p in the £ charged by Water Authorities and about 9·6p in the £ charged on average by Water Companies. Variations in domestic water bills are, however, somewhat less than p/£ charges suggest, since rateable values are generally lower in areas with high p/£ charges, such as the Welsh area. Similarly, the average charge per 1000 gallons for metered water supplies was 36·8p in Scotland compared with 66·2p charged in Water Authorities and 62·3p by Water Companies in England and Wales.

Currently water supplies are allocated largely by administrative rather than economic methods and water supply charges reflect the need to raise revenue to cover costs rather than the need to encourage greater efficiency in water use. For example, with the exception of irrigation, charges for direct abstractions in England and Wales are related to licensed quantities of water rather than to actual water use and there is no financial reward therefore for economising on water use unless licences are revised. About two-thirds of water consumption is unmetered and established policies of charging by property rateable value do not provide an incentive to avoid waste and may be unfair to small consumers living in large houses. A move towards relating charges more closely to cost and measured use is occurring and will continue. The fundamental debate about charges concerns the merits and demerits of allocating water supplies by economic methods and developing charges which encourage economic efficiency. In addition to the pursuit of economic efficiency, charges may be used to achieve financial self-sufficiency or equity objectives and to an extent these objectives conflict with one another (Brown 1978, Water Research Centre 1977).

The economic efficiency objective. Charging structures can promote economic efficiency, and thereby a rational allocation of resources within the water industry, by providing a cost incentive for consumers to avoid waste. In theory, if the price a consumer is willing to pay for an additional unit of water supply (price being a measure of the value of the unit to the consumer) exceeds the cost of supplying it (the marginal cost), then the additional unit should be provided. Supply and consumption of additional units will take place until the price becomes equal to the marginal cost: consumption beyond this point being wasteful because the price consumers pay is greater than the value to them of the water obtained.

The principle of marginal cost pricing is that charges at the margin of supply should reflect the incremental (or marginal) costs of meeting the demand, and therefore to achieve economic efficiency prices should equal marginal costs. Given this argument it is easy to see why existing flat rate charges for unmetered supplies lead to inefficiency and waste. Payment for the water remains the same whatever the quantity consumed so that the charge per additional unit of water supply is zero. Under such conditions there is no incentive to avoid waste and consumers will continue using additional units of water until their marginal value is also zero.

Marginal cost pricing, however, presents considerable practical difficulties. It cannot be used effectively without charges being related to volumes of consumption, and this presupposes metering unless restricted to consumers already metered. Measurement of marginal cost of supply extension may be complex, although not impossible with improved methods of scheme appraisal.

The financial self-sufficiency objective.   Water Authorities are obliged to be financially self-sufficient so that taking one year with another revenue should not be less than outgoings properly chargeable to the revenue account. Water Authorities may also be required to meet other prescribed financial targets (see p.31). However, charges related to marginal costing may not yield sufficient revenue to cover accounting costs or to meet prescribed financial targets. Where prices are set equal to marginal costs and this differs from the average cost of supplying water, financial deficits or surpluses may occur. Deficits require subsidisation while surpluses amount to a tax on water consumption and either may be politically unacceptable. To overcome the possible incompatibilities between economic efficiency and self-sufficiency, pricing policies related to marginal costing would have to be changed to allow financial objectives to be obtained and this inevitably results in a loss in economic efficiency (Webb 1977).

The equity objective.   Unlike economic efficiency and financial self-sufficiency, equity is a social objective and Water Authorities are required under the Water Act 1973 to ensure that their water charges do not 'discriminate unduly' against any group in society. However, equity may be defined in three quite different ways. First, charges may be equitable when consumers are charged the same price for the same amount of water, no matter what the difference in the costs of supply. Secondly, a system whereby all consumers placing the same cost on the public water supplies are charged the same can also be considered equitable. Charges vary between areas in England and

Wales reflecting local differences in the costs of supply due, for example, to variations in the costs of water treatment and regional differences in inherited debt. Lastly, charges may be equitable if they are levied according to ability to pay: the rationale applied generally to our property rating system. Only the second definition of equity is consistent with economic efficiency and the other two involve consumer cross-subsidisation.

Although regional variations in water supply charges traditionally reflect the second definition, as we shall see below, Water Authorities are expected to go some way towards the first definition of equity. They are thus faced with a difficult balancing act: setting prices which are reasonably equitable whilst at the same time reducing diminished economic efficiency to a minimum and satisfying the financial obligations.

Equalisation of water charges.   Some Water Authorities pursued equalisation of water supply charges *within* their regions after the 1974 reorganisation, while others such as the North West Water Authority maintained differences. The impact of the removal of rate support grant subsidies following the Water Act 1973 varied regionally, exaggerating regional inequities. An increase in unmetered supply charges of 121% occurred in the Welsh region, compared to an average increase of 40% elsewhere, because the Welsh local authorities were comparatively heavily subsidised from the rate support grant. Within Wales increases varied from 422% in Anglesey to 59% in the Conway valley (Okun 1977). Welsh anger at these increases led to the Daniel Committee inquiry which recommended equalisation of charges *between* Authorities (Welsh Office 1975).

The Water Charges Equalisation Act 1977 was introduced to reduce disparities in regional water charges for unmetered supplies only. Thus consumption in high cost water supply areas has been subsidised by low cost areas where equalisation levies appear on water bills. Among Water Authorities the principal beneficiaries are the Welsh (receiving £3·3m), Anglian (£2·4m) and South West (£1·1m) while Thames (£2·9m), Severn Trent (£1·0m) and North West (£0·8m) contribute most (1979). Equalisation does little to encourage greater efficiency in the allocation of water supplies – a fact partly recognised in the 1977 Act which only aims to reduce differences rather than eradicate them (Fig. 3.3). Recent evidence suggests that the Act is not working well in practice. Under the Act equalisation was based on the cost of financing the historic debt incurred in providing water supplies – only one of several factors governing water bills. Although in 1977 the Labour government maintained that the Act was working well, in 1980 the Conservative government suggested its repeal because of perverse effects such that many consumers with above average water bills will pay more and vice versa. Political motives have been important in adjusting water charges through the statute law. Although the operation of the 1977 Act may require modification the Act remains fair in principle.

In Scotland water charges are not equalised between regions although there are quite substantial regional differences especially in the domestic water rate. Equalisation has not become a national issue in Scotland partly because of the relatively low cost of Scottish water. However, internal equalisation of water charges took place within Regions following the Water (Scotland) Act 1967 and the 1975 reorganisation.

Some changes in water supply charges in line with the principles discussed above have been made by Water Authorities. The transition from the pre-1974 basis of charging is likely to be gradual and the precise impact of changes is difficult to determine. This is reason enough to proceed cautiously. The pursuit of any single charging objective is most unlikely and depending upon prevailing political, economic and financial pressures future charges are likely to reflect multiple objectives and to that extent will never be optimal with respect to any one criterion.

Alternative plans and schemes

Water supply management alternatives considered in formulating plans can be subdivided into supply extension alternatives (Rodda, Downing and Law 1976) and those which attempt increased economic efficiency and demand management (Rees 1976, Smith 1979) (Table 3.3).

Table 3.3 Water supply management alternatives.

1 *Supply extension alternatives*
   Direct-supply reservoirs
   River regulating reservoirs
   Reservoir enlargement
   Groundwater development/aquifer recharge
   River-to-river water transfers
   Estuary storage
   Desalination

2 *Increased efficiency and demand management alternatives*
   Leakage and other waste reduction
   Dual water supplies
   Re-use and recycling
   Water saving technology
   Integration of supply networks
   Metering and pricing

These are the alternatives generally perceived in Britain. Experiments in alleviating drought through weather modification have been undertaken in countries such as Australia and the United States.

Supply extension alternatives. The Water Resources Board's national water strategy advocated alternatives exemplifying the conventional supply extension approach. The strategy, now largely superseded, recommended inland and estuary source development, groundwater development, enlarging existing reservoirs and river to river water transfer, as well as the combined use of resources. Re-use of water and effluents was also suggested, however, indicating some concern for greater efficiency. Most existing reservoirs are direct-supply ones but wider development of regulating reservoirs, already used in the Dee catchment, was recommended. With direct-supply reservoirs, water is transported to the demand centre by aqueduct, but with regulating reservoirs water is stored during high river flows and released into the river during low flows, smoothing out river yield over the year. The river channel provides a natural aqueduct and cities downstream of the reservoir and close to the river abstract water directly from it. River regulation both reduces the costs of water transportation, and enhances opportunity for successive re-use of water in the channel before abstraction; the reservoirs can also be used to control floods. However, the water often requires more sophisticated treatment prior to use in the public supplies. Reservoir enlargement has been suggested mainly because it minimises environmental disruption and can be cheaper than building new installations.

Maximum use of groundwater was also suggested in the Water Resources Board's strategy. The strategy recommended aquifer recharge, recognising the tendency of aquifers, like the London chalk, to be overpumped and the need to adopt sustained yield resource management principles. Aquifer recharge can sustain aquifer yield by diverting excess river flows down boreholes (Porter 1978) but one problem is that groundwater, for example from the Cotswold limestone, may be too hard for use.

River-to-river water transfers allow water to be moved from water surplus areas to areas of need. The regional scale Kielder water scheme in the Northumbrian region is a good example. The Tyne will be regulated by the Kielder reservoir and water will be transferred southwards by means of aqueduct to the industrial demand centres in the Wear and Tees areas (Conlon 1977).

Estuarine storage received attention in the 1960s and 1970s, with feasibility studies for storage in Morecambe Bay, the Solway, Dee and Wash estuaries (Central Water Planning Unit 1976d). Estuarine storage avoids the loss of land and disruption which inland storage creates, but the ecological side-effects and the higher cost of water offset these gains. The Water Resources Board suggested that the Dee estuary scheme should be implemented by the end of the 1980s, although with downward revisions in population forecasts the need has receded.

The Water Resources Board's strategy can be criticised because of its reliance upon using rivers as aqueducts and assuming that the problems of abstraction from lowland polluted rivers can be overcome. Largely because the Board's strategy was produced before reorganisation it failed to capitalise upon the potential of integrating the management of water supply, pollution control and effluent disposal which make it possible to plan effluent disposal and pollution control with the intended use of a river for supply in mind. The strategy also displays some of the weaknesses inherent in the supply extension approach – the lack of proper cost-benefit analyses, over-generous forecasts which would lead to excess capacity and inefficient water use (Rees 1978).

Desalination. Although desalination may eventually be used on a significant scale to provide fresh water in Britain, it was rejected by the Water Resources Board (1973) which considered that it was 'unlikely to contribute substantially to water resources in this century'. Desalination techniques are well established in Guernsey and Jersey and elsewhere, but following experimentation with a desalination plant at Ipswich in the early 1970s, the Board concluded that desalination was too costly (Water Resources Board 1972). Water from a plant operating to meet normal base-load demand for public supplies would cost two and a half to fifteen times as much as water from conventional sources, making base-load operation unlikely. However, desalination might be used initially in conjunction with other water sources and to overcome peak water demands perhaps in summer holiday areas.

The case for desalination is as follows. First, saline water sources are inexhaustible and more dependable than fresh water sources affected by rainfall uncertainties. Secondly, the energy requirements of desalination can be partly derived from waste energy from power generation plant which can be combined with desalination plant. Thirdly, the failure of the Ipswich experiment was due to concentration upon the freezing process and the exclusion of other well-tried techniques, particularly multi-stage flash distillation. Finally, it is argued that desalination is attractive when the wider social costs of developing inland reservoirs are taken into account (Silver 1974).

These arguments are challenged in several ways. First, being technically complex, desalination plants are prone to break down making water from this source less reliable than from conventional sources. Secondly, combined desalination and power plant operation may increase energy production costs. Lastly, the social costs of unsightly desalination plants on the coast may well be greater than constructing inland reservoirs which, though socially disruptive, may be recreationally attractive.

Desalination might become economically competitive as the cost of conventional sources rises, or if the cost of desalination falls through some technical breakthrough. However, the steep rise in energy costs during the 1970s moved the economic cost comparison further against desalination (National Water Council 1977a).

Increased efficiency and demand management alternatives. Leakage has already been shown to be high and opportunities for reduction are related to programmes to replace aging water mains and to advances in leak detection technology (Pullin 1976c). Dual water supplies which use one system of supply for potable water and another for non-potable water, offer opportunities for greater efficiency and possibly for greater safety in water supplies. Only about 10–20% of the water used in industrial societies needs to be of high purity. However, potable supplies with their associated extra treatment costs are used for lavatory flushing and in industrial processing where high purity is not required. In Britain non-potable supplies are already provided for a few large industrial concerns. Separate supply systems increase costs but may be less costly than building new potable quality reservoirs. The main potential for dual supplies appears to be in new housing projects and it is unlikely that their introduction into existing built-up areas is economically feasible (Rees 1976). The safety of water supplies might be enhanced if the demand for potable water is reduced and potable supplies can be limited to protected sources. However, dual domestic supplies may introduce the possibility of inadvertant use of non-potable water (Okun 1977).

Water re-use can be achieved either by reclaiming sewage effluent to provide supplies of low quality, perhaps for dual-supply systems, or by recycling water in homes and factories. Re-use of sewage effluent for irrigation and industrial processing is most likely to increase. Direct re-use of sewage effluent for potable water supplies is regarded as unacceptable in Britain, although the proportion of sewage effluents in lowland river sources is increasing making higher treatment standards necessary.

Industrial recycling of water has grown as the price of metered water has risen and some domestic water re-use occurs during water shortages. However, little serious attention has been paid to recycling in Britain particularly in homes where, for example, wash-basin water could be stored and used for lavatory flushing. The same is true for the redesign of water using equipment such as dual-flush lavatories. These produce savings of 25% over conventional systems and atomised heads on showers and taps can produce even larger savings. The question of whether such devices should be compulsory in new houses is debateable.

Domestic water metering.   Metering domestic water supplies and charging by volume is a focus of considerable debate and research (Jenking 1973, Lingard 1975, Dugdale 1975, Rees 1976, 1978, Okun 1977). The opponents of metering argue that domestic metering is incompatible with public health maintenance because the less well-off may reduce their water consumption below hygienic levels. This argument is sometimes associated with the view that almost limitless supplies of water are a basic human right.

Proponents of metering emphasise that only a small proportion of current per capita consumption is necessary to maintain public health and that luxury use of water is costly and wasteful and should not be regarded as a human right. A second argument against metering is that water demand is unresponsive to price rises. Apart from contradicting the public health argument, this point ignores evidence from North America and Europe suggesting that domestic consumption is price responsive. A third argument is that metering is not worth the expense because although consumers will reduce consumption, the savings which result from delaying the development of new capacity will be outweighed by the cost of installing and operating a metering system.

The central issue in the metering debate concerns the price elasticity of demand for water (Russell 1974). This is the extent to which a price change is reflected in a change in consumption. Research in America and the Netherlands indicates water demand to be price sensitive with a 10% price rise bringing up to 12% reduction in consumption in parts of the United States. However, much depends on whether or not water charges are small. If they are trivial demand tends to be unresponsive to price changes and vice versa. Experience of domestic metering in Britain is mainly limited to Malvern where meters have been in operation since 1872, following a local water shortage, and the Fylde and Mansfield areas where metering research was initiated in the 1970s. British experience suggests that the likely impact of metering may be about a 10−15% reduction in household use in some areas.

The metering debate is not only about universal metering because it is likely that metering will be economic in some parts of the country before others, making partial metering probable. Some domestic metering is not ruled out by the National Water Council and was legalised by the Water Act 1973. Domestic metering is unlikely in Scotland for several reasons. It is precluded under the Water (Scotland) Act 1967. In Scotland, where the cost of water is so low by comparison with England and Wales, there is a strong argument against metering because of the comparative size of increase in water bills due to meter installation and reading. The future of domestic metering in England and Wales depends heavily upon political as well as economic arguments. For example, the Labour Party has rejected domestic metering, believing water to be too vital to family life to be restricted through charges. Given these difficulties the whole question of demand management becomes problematic, yet it is by no means certain that the public is willing to see regional water authorities spending more on supply extension.

Current trends in policies, plans and schemes

Since 1974 there has been a shift in Water Authority policies, plans and schemes towards pursuit of increased efficiency and consideration of methods of controlling water demand. The reasons are complex but include the opportunities created by reorganisation for integration and scale economies and the continued downward revisions in water consumption projections. Also the 1975−76 drought, the pressures created for greater efficiency by the Water Act 1973 and the economic recession encouraged policies to be reconsidered.

Following reorganisation all Water Authorities made progress in regional integration of water sources and distribution networks. The Yorkshire Water Authority's 'water grid', discussed below, is an example, and many other annual and medium-term plans show a fresh concern for leakage loss reduction. A reduction in future losses to a level compatible with economic detection and repair is assumed in the demand projections of the South West Water Authority (1978). Loss reduction programmes are also underway in the Wessex region. Water Authorities also recognise the growing importance of demand management. By March 1979 six Water Authorities had made byelaws requiring dual-flush cisterns to be installed with lavatories in dwellings. The remaining Water Authorities were preparing similar byelaws. Publicity on water wastage is also seen as a method of demand management, although publicity campaigns tend to be limited to drought periods. Some Authorities, including Wessex and the Severn Trent, are also experimenting with domestic metering although these experiments are concerned with consumption research rather than with restraining demand. The Authorities are taking greater interest in efficiency of use and demand management, but there are few signs of serious consideration of re-use, particularly of sewage effluent and re-use in homes and factories or the development of more dual-supply systems (Rees 1978).

The issues concerning appropriate policies for water supplies in Britain are illustrated in more detail by two further examples. The first is the experience of the 1975–76 drought which demonstrated the effectiveness of the 1974 reorganisation and showed that heavy public spending on new water supply extension schemes is probably not required in England and Wales. A major supply extension scheme – Carsington reservoir – which is expected to come into operation in the mid-1980s is the second example. Carsington demonstrates the arguments for and against supply extension and the opposition facing new supply extension proposals as well as providing some insights into the public inquiry process and pressure group effectiveness in the context of water supply planning.

Example One:

The 1975–76 drought and water supply policy

The capacity of Britain's developed water resources to yield a reliable supply in extreme conditions had a severe test during 1976. Over England and Wales the period May 1975 until August 1976 was the driest sixteen-month period since records began in 1727. In the nine months to August 1976 including the winter of 1975–76 only 55% of average rainfall fell and in the three months prior to the same date the proportion for the country as a whole was only 35% (Perry 1976). Ascribing probabilities to such rare events can be misleading but the probability of recurrence is reckoned to be once in 1000 years on average. Fortunately heavy rains fell throughout September and October 1976, with virtually double normal rainfall in these months, but groundwater deficiencies still remained even many months later (Economic Intelligence Unit 1977). In Scotland, although there was a serious rainfall deficiency in 1974, there was no appreciable drought during 1975–76. Our ability to predict climate change reliably is limited, but by itself the drought does not appear to herald a significant climatic change. The event can be explained within the variations which can be observed in the available long-term meteorological data.

The response to the developing crisis.   Emergency legislation to meet water shortages has been passed in previous droughts. For example, the Water Supplies (Exceptional Shortage Orders) Act 1934 and the Water Act 1958 were both passed to meet water crises. However, although hosepipe bans could be made under the Water Act 1945 for private gardens and motor car washing, previous emergency legislation required extension to allow rationing in 1976. Parliament therefore passed the Drought Act 1976 during August of that year to extend the powers of control already contained in earlier legislation.

The Drought Act allowed Water Authorities to prohibit or limit the use of water for parks, recreation grounds, golf courses and lawns – whether privately or publicly owned – filling swimming pools, operating car washing plant, cleaning buildings and the operating of ornamental fountains even where the water was recycled. Such bans were imposed not simply to save water but sometimes to placate domestic consumers suffering rationing and who were concerned about what they perceived as 'wastage'. Water Authorities used their powers discriminately, for example allowing watering to avoid damaging cricket pitches or bowling greens.

Water use was reduced through staged implementation of increasingly severe water saving measures. The timing of staging differed between regions because the impact of the drought was not uniform. Initially reductions could be gained with little inconvenience by reducing pressure in the mains and through greater vigilance in correcting leakages. All the Water Authorities undertook intensive publicity campaigns to urge economy. Although consumers responded to local appeals for economy at the same time the hot weather increased the tendency for water use. Domestic hosepipes were banned at an early stage in most regions.

In the worst hit areas greater reductions in use were needed than voluntary savings achieved and therefore either properties were cut off from supplies and districts provided with standpipes, or water use was reduced by cutting off supplies by rota-cuts. In north Devon, one of the most vulnerable areas, 65 000 people experienced rationing by standpipes for one to three weeks in September 1976 forcing them to carry water from the streets. In south Wales one million people suffered rota-cuts for seven to eleven weeks for up to 13 hours daily. Although other Water Authorities were similarly prepared, north Devon was the only area to use standpipe rationing.

A major feature of the drought response was the adoption of priorities for water supply. The traditional approach reflected in the Water Act 1945 was to give priority to domestic consumers but in 1976 the government accepted representation from the Confederation of British Industry and the Trades Union Congress for priority for industry. The shift in emphasis was related to fears for industrial productivity during the recession. As a result water savings were made to protect industry, agriculture, health and safety and essential domestic supplies.

A further response to the drought was the augmentation of supplies. As a result of reorganisation the Water Authorities had already embarked upon regional water source and distribution system interconnections, and when the crisis came previously inadequate systems were able to draw upon other systems less heavily affected by shortages. For example, on reorganisation the Yorkshire Water Authority began a vigorous programme to integrate the water resources in its area into one operational unit. By the summer of 1976, given some contingency planning, all 54 reservoirs in the Authority's south west division were interconnected forming part of a regional water grid serving the Yorkshire conurbations (Baldwin 1977). Water Authorities effected emergency connections where possible, increasing the flexibility and thereby the security of supplies. New water sources were also tapped (Andrews 1976).

The short-term water savings and the effect of the drought.   The drought showed that the potential for voluntary savings with hosepipe bans can be substantial. Savings can reach 25 – 30% in limited areas but for whole Water Authority areas figures of 20% or less can be expected. Rationing of domestic consumers with rota-cuts or standpipes may increase overall savings to 40%, while savings from pressure reduction appear generally less than 10%, most of which is reduced leakage. In the Welsh Water Authority area the reduction in per capita water consumption was about 16%: a reduction similar to that in Yorkshire (National Water Council 1977b).

Industrial water savings during the drought were clearly considerable but are less easy to estimate because in most of the worst affected areas Water Authorities gave industry priority and took action to enable industry to use alternative sources. In south Wales a sample of 58 businesses are estimated to have saved nearly 70% of normal usage by 'good housekeeping' and 'domestic' savings (Biggs 1977). The largest water users were able to economise least. South west Yorkshire food manufacturers saved only 2% of normal consumption while smaller users such as electrical engineering plants saved as much as 34% and figures for individual factories were higher (National Water Council 1977b). Some of these savings were made under threat of restrictions and rota-cuts and many schemes involved capital investment in alternative supplies or alternative cooling systems.

Although disruptive and inconveniencing the drought had no serious long-lasting effects. With one or two exceptions industrial employment and output was not adversely affected and although some businesses such as car washing concerns suffered financially (Doornkamp and Gregory 1980) there was no significant adverse effect on the national economy. By emphasising the potential for savings the drought may well have had important positive effects and in some cases industrial consumption has not reverted to pre-drought levels. The cost of the drought in terms of capital works undertaken by Water Authorities, both permanent and temporary, was £68millions whilst the cost of the national publicity campaign plus local campaigns probably did not exceed £2millions.

Assessment. There is no doubt that the 1974 reorganisation contributed significantly to the water industry's ability to cope satisfactorily with the stiff test presented by the 1000 year drought. The Water Authorities were advantageously organised to enhance the flexibility and security of their supplies by developing regional water grids and other schemes of this type were already well underway before the 1976 crisis and provided a considerable benefit.

Although the drought identified some areas of vulnerability it also proved that, given water use reduction and supply augmentation, sufficient supplies could be maintained in most areas so that a water shortage as rare as the 1975–76 event could be overcome without undue hardship. Given recent trends in water demand, and apart from schemes necessary to increase security in vulnerable areas, the drought emphasised that the water supply system in England and Wales is currently sufficiently robust to warrant few major additional reservoir storage schemes until the end of the century. Extension of regional water supply connections to form a national water grid also seems unwarranted at present. However, against this it must be remembered that shifts in climatic conditions and in water demand trends or in public expectations of supply reliability could change this situation in the future.

The drought illustrated that water demand can be managed, at least in a crisis. However domestic consumption has returned to pre-drought levels. The potential saving on non-essential water use demonstrated during the drought will not be realised without widespread introduction of domestic equipment that uses less water. However, it must be remembered that if economies are achieved during 'normal' periods, then the scope for economies during future droughts is reduced. The experience raises important questions about society's desired standards of reliability of water supplies and the possibility of reducing water wasted during non-drought periods. Given the performance of the water industry and consumers in 1976, increasing supply security does not appear to make economic sense. Increments of investment required to provide extra capacity to insure against progressively rarer droughts impose unacceptable opportunity costs.

Example 2 :

The Carsington Reservoir Scheme

In May 1978 the Carsington Reservoir Scheme – a major supply scheme in the North Midlands – received Ministerial approval. The complex preceeding events exposed the clash between local and national amenity interests which reservoir proposals create. Under the public inquiry procedure the local conflict sharpened as alternative arguments were advanced, drawing in wider national issues about the respective merits of supply extension schemes versus increased water use efficiency and demand management. The events also illustrate how through the public inquiry process interest and pressure groups seek to influence decision making, how decisions concerning the public interest are made about complicated technical, social and economic issues and the time and administrative costs involved when reservoir proposals are publicly opposed.

Carsington is on a tributary of the Dove which itself flows into the Trent. The reservoir site is 4 km from the Peak National Park boundary and 15 km from Derby. Plans involve flooding medium-grade farm land in an attractive valley containing several villages. A few houses will be flooded and land divided amongst 24 holdings will have to be compulsorily purchased. The reservoir will regulate the River Derwent and will provide about 240 Ml/d.

The Carsington proposals have involved three public inquiries, the last being adjourned and reopened. In 1970 the Trent River Authority shortlisted three sites for a regulating reservoir: Carsington, Brund and Hassop. Only Carsington is outside the National Park and following the first public inquiry in 1971 the Minister refused further investigation of Hassop. There were doubts about the suitability of the site owing to old mine workings and its location in the Park close to Chatsworth. A second inquiry in 1973 considered the Trent River Authority's proposal to build a reservoir at Carsington to cost £11–£12millions at 1972 prices.

The 1973 public inquiry.   The Authority's case bears considerable resemblance to supply–fix reasoning. It argued that forecasts revealed a need for extra water in the north and east Midlands and that inland storage was the only practical means. Carsington created the least damage and an opportunity for new recreational facilities to ease pressure on the National Park. Evidence provided by local water undertakings showed that by 1978/79 consumption in the Potteries and north and south Derbyshire would exceed supplies. By 1991 the entire area, with a population of 2·7 million, would be in deficit.

All the main alternatives considered by the Authority were for developing the area's water resources to meet further needs. The development of ground and surface water resources, including the possibility of aquifer recharge and direct abstraction from the Trent, were all assessed, and all but additional storage were ruled out. Aquifer recharge required further feasibility studies and the problems of using Trent water, heavily polluted by effluents and organic compounds, remained unresolved. Desalination and water imports from an adjacent region were also rejected on economic grounds. Alternatives for increasing water use efficiency, dual supplies and managing demand appear to have received scant attention, metering being dismissed as being uneconomic.

Both Brund and Carsington were geologically suitable as reservoir sites. On economic grounds Brund was more favourable but on environmental grounds the Authority argued that the advantage lay with Carsington, Brund being in the National Park. The Authority accepted that Carsington would cause some disruption but that gains from recreational potential and trade and employment generation would accrue. Plans to provide for 750 sailing boats and other recreation existed. Rock for the dam would be obtained from opening local borrow pits.

The objectors to the Carsington proposal included Derbyshire County Council, the Henmore Valley Preservation Society – formed to fight the scheme – amenity societies and other local interests. Some objections concerned the local impact of the reservoir, while others concerned the merits of supply extension, but the demand forecasts of the Authority were not seriously challenged. Derbyshire County Council's objection was to the opening of borrow pits. The Henmore Valley Preservation Society argued strongly that supplies of water could be obtained by abstracting water from the Derwent, by raising the height of Ogston reservoir (on a tributary of the Derwent) and by reallocating existing resources more efficiently. The Society felt that the dam would be an ugly scar on the valley and that if the full social and environmental costs of the scheme were quantified, the balance would be against Carsington.

The Council for the Protection of Rural England and the Conservation Society both argued strongly in favour of options which they felt the Authority had not properly considered. These included options designed to improve efficiency in water use and to control demand. Installation of dual-flush lavatories and rain water tanks in houses were suggested, as were dual supplies, domestic metering and leakage control. Pleas were also made for more progress in treating industrial waste before it entered the Trent. Desalination was not ruled out, a point also made by the Voluntary Joint Committee for the Peak National Park which was opposed to a reservoir so close to the Park. The Ramblers' Association argued that the provision of an abundant water supply was against the public interest since it implied misuse. One objector stated that the lack of cost-benefit analysis of the scheme was a major weakness in the case.

Responding to objections the Authority accepted that changes in the operation of the Derwent reservoirs and some reallocation of resources could make some water available but only at increased cost. The Inspector concluded that the scheme would have a drastic impact on the locality, that the effect of the recreation proposals would be 'catastrophic' because of the influx of visitors to be expected, and that he was not satisfied that the full range of alternatives had been examined. The Inspector's main reasons for rejecting the proposal were that the independent Engineering Assessors report suggested that a redistribution of resources based partly on a modified version of the Henmore Valley Preservation Society's suggestion to take water from the Derwent, the raising of Ogston dam and a change in the operation of Derwent reservoirs, might well yield the extra resources required until the mid-1990s.

The acceptance of these views represented a victory for the Henmore Valley Preservation Society. On the question of the merits of supply extension schemes the Inspector also commented 'I am left with the firm impression that as a matter of policy the Authority is somewhat wedded to the

principle of providing new impounding reservoirs as a solution to the problem of water supply, and I feel that perhaps insufficient attention and consideration has been given to . . . other ways of meeting present and future difficulties.' Finally, the Inspector recommended that if the scheme was
reappraised in the future permission to open borrow pits should not be
granted and that the recreation provision be reduced drastically.

The 1976 public inquiry.   A new inquiry was opened in May 1976 to review
the alternatives suggested in 1973 by the Engineering Assessor and because
circumstances had changed with the creation of the Severn Trent Water
Authority.

Presenting its case the Water Authority maintained that water demand
forecasts still showed a need for extra resources and held that, even when the
Assessor's alternatives were considered, Carsington remained preferable.
The case continued to be based upon the assumption that forecasted requirements must be met by increased water supply capacity. A benefit of the new
regional Water Authority was that water resources and their use could be
integrated over a wider area so that surpluses and deficits which were not
interchangeable under the former water undertakings were now transferable
thereby reducing aggregate water supply capacity needs.

However, the Authority had now changed the supply boundaries of the
proposed reservoir and although the population involved was now less (2·57
million) existing and authorised resources of the new area now only yielded
809 Ml/d compared with the Trent River Authority's estimate of 928 Ml/d
for the old area in 1973. The Potteries were now excluded and central
Nottinghamshire added. The Authority's new forecast for the Potteries indicated a demand of 168 Ml/d for 2001 rather than the 241 Ml/d estimated in
1973, and furthermore this demand could now be met by groundwater
resources.

Fresh demand appraisals for the new supply area also showed how sensitive forecasts over a short period were to change. In this case change was due
mainly to the downward revision of official population forecasts, because
new forecasts up to 2001 resulted in figures substantially lower than those
given in 1973. However, the Authority concluded that even with greater flexibility and lower demand forecasts, Carsington was still needed because the
new supply area had substantially fewer resources than the original. The
Authority calculated that the area would run into deficit sometime between
1983 and 1988.

In making its case the Water Authority accepted recommendations made
by the 1973 Inspector among which were that borrow pits should not be
opened and that recreational provision be reduced. Shale instead of rock
would now be used for the dam, the shale being derived from reservoir exca-
vations. Reviewing the Assessor's alternatives the Water Authority stated
firstly that there were serious amenity and other objections to raising Ogston
dam. Secondly, changing Derwent reservoir operations would not work

because of an error in the Assessor's calculations and because there were serious amenity objections to a necessary pumping station and pipeline. Thirdly, water abstracted from the Derwent would have to be replaced from untreated Trent water and this would lower river water quality causing a deterioration in fisheries and difficulties for industrial abstractors. Both the anglers and the industrial abstractors concerned supported this view at the inquiry. Variants of the Assessor's suggestions were also considered by the Water Authority but all proved more costly than Carsington, now estimated at £45millions.

Objections to the Carsington scheme were heard from individuals, the Henmore Valley Preservation Society and amenity groups. The Council for the Protection of Rural England and the Conservation Society reiterated that alternatives based on greater economy in water use, demand management and water quality improvements on the Trent could produce substantial water. They also argued that the Water Authority's demand forecasts were seriously inflated, official population forecasts being consistently over-estimated, and that increased per capita water consumption should not neces-sarily be accepted. At this point the Henmore Valley Preservation Society made a major new proposal: a new high Derwent dam should be built instead of Carsington, to regulate the Derwent and to allow for downstream abstrac-tion. The Society gave results of a preliminary investigation of the proposal undertaken by consultant engineers. These indicated that no agricultural land or dwellings would be flooded. So that this new proposal could be studied the inquiry was adjourned in May 1976. Other proposals were also considered concerning raising Ogston dam and a suggestion from the Central Water Planning Unit that some water could be imported from the new Anglian reservoir at Empingham but this was considered to be more costly than Carsington water by the Authority.

The 1977 reopened public inquiry. At the reopened inquiry The Peak Park Joint Planning Board, the High Peak Borough Council and others including the National Trust, all opposed the new proposal for a new high Derwent dam. The Park Board's policy was that new reservoirs within the Park boundary, as the new dam would be, were only acceptable in the most compelling national need. The Board argued that such a need had not been demonstrated and was therefore strongly against the dam because of the landscape and other intrusions it would create. This view was broadly supported by other objectors. Responding, the Henmore Valley Preservation Society argued that the cost estimates made by the Water Authority for the new high Derwent dam were inflated and that as Empingham water was avail-able the Water Authority ought to negotiate for its use with the Anglian Water Authority.

In finally weighing all the arguments the Inspector agreed with his Engin-eering Assessor that the Water Authority's demand forecasts should be accepted and that a new water source should be developed. Raising Ogston dam and revising the operation of the Derwent Valley reservoirs were, he concluded, too costly in financial and amenity terms to be accepted. A new high Derwent dam was also unacceptable because of the damage to the Peak National Park environment. The Inspector therefore recommended that the Carsington scheme be approved subject to the earlier conditions.

Assessment.   Carsington illustrates the case which Water Authorities can make for major supply extension schemes and how financial arguments often win over social and environmental ones. Usually a proposal has a long history and once finally formulated it develops a considerable momentum which is difficult to resist. Until the public inquiry stage a Water Authority, with its substantial professional expertise, has considerable control over knowledge of its plans and it is difficult therefore for objectors to find experts who can develop an effective rebuttal. Once formulated the impact of pressure groups' arguments may well be weakened by each arguing its own particular case.

Between the adjourning of 1976 inquiry in May and the reopening in July 1977 the serious drought occurred. Pressure groups like the Council for the Protection of Rural England were unable to capitalise upon the drought experience in showing how effective water economy measures could be. Unfortunately they had already given evidence leaving cross-examination of witnesses as the only procedural possibility, and therefore some valuable evidence may have been lost to the inquiry.

Carsington also raises questions about the adequacy of the public inquiry process which have also become apparent through experience at recent motorway inquiries (Levin 1979). Public inquiries are set up to consider *local* views, and criticisms of government *policy* are considered to be beyond their terms of reference. However, the objectors' case at Carsington rested on two interrelated arguments – at the local and national policy levels. The Henmore Valley Preservation Society was concerned about local impact whilst other groups, like the Council for the Protection of Rural England, were concerned more with broader policy issues of the *need* for new water supply exension schemes. Arguments in favour of increasing the efficiency of water use and demand management were therefore largely beyond the allowable scope of the inquiry. Although the Inspector at the 1973 inquiry was sympathetic to these arguments they could not, in the end, be expected to defeat the Carsington proposal. The existing public inquiry process is inadequate in not allowing full scrutiny of the policies which lead to proposals such as Carsington. Largely as a result of bitter motorway inquiry disputes the public inquiry procedure is under review. Apart from emphasising the inadequacies of the public inquiries, the main impact of opposition to the Carsington proposal was, nevertheless, a more comprehensive review of alternatives and the delaying of the scheme.

Finally, it is worth reflecting that after three lengthy public inquiries spanning six years, the Carsington reservoir will come into operation about

16 years after the Trent River Authority completed a survey of possible sites for a new source.

Evaluation

Any evaluation of water supply planning in Britain must begin by reiterating that the British public supply system has few equals elsewhere in the world. However, this does not imply that fundamental issues do not still face the water industry. There are significant technical problems associated with maintaining drinking water quality – requiring continuous research – and financial limits which call into question the assumptions on which our water supply provision is traditionally based.

Does society provide water planners with an adequate framework of legislation, institutions and financial provision?
With the integration of water supply and sewerage services the Scottish Regional Councils provide generally adequate institutions for water supply planning. Satisfactory institutional arrangements for water supply planning were also provided by the 1974 reorganisation in England and Wales. At present many of the water supply problems facing the water industry are of a regional nature and increasingly involve water quality control. The value of regionalisation in England and Wales was demonstrated by the 1975–76 drought and integrating the management of clean and dirty water offers the best solution for maintaining potable water quality standards and sufficiency of supplies. However, there is no national water strategy. The National Water Council has so far taken a limited role in national planning and there is no national coordinating organisation other than the Ministries responsible for water supplies. Recent legislation especially in England and Wales reflects society's support for greater economic efficiency and for equity. Despite the Water Authorities' financial self-sufficiency obligation financial provision is basically adequate.

To what extent do public attitudes and preferences towards water and associated land resources affect policies, plans and schemes?
Without monetary incentives society finds it difficult to avoid waste and by wasting water it encourages the extension of water supplies which are increasingly costly in social, economic and environmental terms. Social attitudes are ambivalent: society continues to waste water yet is often indignant at price rises necessary to meet growing demands. Growing conflicts over reservoir proposals emphasise the need for greater economy and stimulate debate about reducing water consumption, including domestic metering and pricing, as the Carsington case shows. Society is understandably unwilling to allow potable water quality standards and reliability of water supplies to fall. Indeed medical research may well bring fresh demands for higher quality standards.

How do the inherent characteristics of water in Britain influence the choice of alternative policies, plans and schemes?

Britain is a small densely populated country, yet overall it has ample water resources. Scotland especially has a very favourable ratio of resources to population. The main problems exist in England and Wales. Here the density of population is inversely related to precipitation and increasing dependence upon polluted lowland river sources places a premium on river water quality protection, emphasising the technical problems of water treatment and re-use.

To what extent are resource management principles incorporated into water policies, plans and schemes?

Water supply planning is basically about sustaining water yields and the water industry is well organised to achieve this. The management structure is catchment-based allowing source to mouth planning and multi-functionalism enhances the opportunity for more productive use of water through re-use and recycling. The position of Scotland is similar although some incompatibilities arise because the Regional Councils are not catchment-based.

How well is water planning integrated with other forms of public planning?

To ensure that the statutory responsibilities of regional water authorities are met, effective liaison between water supply and land use planning is vital. Except in Scotland some difficulties are presented by different areal units. Other problems are presented by the vagueness in structure plans and by integrating the goals of land use and water development plans so that decisions are not pre-empted. Nevertheless, liaison is developing well.

Is water planning comprehensive and systematic and are all relevant interests adequately involved?

The assumptions on which the traditional supply extension philosophy of the water industry are based have been increasingly called into question on economic, social and environmental grounds. Past needs and the professional bias of the water industry led to reliance on a narrow range of options but a wider, more systematic and discriminating approach is now required to ensure that future developments are worthwhile to society. Since reorganisation and the financial pressures of the 1970s the water industry has responded by introducing waste control measures although considerable potential for savings still exists.

Pressure groups have successfully influenced policy concerning reservoir developments and, although most of the relevant interests are adequately involved in the planning process, the public inquiry process which has generally proved to be robust does not allow adequate challenge of government policy.

Selected further reading (for full bibliography see pp. 254−66)

For an outline of British hydrology and water resources see:

Smith, K. 1972. *Water in Britain: A study in applied hydrology and resource geography*. London: Macmillan.

A useful survey of Scottish water resources is:

Scottish Development Department 1973. *A measure of plenty, water resources in Scotland: a general survey*. Edinburgh: HMSO.

Apart from detailed data on surface water, groundwater and water demand (Department of the Environment Water Data Unit, 1974, 1975 and 1976 respectively) the principal annually published data source on water in Britain, which includes data on water resources, finance and charges and information on principal water planning institutions, is:

Department of the Environment Water Data Unit 1977. *Water data 1975*. London: HMSO.

For a concise history of water supply legislation and development in Britain until 1950 see:

Dracup, S. B. 1973. 'Water supply in Great Britain 1690−1950, A brief history in six parts,' *British Water Supply* Jan. to June. London: British Waterworks Association.

An excellent illustration of the conflicts of interest associated with a major water supply proposal is:

Gregory, R. 1975. 'The Cow Green reservoir.' In *The politics of physical resources*, P. J. Smith (ed.), 144−201. London: Penguin/Open University.

The supply−fix approach and water demand management alternatives are discussed in:

Rees, J. A. 1976. 'Rethinking our approach to water supply provision.' *Geography*, **61**(4), 232−45.

For detailed case studies of water supply development see:

Porter, E. A. 1978. *Water management in England and Wales*. Chs 3, 4 and 5, Cambridge: Cambridge University Press.

A useful review of problems and policies associated with water supplies in England and Wales is:

National Water Council 1978a. *Water industry review 1978*. London: NWC.

The financial and economic policies associated with water supplies are reviewed in:

National Water Council 1976. *Paying for water*. London: NWC.

4 *Effluent disposal and pollution control*

Waste water treatment and disposal, and the control of pollution, dominate the expenditure of the British water industry, with annual revenue and capital budgets exceeding £750millions (1978). This high priority is because pollution forecloses options on most uses of water and can constitute a serious threat to public health.

The quality of water in streams, lakes and canals, estuaries and rivers controls their use as sources of supply for essential human consumption and industrial use, and may affect their potential for water-based amenity and recreation. In addition water-based wildlife is impoverished or eliminated by low water quality of inland sites, estuaries and at the coast. In all cases pollution is a 'negative resource' reducing the economic, life-supporting or aesthetic value of water and related land resources, although to an industrialist the availability of a watercourse for waste disposal is a positive asset.

In this context the role of effluent treatment and pollution control is to adjust water quality to suit the demands for those resources which pollution can adversely affect, while minimising the economic, social and environmental costs of the policies and schemes themselves. Consequently water quality improvement is affected by the role of pollution sources within society. For example, industrial pollution may only be reduced at the expense of profitability or employment or with higher prices for industrial products. These are costs which society may be unwilling to pay. Therefore by aiming to raise water pollution standards by more efficient effluent disposal in response to some general social goal of higher environmental quality, the water planners may threaten some other more valued goal of society, such as full employment.

Water quality planning in Britain today is hampered by an historical legacy of neglect marked by substantial underinvestment. This neglect was partly because of the low political appeal of pollution treatment and partly because industry did not pay for effluent disposal which, prior to 1937, was virtually uncontrolled. Adequate sources of clean water and inadequate appreciation or indifference to the effect of pollution on the natural environment encouraged low effluent disposal standards, exacerbated in England and Wales prior to 1974 by the fragmentation of this responsibility between many small local authorities. The current combination of higher standards, the immense investment needed to raise water quality where it is still too low and the increasing dilapidation of much of the late-nineteenth-century effluent disposal system on an enormous scale means that the effluent disposal and pollution control function of the water industry in Britain today is a major task, not just for the water planning system but for the country as a whole.

The water pollution problem defined

In the natural environment water is never truly clean in the sense that distilled water is free from all impurities. Even a 'crystal clear' mountain stream can contain harmful bacteria from animal excreta and small quantities of toxic chemicals such as arsenic and lead dissolved from underlying rocks. But the term 'polluted' is generally reserved for water with its quality modified by human interference making it less useful or attractive than in its original state and less able to support the flora and fauna of the water, the river bed and the bankside.

It is often wrongly assumed that harmful water pollutants are exclusively waste chemicals and other by-products from industrial processes. In fact the majority of water pollution is domestic sewage and waste products from lavatories and canteens in factories and offices. As such, this pollution is not generally the result of accidental spillage of contaminants into watercourses but the deliberate discharging of below-standard effluent from sewage treatment works, as well as effluent from farms and factories with inadequate treatment facilities.

Pollutants commonly found in water include pathogenic bacteria or other micro-organisms, rotting organic matter which causes unpleasant smells and absorbs oxygen from the water thereby killing fish and other wildlife, and inorganic salts such as potash, phosphates and nitrates. These chemicals increase weed growth in water thereby also absorbing oxygen indirectly, a process known as eutrophication. Also there are oil-based pollutants generally from industrial plants and roadways and a large variety of toxic chemicals, for example compounds of lead, nickel, copper and zinc, as well as complex synthetic chemicals such as detergents (Fish 1973).

Measurement problems and controversies

Water pollution, then, is highly complex. Measurement of the concentration and extent of this pollution is similarly complex and controversial (Dart 1977a; Ross 1977) although conventionally three main methods are used, based on the chemical and physical characteristics of polluted water. First, and arguably most important, is the Biochemical Oxygen Demand (BOD) of the pollutants in the water. The rationale for this measure and the allied Chemical Oxygen Demand (COD) is that the more oxygen a pollutant uses from the water the more it 'kills' the water and inhibits the river or lake's ability to purify itself. This self-purification is a continuous natural process through bacteria and other micro-organisms feeding on organic waste in the water and making it harmless. The process consumes oxygen which is replaced only slowly by absorption from the atmosphere. An abnormal pollution load in a stream or lake consumes large amounts of oxygen and can cause the total dissolved oxygen concentration in the water body to fall dramatically. The micro-organisms involved in the self-purification process then die so that the water becomes completely lifeless and unable to purify itself. The BOD test records the amount of oxygen used by a sample of polluted water incubated at 20°C for five days, and as such is a simulation of natural river conditions at mean summer temperatures rather than a measure of any specific constituent of the polluted sample. The test is therefore not useful as a measure of pollution in water supply where specific toxic elements need identification.

A second measure of pollution is the concentration of suspended solids (SS) in the water, such as faecal matter from humans and animals or grit and coal dust in colliery waste water. Thirdly, it is customary to measure the amount of dissolved toxic metals and other chemicals such as cyanide which can be dangerous even in low concentrations.

The levels of biological pollution by pathogenic micro-organisms such as bacteria, viruses and protozoa are also important to water quality, particularly in water for public supply. It is technically possible to test for all the many hundreds of different organisms found in polluted water but this would be time-consuming and expensive. Instead a standard test is regularly carried out by all water undertakers as an indicator of total micro-biological contamination. This is the colliform test which measures concentrations of just one type of bacteria, the colliform group, which are excreted in large numbers by warm-blooded animals (Department of Health and Social Security 1969).

Obtaining universal methods of measuring pollution levels is desirable but problematic. Both the efficiency of the individual measures of pollution levels and the use of composite water quality indices which weigh and combine such individual measures to give a single figure are open to criticism (Brown *et al.* 1970). All measurements need to be relatively simple to allow large numbers of samples to be analysed quickly and cheaply. Yet this simplicity is virtually impossible, as is the standardisation of measurements subsequently used for different purposes. For example, BOD is useful to a sewage works manager monitoring effluent discharges but some substances have no oxygen demand yet are toxic to fish or may be harmful when consumed over long periods. Identification of these pollutants rather than BOD – which in moderation can improve fisheries – will be crucial for water supply safety and fishery protection or everyday anglers. With measurement problems such as these increasing emphasis is being put on biological indices of pollution, such as the presence of fish in receiving water bodies, thus combining technical efficiency with public expectation of fish life in rivers and lakes (Garland 1979).

The sources and significance of water pollution

Water pollution today comes mainly from four sources. These are sewage treatment works, direct discharges of industrial waste water, urban storm water runoff and untreated farm waste and agricultural fertiliser.

Domestic and industrial pollution. It is ironic that most water pollution in Britain comes from sewage works designed to prevent river contamination and also that the main water polluters today are therefore the regional water authorities themselves, despite their statutory duties to control pollution. This situation has arisen because sewage treatment capacity has not kept pace with increasing waste flows from increased water consumption, new housing and industrial developments. Despite substantial expenditure such that the real value of investment in sewage treatment increased five-fold between 1951 and 1971 (National Water Council 1979), many sewage works are still old and inefficient and cannot deal with effluents from modern industrial processes or the effluent volumes they receive (Wiseman 1974). Either a lower standard of treatment is given to all incoming effluent or part of the crude sewage is discharged into nearby watercourses with no treatment at all. In many cases 'foul' water from lavatories and industrial premises is not separated from 'storm' runoff from roads and roofs and both use 'combined' sewerage pipe systems. During storms total flows into sewage works can far exceed storage and treatment capacity. Then a storm overflow system usually discharges the excess straight to the river outfall and considerable pollution of river water, banks and flood plains ensues despite the dilution by flood water.

About half the flow into sewage works is from industrial plants and half is domestic waste, although the proportion is highly variable. Works in industrial areas naturally take more 'trade effluents'. These comprise waste from food processors and drink manufacturers, containing mainly organic compounds, and other organic effluents from industries such as paper, leather and wool processing. These normally pose no treatment problem, provided adequate capacity is available. However, both effluents containing metals or cyanides – produced largely by engineering industries – and the large variety of chemical effluents from chemical processing plants and industries using acids, alkalis and synthetic detergents can damage or inhibit the biological treatment processes used at sewage works and if discharged to rivers they can be toxic to fish. Chemical pollutants from sewage works can comprise complex organic compounds such as highly dangerous pesticides which have passed right through the treatment process and at the other extreme they may be quite harmless.

Detection of low concentrations of toxic substances in trade effluent is problematic, especially as many sewage works are not permanently manned. It is not practical to test for all known contaminants and the cooperation of local industry is critical in preventing toxic pollutants passing through a sewage works and discharging to the river. The Jeger Report (Ministry of

Housing and Local Government 1970) describes an accidental discharge of cyanide from an industrial plant which killed some 35 000 fish in a river used for drinking water. A warning sounded by anglers luckily allowed the public supply intake to be closed in time. The manufacturer was fined a mere £25 for a breach of the Salmon and Freshwater Fisheries Act 1923.

Water Authorities and River Purification Boards allow direct industrial effluent discharges to rivers and other watercourses although each discharge should conform to standards laid down by these agencies concerning strength (BOD, SS and toxic chemical content) and considerable pre-treatment may be necessary within the factory. Pollution prevention officers make intermittent tests on these standards but until recently test results were not published, and there is ample evidence from many areas that industrialists have failed to conform strictly to these standards with resulting high river pollution (Tinker 1975). In the past fines for non-compliance have been generally low, such as a maximum of £100 under the Rivers (Prevention of Pollution) Act 1961 for an individual who 'knowingly causes or permits to enter a stream any poisonous, noxious or polluting matter without consent'. Also intermittent testing cannot prevent occasional large discharges of noxious effluents, perhaps even at night.

Pollution from agriculture and other sources.   Water pollution from agricultural wastes occurs where modern farming practices have concentrated animals in sheds and yards throughout the year. Few farms are connected to public sewers and some such as broiler units may have insufficient land to dispose of wastes as manure. Therefore much farm waste is discharged into watercourses direct, although agricultural enterprises are in theory controlled as with other direct discharges. Some wastes are treated in oxidation ditches to reduce pollution concentrations before discharging and in other cases wastes are diluted forming a slurry which is then pumped or transported by tanker, mainly on to agricultural land. This slurry can be more dangerous than farmyard manure as in this case storage produces self-sterilisation through composting. Therefore the seepage of slurry into watercourses can cause de-oxygenation and health hazards through the spread of bacterial, parasitic and viral diseases.

Particular pollution problems can arise from chemicals used as animal growth stimulants. Copper is used in pig rations, for example, but most is excreted and pollution can be caused if pig waste is concentrated near watercourses (Yorkshire Water Authority 1978b). Also sheep dip chemicals and pesticides and fertilisers applied to agricultural land can seep into rivers contaminating supplies and causing eutrophication. The waste water from pea vining is also strongly polluting as is the seepage from silage. The large quantity of effluent from farm food processing plants and slaughter houses can overload small rural sewage works or cause serious pollution if discharged to streams (Royal Commission on Environmental Pollution 1979).

A source of water pollution of growing importance is the run-off from densely populated urban areas. In contrast to 'point source' sewage treatment and direct industrial discharges, which in general can be traced fairly readily, 'non point source' surface water discharges from roofs, roadways, garages and industrial premises or from do-it-yourself motorists who discharge oil and other polluting substances into drains are diffuse and therefore more difficult to control (Ellis 1979). During storms these pollutants can pass straight into watercourses if sewerage systems are separate, as they are in many new housing and industrial developments. In contrast at least some treatment may be given to the pollution if the sewerage system is 'combined', and therefore the discharge passes through the treatment works, although overflows to watercourses generally operate at between two and five times normal dry weather flow. In this respect the modern ethic of separating 'storm' and 'foul' sewers is coming under review (National Water Council 1978a). A return to combined sewers is gaining some popularity as are techniques of catchment quality control whereby all potential sources of pollution in a catchment are anticipated and investigated rather than pollution control being based on effluent discharge and river water analysis followed by the problematic tracing of pollution sources (Fish and Torrance 1978).

Although not a major national source of water pollution, accidental and 'accidental' spillages may contaminate watercourses and groundwater, for example when tankers are involved in road and rail accidents and spillages occur from oil installations and other industrial plant. Toxic and corrosive chemicals from these accidents are usually swilled away to the nearest watercourse without thought as to the consequences. The Thames Water Authority reported 925 incidents in 1975/6, mostly oil spillages. In one incident a tanker spilt 23 000 litres of petrol in Ealing, London, causing a potential hazard of explosion in the sewers as well as a major pollution problem. Such sudden polluting discharges can have severe long-term effects on wildlife of water affected. The biological processes of sewage treatment can also be seriously harmed by sudden overloading and water supplies could be severely contaminated, although as yet there has been no major accident in Britain. Illegal 'fly' tipping of industrial wastes into sewers and watercourses also occurs and can be difficult to detect and prevent.

Most industrial waste abstraction is for cooling and thermal pollution can occur. The water is returned unchanged except for the higher temperature, and with the accelerated building programme for new and larger power stations this thermal pollution has increased over the last 10–15 years. Heat speeds up the natural decomposition of the water's organic content, consuming more oxygen from the naturally scarce supplies dissolved in hot water, thereby killing fish and other wildlife in the water thereby further limiting its self-purification potential. Britain has kept nearly all river temperatures well below 30°C through complementary use of cooling towers with river water cooling, as at the Ferrybridge power station on the river Trent. The worst effects of thermal pollution found in other countries have therefore been avoided but this use of cooling towers results in a net abstraction of river water leaving the remaining water pollution more concentrated.

The effects of water pollution

Pollution from all sources can be damaging and disagreeable, affecting both the essential and the non-essential or materialistic water resource roles.

Historically the motivation for pollution prevention was the conservation of fish stocks and the health hazard of polluted supplies. Now that the cheaper clean upland water resources have been mainly exploited, and an increasing proportion of supplies in England and Wales are now taken from lowland rivers and lakes, further demands for water cannot be met without improving the quality of effluents discharged to these lowland sources. In Scotland, despite abundant supplies of clean upland water, the use of the clean upper Clyde for water supply is made problematic by the need for this water for dilution of effluent from the urban areas downstream (Clyde River Purification Board 1978). In contrast the river Lee is used to supply water to 600 000 people and numerous industrial plants in north London despite containing large amounts of sewage effluent from numerous sewage works at Luton, Hatfield and other Hertfordshire towns which, in dry weather, comprises approximately 90% of the flow. Most British cities, however, are not so well served by upstream sewage works and therefore the cost of meeting future demands by treating polluted river water for supply, or obtaining alternative sources, will be greater without stringent river pollution control which of course is itself costly.

Water use for amenity and recreation also suffers through water pollution. Angling is the sport most obviously affected since contaminants lower fish stocks by reducing the amount and variety of fish food and by reducing resistance to disease. Hazard to public health may arise from bathing and paddling in polluted water. The risk is probably very low except from accidental immersion in heavily polluted water when considerable quantities can be swallowed and serious diseases can result, such as leptospirosis (Weil's disease) originating from substances in rats' urine. Nevertheless overt pollution and objectionable smells spoil riverside walks, picnics and boating and polluted waters near urban areas are just those where recreation use could otherwise flourish.

The official water pollution surveys

Progress in river pollution control since the second world war has been considerable but recognition of a continuing problem has led to a series of national surveys of river and estuarine water pollution (Department of the Environment and Welsh Office 1971; Scottish Development Department 1976). Rivers and estuaries are classified on the basis of their dissolved oxygen content, BOD, biological data and the presence of toxic compounds where

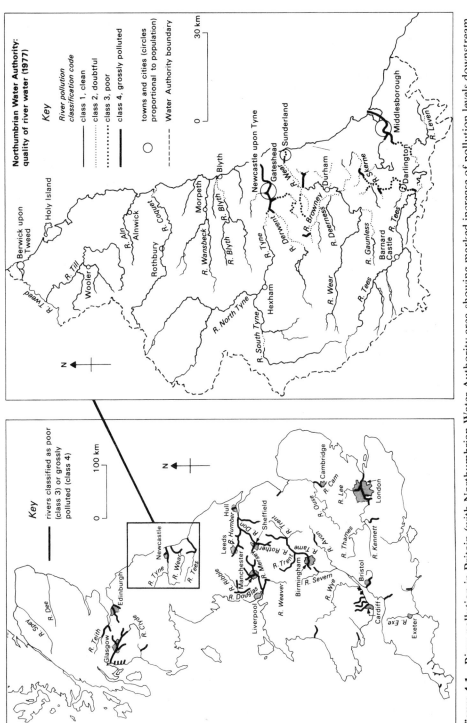

Figure 4.1 River pollution in Britain (with Northumbrian Water Authority area showing marked increase of pollution levels downstream of urban areas).

information is available (Table 4.1; Fig. 4.1). The surveys in England and Wales have also considered the extent of substantiated complaints by the public.

Table 4.1 Summary of river pollution survey classification.

1 Rivers unpolluted and recovered from pollution (e.g. BOD less than 3 mg/l);
2 Rivers of doubtful quality and needing improvement (e.g. those not in class 1 on BOD grounds and which have a substantial decrease in oxygen content at normal dry summer flows);
3 Rivers of poor quality requiring improvement as a matter of some urgency (e.g. containing substances which are suspected of being actively toxic at times but with BOD less than 12 mg/l);
4 Grossly polluted rivers (e.g. average BOD more than 12 mg/l and incapable of supporting fish life).

Source: Royal Commission on Environmental Pollution 1974. For a more detailed version of the slightly revised classification in current use see National Water Council 1978.

Table 4.2 shows some improvement in water quality in Britain since 1958 using this classification, particularly the continuing reduction in the amounts of grossly polluted rivers. However, the state of our estuaries is cause for considerable concern (Porter 1973). Here pollution levels reflect a shift of effluent discharge from inland rivers to tidal waters rather than a solution to the problem as a whole. Moreover the data from these surveys should be viewed critically since what is measured is the lengths of rivers and estuaries. Therefore a kilometre of a small clean upland stream contributes as much to the results as a kilometre of the highly polluted river Tees or Clyde, both with high discharges flowing through heavily populated areas. Indeed a large proportion of rivers passing through the major towns and conurbations of Britain are Class 3 or worse (Royal Commission on Environmental Pollution 1974). In these areas population densities are too high for normal treatment standards to provide adequate eventual effluents and hitherto higher treatment standards have been considered too expensive. This indicates a continuing problem not well demonstrated by the high percentage of unpolluted river lengths as shown in Table 4.2 and Figure 4.1.

Indeed these national water pollution surveys are highly generalised and subjective (Lester 1977) and detailed analyses by Water Authorities and River Purification Boards reveal other problems and the considerable geographical variation in pollution levels. Wessex Water Authority (1978b) reports no significant pollution problems and away from the Clyde region most pollution problems in Scotland are local (Highland River Purification Board 1977). Surveys of the Anglian Water Authority (1976) show pollution problems from nitrate concentrations probably resulting from fertiliser runoff not adequately identified by the broader scale national survey which fails, in addition, to take account of acute but local problems and seasonal variation in pollution load. For example, the flow of the Tyne at Newcastle during the 1975–76 drought was reduced from 4·4 to 0·318 million m^3 per day. Given

Table 4.2 Results of official river pollution surveys in Britain (1958–75).

England and Wales

	1958		*1970*		*1975*	
	km	%	km	%	km	%
1 *unpolluted*						
non tidal	23 500	72·9	23 370	76·2	28 037	77·6
tidal	1 160	40·7	1 383	48·1	1 422	49·6
canals			1 127	45·4	1 223	50·7
2 *doubtful quality*						
non tidal	4 611	14·3	5 297	14·7	5 458	15·1
tidal	935	32·8	675	23·4	720	25·1
canals			968	39·1	925	38·3
3 *poor quality*						
non tidal	2 058	6·4	1 724	4·8	1 449	4·0
tidal	400	14·1	485	16·8	424	14·8
canals			219	8·8	177	7·3
4 *grossly polluted*						
non tidal	2 057	6·4	1 533	4·3	1 178	3·3
tidal	355	12·4	336	11·7	301	10·5
canals			166	6·7	88	3·7

Scotland

	1968		*1974*	
	km	%	km	%
1 *unpolluted*				
non tidal	3 851	81·7	30 096	93·2
tidal	198	63·0	192	53·5
canals	0	0·0	35	21·8
2 *doubtful quality*				
non tidal	561	11·9	1 615	5·0
tidal	59	18·8	98	27·3
canals	72	80·0	121	75·6
3 *poor quality*				
non tidal	166	3·5	407	1·3
tidal	27	8·6	31	8·6
canals	7	7·8	2	1·3
4 *grossly polluted*				
non tidal	135	2·9	161	0·5
tidal	30	9·6	38	10·6
canals	11	12·2	2	1·3

Source: Department of the Environment 1978, Scottish Development Department 1976, Department of the Environment and Welsh Office 1971. (Figures differ marginally in these owing to revisions and redefinitions).

the very large volumes of only partially treated sewage effluent in the low flow the pollution nuisance was considerable and emphasises the benefits of multi-purpose river regulation schemes to pollution control through the provision of adequate dilution.

Further indication of continuing problems comes from high pollution levels in canals. Furthermore no comparative surveys exist of lakes, which can show considerable pollution problems, or of coastal pollution levels. It is generally assumed that the sea has an almost infinite capacity to purify biodegradable pollutants yet very little data exists on the biological effect of the 1300 sewage outfalls to the sea. One thousand of these are of crude untreated sewage, providing effluent disposal for 5 million people in England and Wales or 11% of the population. Therefore while there has undoubtedly been substantial improvement in effluent disposal and pollution levels in the last 20–30 years, there are significant problems to be tackled which, in general, are likely to be more difficult and expensive to solve as diminishing returns to pollution abatement expenditure set in.

Pollution treatment

Most pollution can be treated at regional water authority sewage works which receive sewage through an immense network of sewers from over 90% of British households and in England and Wales remove approximately 77% of the pollutant load.

In 1978 there were in England and Wales just 22 discharges of crude sewage but 4056 discharges of treated effluent from 30 million people to non-tidal waters, of which treated sewage from 9 million people goes to rivers used for public supply (Garland 1979).

Treatment at modern sewage treatment installations comprises primary, secondary and tertiary stages, leaving effluent for discharge to a watercourse and sludge for disposal (Fish 1973). With primary treatment incoming sewage and industrial waste is screened to remove large debris such as wood or rags. Grit is then removed and the sewage passes through large tanks allowing solids to settle out by gravitation for removal as sludge. Effective primary treatment can lower BOD by one third and remove between 60% and 80% of settleable solids.

Liquor from the primary stage would slowly convert itself into harmless substances through the action of bacteria and other micro-organisms. With secondary treatment this process is accelerated. Either the liquor passes through 'filter' beds of inert slag or gravel where a film of bacteria and fungi develops which oxidise the sewage rapidly on the large surface area, or the sewage has oxygen blown through it or is mechanically aerated in tanks. The liquor with suspended solids from the oxidisation passes through further settlement tanks separating sludge from the final effluent.

Each increment of treatment involves increased capital and revenue costs. For a higher effluent standard a tertiary or 'polishing' stage can remove suspended solids which escaped the secondary sedimentation by passing liquor over grass plots, slow filtration through sand, long retention in lagoons or microstraining. Effluents of 10 mg/l BOD and SS can be produced, while grass plots and lagoons reduce the bacteria content of the effluent. Tertiary treatment can remove nitrates which would otherwise cause eutrophication of the receiving watercourses.

Critical to the economics of sewage treatment, amounting to 40% of total costs, is the disposal of sludge from the sedimentation tanks. This is an evil-smelling thick liquid full of pathogenic bacteria, in total less than 1% of the initial sewage, amounting to 26 kg of dry solids per head per annum. Most sludge is treated prior to disposal and a common treatment method is 'anaerobic digestion' in sealed tanks heated to 35°C for several weeks. Bacteria which flourish without air transform the sludge into a humus-like substance, which can be used as a manure, and gas including methane which can be used as a fuel. The Northern Outfall works at Barking in London is almost self-sufficient in electricity generated using this method. The majority of sludge is now spread on farm land following treatment, although the harmlessness of untreated sludge is becoming appreciated (Brown 1977) as well as its value, not least as a substitute for oil-based artificial fertilisers. Problems do occur when sludge contains toxic metals, as from many works in industrial areas, and in these cases sludge is also dumped at sea, either pumped beyond tidal limits or dumped from special vessels, with apparently few harmful consequences. Incineration has proved costly and unsuccessful – with the Leeds plant a total failure – and with incineration water pollution may be lessened at the expense of greater air pollution.

With the discharge of sewage to the sea the need for treatment is considerably reduced. Sewage in the sea undergoes natural chemical and biological processes of purification to the extent that no change in the character of the sea can be detected. Screening is generally desirable as is discharge below low water with long outfalls, which has not been the case in the past (Consumers' Association 1975, Department of the Environment 1978).

There are, therefore, few technical problems with pollution control, simply economic constraints concerning treatment standards. In the past technical problems have arisen, such as with treating the 'hard' detergents developed in the 1950s which passed right through treatment works causing serious pollution and foaming effluents. Furthermore, our chemical environment is constantly changing and there is a major uncertainty as to the long-term effects of low concentrations of toxic pollutants for which there can be no guarantee of elimination by conventional sewage treatment.

The historical and social context of water pollution control

Water pollution control is fundamentally about standards. The standards that society sets for the quality of water in its rivers and lakes depend on the public attitude prevailing towards the environment which in turn either allows goals to be set and funds allocated for environmental improvement or alternatively the acceptance of the *status quo*. The process of setting standards involves either this acceptance or arriving at a consensus of all those concerned as to some future desired state or the enactment of legislation and local regulations which attempt to encourage or force individuals and groups to comply with some desirable level of environmental care.

The setting of standards is easy, but the implementation or enforcement of these standards in our democratic society is not. Such problems are possibly related to the public's perception of water as a common property resource which all individuals have the right to use but no one in particular has inherent interest in care and conservation. Implementation of standards may involve limiting the individual's right to pollute water on privately owned land or necessitate restrictions on the uses of water which lead to pollution, such as prohibiting pleasure craft on inland waterways without sealed sanitary equipment. As such pollution prevention and control measures may infringe the liberties of the few to promote the wellbeing of the many and, even within a democratic society, such egalitarian practices do not always carry the popular support one might expect and often promote considerable sectional opposition. Legislation often fails in its purpose not on account of inadequate laws, nor through lack of technical knowledge, but because the laws are not being enforced, sometimes through indifference but usually because those responsible are unable (or unwilling) to meet the costs of controlling pollution' (Royal Commission on Environmental Pollution 1971). Therefore to complement legislation curbing rights and setting restrictions, pollution prevention can be encouraged through grants to industry for pollution treatment facilities, through penalties for illegal pollution and through charges for effluent discharge and treatment, all of which discourage pollution if properly planned and adequately enforced but all of which bring their own problems, not least that of uncertainty as to effect.

The historical evolution of legislation and practices in the water pollution field illuminate society's evolving attitudes which in turn helps to explain attitudes and policies today. This historical picture in turn raises the central question of who within society sets standards. The answer to this question is not simple, but differs at different times. Sometimes, for example, standards are set within the water industry, by the scientists and engineers concerned both with water pollution prevention and with other areas, when water planning goals in these other fields become threatened such as the high quality standards of those concerned with river abstractions for public supply. At other times independent interest groups appear to force the setting of standards, perhaps through dangers to wildlife caused by toxic or other pollutants, as in the case of pollution standards for the Norfolk Broads.

The public at large seems not to be interested in promoting higher pollution prevention standards, perhaps through lack of appropriate education, but to follow certain key leaders, professionals or groups who initially perhaps promote higher standards on behalf of just their sectional interest. Parliament and government, in turn, generally follow behind public opinion. Therefore restrictions, legislation and incentives tend to lag behind the need for pollution prevention, reflecting perhaps inherent weaknesses in democratic processes. Legislation may, however, have the function of encouraging or forcing uniformity of standards pioneered by the few and so raising overall standards through focussing attention on particular areas and problems where ignorance or negligence has caused slow progress. In this way the Control of Pollution Act 1974 is focussing attention on the continuing problems of polluted estuaries such as the Humber and the Mersey and away from the successes such as the improved non-tidal Thames.

The evolution of the problem and of pollution control legislation

The raising of standards through legislation has been incremental, as reflected in the large number of Acts of Parliament which have attempted in the last 130 years to control polluting discharges into water bodies. Many of these Acts have deliberately exempted pre-existing discharges from control and therefore have only attempted to tackle the growth of pollution, rather than the problem as a whole. Not until the Control of Pollution Act 1974 has comprehensive legislation for pollution prevention been enacted, although as yet the effect of this more systematic planning of water quality management cannot be judged as much of the Act has still to be implemented.

Early history: administrative fragmentation and indifference.   The eighteenth and nineteenth centuries left a legacy of severe pollution in many rivers and canals. During the eighteenth century the state of British towns by today's standards was disgusting, since the lack of any proper sewerage system meant garbage and excrement simply accumulated in the streets. Early in the nineteenth century the introduction of sewers carrying wastes to rivers lessened the more obvious problem on the streets (in front of people's noses one might say) but created a no less serious problem of polluted watercourses, because the sewage was discharged into the rivers and canals completely untreated. As the British population grew, new industries arose and urban agglomeration continued, more and more contaminants found their way into rivers, canals and estuaries.

Nineteenth-century legislation went some way towards controlling the worst abuses, mainly through the Fisheries Acts 1861 and 1865, the Public Health Act 1872 and the Rivers Pollution Prevention Act 1876 in England and Wales, and the Public Health Acts 1867 and 1897 as well as many local Acts of Parliament specific to Scotland. However, a problem of enforcement remained and standards in many cases were very low indeed. The numerous small local authorities, dominated by industrialists, were supposed to police their own standards yet their motivation in pollution control was somewhat low, in part because they were not required statutorily to treat sewage in their area and any treatment undertaken voluntarily only benefited people living downstream rather than the local authority's own ratepayers.

The 1912 Royal Commission report.   At the end of the nineteenth century concern for the state of British rivers led to the appointment of the Royal

Commission on Sewage Disposal (1912). Since then a standard has been set, despite all the complexities of water pollution, for the level of pollution in discharges into water bodies which can be tolerated and will not upset the self-purification processes. This '30/20 Royal Commission standard' sets the level of suspended solids at 30 milligrams/litre (mg/l) and the BOD at 20 mg/l for discharges where the 'dirty' effluent is diluted with at least eight times as much 'clean' water flowing in the stream. A modern sewage works with secondary treatment facilities should produce this 30/20 effluent.

This is clearly a generalised standard, ignoring both toxic chemicals and bacteriological pollutants. Also the efficiency of the self-purification process is more rapid in shallow fast-moving water than in deep rivers where the water surface area for oxygen absorption is small in relation to discharge. This difference in oxygenation rates will influence the effect a 30/20 effluent will have on a water body. Therefore many Water Authorities require a higher standard for certain watercourses, especially those for public supply. Nevertheless the Royal Commission recommendation was found to characterise an acceptable general standard for many years (Roberts 1974) although by no means all discharges meet this standard even today. More than 3000 out of the 5000 sewage works in England and Wales produce effluents which do not meet the 50-year-old standard. This demonstrates how standards may be set with ease but implementing the necessary improvement in treatment plant may well not follow.

The development of real powers.　　The Salmon and Freshwater Fisheries Act 1923 established fisheries boards to counteract river pollution but they did little to influence already fishless waters owing to inadequate finance. Not until 1936 did local authorities in England and Wales have a statutory obligation to carry out sewage disposal and treatment and not until 1937 were industrialists allowed to discharge polluted wastes into public sewers. Scotland had to wait until 1968 for similar effluent disposal and pollution control powers.

The Public Health Act 1936 empowered local authorities in England and Wales to construct public sewers and sewage treatment works and required them to undertake their sewerage functions 'without creating a nuisance', that is without discharging an unsatisfactorily polluted – but undefined – effluent. In addition the Act provided safeguards to protect sewers and sewage works, for example by prohibiting discharges of petrol and liquids with temperatures higher than 35°C into sewers. The Sewerage (Scotland) Act 1968 similarly places a duty on Regional and Island Councils to provide 'such public sewers as may be necessary for effectually draining their areas of domestic sewage, surface water and trade effluent'. The Councils also have a duty to treat or otherwise deal with the contents of the sewers, although only in 1972 were the relevant sections on trade effluent powers implemented. Under the Water Act 1945 water authorities in England and Wales could make byelaws preventing discharge of pollutants where water supplies might be contaminated, whether on the surface or underground, and acquire land to protect their water or water gathering grounds. There are similar provisions in the Water (Scotland) Act 1946, although except for the Clyde area through a private Act of Parliament there was here no control over pollution of groundwater.

Control of industrial discharge into sewers in England and Wales originally comes from the Public Health (Drainage of Trade Premises) Act 1937 which gave industrialists the right to use public sewers, and the water authority powers to impose 'consent conditions' comprising upper limits on parameters such as BOD, suspended solids, toxic metals, phenols, cyanide, oil content, temperature and total discharge. The refusal of consent or the conditions imposed could be appealed against and this legislation also empowered water authorities to charge for the conveyance and treatment of trade effluent, powers mirrored in the Sewerage (Scotland) Act 1968.

Control of discharges direct to watercourses has been the subject of many Acts, foremost in England and Wales being the Rivers (Prevention of Pollution) Acts 1951 and 1961. The 1951 Act made it an offence to cause or knowingly permit pollution to enter a stream (including canals), thereby excusing accidental spillages, and prevented new or altered outlets for discharges without water authority consent, again subject to appeal. The 1961 legislation brought under control the pre-1961 discharges for which consent was not previously needed and required periodic reviews of the consent conditions. Also water authorities were empowered to make byelaws to control the discharge of pollutants from vessels on inland waterways. Section 6 of the 1951 Act allowed extension of the provisions to specific tidal waters, estuaries and adjoining parts of the sea, and a few minor estuaries in England and Wales were fully controlled by these orders, while the Clean Rivers (Estuaries and Tidal Waters) Act 1960 established control over new or altered discharges to tidal rivers and estuaries. The Water Resources Act 1963 gave power to prevent pollution of underground water in England and Wales by discharge into wells, boreholes and pipes, as well as giving emergency powers to water authorities to clear accidental pollution of rivers. The tidal area of the Thames has been cleaned up considerably since 1968 through special legislation, and points the way to possible improvements elsewhere (Harrison and Grant 1976).

In Scotland the Rivers (Prevention of Pollution) (Scotland) Acts 1951 and 1965 gave the Secretary of State for Scotland and the River Purification Boards the duty to promote the cleanliness of Scottish rivers and lakes by regulating new or altered discharges (1951 Act) and subsequently all discharges (1965 Act). Also tidal water Orders could be made by the Secretary of State to control new discharges to certain tidal areas (1951 Act) and to all tidal areas (1965 Act). In contrast to England and Wales these orders covered the main estuaries of the Clyde, Forth and Tay as well as minor areas sensitive to pollution such as the Findhorn and Wick bays.

The legacy of history.   Legislation since 1945 has progressively tightened control over discharges to sewers, watercourses and to the sea. Nevertheless a pollution problem still remains because of continuing difficulties of enforcing the all-important consent conditions set by the Water Authorities in England and Wales and by the River Purification Boards in Scotland, partly because of the substantial costs of required treatment facilities. This, together with an ever-increasing volume of effluent from increasing water consumption, has meant that pollution control authorities have been working hard to prevent deterioration of existing unsatisfactory pollution standards.

These low standards were all too clearly revealed when the new Water Authorities in England and Wales took over the sewage treatment plants from local authorities, thus integrating water quality management with other water service planning. Before reorganisation sewage treatment was probably the most neglected of all parts of the water cycle; the legacy inherited by the Water Authorities was one of 'insufficient, inadequate, outdated works, coupled with a heavy burden of loan debt' (Southern Water Authority 1976). In 1973 central government estimated that massive capital expenditure of around £1200millions at 1970 prices (perhaps £3500millions at 1980 prices) was needed to bring all discharges of sewage and industrial effluent up to the standards expected to be imposed with full implementation of the Control of Pollution Act 1974. Half of this capital was needed for sewerage and replacement of worn out equipment and half for new sewage treatment works. The North West Water Authority area, for example, has some 30 000 km of public sewers, one sixth of which are more than 100 years old, in poor structural condition and probably close to collapse. Sixty per cent of the sewage works (245 out of 411) taken over by the Authority were in an unsatisfactory condition on 1 April 1974 (Wiseman 1974). Again, the Horsham sewage works in Surrey were only built in 1931 but by 1976 were grossly overloaded due to the large increase in population. Many local authorities neglected their statutory responsibility for keeping maps of sewers and details of their condition: basic information required for planning the maintenance and phased replacement of the aging public sewers. In the Anglian Water Authority area in 1974, for example, less than 50% of the area had proper records and 10% had none at all. The early annual reports of all the other Water Authorities give similar examples of the legacy of 120 years of piecemeal and underfinanced effluent disposal and pollution prevention.

Social attitudes to water pollution and the policy implications

There is no doubt that British society is more environmentally conscious today than at any previous time in its history. The fundamental reason for this is not clear but it is perhaps because other social needs have been increasingly satisfied so that concern about the environment has moved up our list of priorities. This new attitude is shown by a greater awareness of the damaging effects of pollution of all kinds. Other manifestation of similar attitude shifts is the greater interest in 'natural' and 'health' foods, encouraged by advertising linking such products with a healthy body and a clean environment. Although this is still not an area where there is general public debate, more and more sectional interests are concerned about environmental quality and these groups embrace more and more of society.

As a result of these and similar shifts in attitudes the public has accepted some higher costs in the interests of environmental protection, for example in the use of smokeless fuel rather than cheaper alternatives. This acceptance is partly as a result of a greater appreciation of the social costs of poor environmental standards, perhaps best exemplified in the antipathy now felt towards high-rise flats. Such acceptance of the principle of higher commodity or property costs on the one hand and of the social costs of degradation on the other has been significant in allowing progress in all areas of environmental planning and pollution control.

The rise in the national and local amenity societies has both reflected and generated interest in environmental quality (Lowe 1975a, 1975b, 1977). These societies are mainly focussed on urban residential issues, associated with conservation area designation or neighbourhood improvement schemes. Nevertheless this greater awareness of environmental quality and, perhaps more important, of the power of the public voice when raised, has spread rapidly to other issues. We cannot separate cause and effect in the shift in public attitudes but the general increase in interest in environmental education, of which the reader is probably part, reflects a significant shift in social attitudes and priorities. Given the interdependence of the water planning system with its social context this shift has had and will continue to have a profound effect on water pollution prevention policies.

However, while these changing attitudes are complemented by some public dissatisfaction with economic advancement coupled with excessive environmental degradation, this dissatisfaction is not always translated into action. Both individual members of the public and sectional interest groups on both sides of industry may well be more concerned with raising their own standards of living than with controlling effluent discharges from the factories, farms and offices in which they work. Economic advancement with its associated technological development affects pollution levels simply because with increasing industrial production come increasing volumes of waste products. Also in our society up until now the 'costs' of pollution are not borne by the polluter but by someone else. Therefore there may well be little or no incentive for the industrialist to create less pollution, thereby raising costs and therefore, in a competitive market, reducing profits. For example, the Yorkshire wool-scouring firm, faced with keen competition from imported goods from countries with less concern for environmental pollution, has little motivation to reduce its seriously polluting effluents discharged direct to rivers since to remain competitive it cannot afford either the necessary pre-treatment plant or the charges that might be levied by the Yorkshire Water Authority for treatment at its sewage works (Yorkshire Water Authority 1978a).

Complete elimination of pollution is technically impossible and economically undesirable: waste from industrial processing is inevitable. Water dispersal, with its useful natural self-purification processes, could only be eliminated at the expense of increasing air pollution or dumping more wastes on land with resulting landscape erosion, although these fields of environmental management are the concern of different agencies in this country and therefore each considers its own resource and attention is rarely paid to reducing the total waste load received by the environment as a whole (Rees 1977a).

In theory pollution should be reduced to the point where the costs of doing so are covered by the benefits from the reduction in pollution although in practice such a cost-benefit calculation is virtually impossible. Moreover the more we spend on pollution abatement the less we have to spend on other social needs such as hospitals and schools. The question facing society, then, comes back to what standard of environment is acceptable and to what levels should water pollution be reduced? For the individual this question becomes one of how much of his current and future personal prosperity he is willing to forgo in the interests of communal environmental quality, given competing demands for his finite resources.

Therefore while attitudes towards pollution may be shifting over time these shifts are slow and incremental. At times of economic progress individuals may be content to see an increment of their increasing income diverted into pollution control and other forms of environmental improvement. At times of economic recession, however, this may not be acceptable and in our society where decisions are largely made to satisfy public opinion and industrial profitability this recession will result in the slowing down of environmental expenditure as personal incomes or industrial profits are stretched and tax increases are politically unacceptable. It may be inappropriate at these times to criticise the policy-making and executive agencies for negligence since they are merely responding to society's priorities. However, it may be appropriate to evaluate at a less basic level the mechanisms of pollution prevention adopted by these agencies and their effects on different sections of society. Critical here is whether standard-setting, incentives or penalties and charges are sufficiently sympathetic to the complex economic forces in operation and whether they make, for example, the industrialist realise and react to the social cost of pollution and to include this with his other production costs rather than transferring them via the water authority pollution prevention budget on to the public at large. Also not insignificant is the erosion of rights the individual may suffer such as inspection of property to locate pollution sources. In each of these cases unpopular pollution control measures may, through exciting public opposition, prove counterproductive and adversely affect the pace of progress.

The financial context of pollution prevention

Given the implementation of the Control of Pollution Act 1974, discussed below, there will be no legislative constraint to restoring our rivers, lakes and estuaries to the healthy conditions prevailing before the industrial revolution. The technical problems are minimal (Ministry of Housing and Local Government 1970) but the main impediment to progress is shortage of money both for sewage treatment and for industrial pre-treatment capacity before discharging to sewers or rivers. This financial problem has two components, shortage of capital and shortage of revenue, both of which are interrelated and subject to political control.

The water industry as a whole is highly capital intensive and the effluent treatment and pollution control side of Water Authority work takes a disproportionate share of available capital. To up-grade programmes of sewage works and sewerage investment would involve either taking capital expenditure from other fields, such as water recreation or water supply – contrary to the spirit of the Water Act 1973 which encourages Water Authorities to operate each service on a self-sufficiency basis – or increasing the total level of capital expenditure and such increases can only occur with government sanction. Therefore what should be long-term investment programmes are disrupted by shorter-term fluctuations in national economic fortunes. Cost is a further deterrent to increased capital expenditure. Already the Water Authorities spend about one third of all their revenue in interest charges on capital borrowed and to increase this further is politically difficult as the public sees the proportion spent so apparently unproductively as already too high. The North West Water Authority sewage treatment budget, for example, is already dominated by 47% in loan charges and for sewerage the figure is a staggering 76% (North West Water Authority 1976b).

Historically revenue from sewage treatment and pollution control services has been too low, because of short-sighted local government political control and little rational costing of services. This legacy again is a major constraint on achieving higher standards today. More revenue is needed to pay staff sufficiently to attract more highly qualified pollution prevention officers, laboratory chemists and sewage works managers to man the increased numbers of treatment works, and also to recruit, train and retain the manual labour in sewerage services doing an unpleasant and dangerous job for relatively low pay. More revenue is also needed to finance the enlarged capital programmes.

The effluent quality from a sewage works and the processes used also affect running costs directly. Tertiary treatment adds some 15–25% to the costs for the 30/20 standard. To achieve potable supply quality the costs rise very rapidly although here different processes can have markedly different costs (Truesdale and Taylor 1975). However, as an example of how little difference is caused by quality differences towards the bottom end of the scale, partial treatment to an 80/60 instead of a 30/20 standard saves only some 15% of costs. This however assumes sufficient capacity to treat to 30/20 already exists. Extension of capacity to treat an excessive sewage inflow to this as opposed to the lower standard will involve capital expenditure constraints not just increases in running costs.

Revenue comes from charges for sewage and sewerage services which historically have been too low in many ways. The general charges levied through local authority rates before 1974 often covered the running costs of sewage works but not depreciation, that is nothing was charged for the replacement of the works which, when needed, require further capital borrowing so increasing the loan charge burden on revenue resources: a financial vicious circle!

Industrial organisations should pay for the disposal of their wastes through public sewers but in 1974 a fifth of all local authorities in England and Wales made no charge over and above the normal rates for industrial premises and few local authorities in Scotland made charges for trade effluent discharges (Woodward 1976). Where local authorities did levy charges they were very low, perhaps in the hope of attracting or retaining industry. Another revenue source involving low charges is fishing permits. Much of the direct benefit of pollution prevention, which in 1975/6 cost some £6·7millions in England and Wales, is gained by the angler yet fishery revenue for all the Water Authorities amounted in the same year to only £2·4millions. This is probably an unfair comparison as there are clearly many other beneficiaries of clean water, but perhaps the £3 per annum fishing licence is too good a bargain for the national good.

The water pollution control system

Within the overall water planning system two features concerning pollution control warrant further attention. These are, first, the inherent problems in the administration of sewage treatment and pollution prevention – the institutional problem – and, secondly, the strength and diversity of the pressure groups in the pollution control field.

The institutional problem

Pollution prevention has far-reaching social and economic implications. The enforcement of standards and the prosecution of offenders necessitates scrupulous objectivity and honesty on the part of pollution control agencies in the face of strong economic pressures. Herein lies an institutional problem: whether to include the all-important monitoring function within truly multi-functional water authorities, who must necessarily be polluters through their own sewage works, or whether to have separate and therefore possibly more objective agencies. In this respect Scotland has taken a different path to England and Wales.

In Scotland the River Purification Boards have the separate pollution control function and they therefore monitor river quality, effluent discharges and set consent conditions for both sewage treatment works and direct discharges. It has been argued in favour of this system that pressures by the Boards on the Regional Councils has resulted in extra expenditure being sanctioned by the Scottish Development Department. In reality all except the Clyde Board are relatively weak but then their pollution control problems are more minor. The Clyde Board has 51 members drawing on 17 different interest groups and has through its publications and an energetic chief executive pioneered higher river quality standards (Pullin 1977). However, the Regional Councils should not be depicted as the villains and during a period of financial stringency in the middle 1970s one chief engineer publicly threatened to close down sewage treatment works if a larger financial allocation was not made, which it was. The natural tension created by this institutional separation might create more problems of cooperation if staff in both sets of agencies did not have a strong professional commitment and interest in higher standards.

In England and Wales all effluent disposal and pollution control functions are combined within the Water Authorities who thereby are both polluter and pollution control agency, or both 'poacher' and 'gamekeeper'. Recognising this problem most Water Authorities have set up Water Quality Advisory Panels, or similar, comprising members of the Authority, to oversee the officers' work in this field and to publish results of surveys. Furthermore at officer level most Water Authorities have a water pollution officer who is free to report to the Water Quality Panel and thus directly to the Authority rather than through the Chief Executive. In general he is the Director of Scientific Services, where this post exists, or is an Assistant Director within the resource planning directorate in smaller Authorities, as recommended by the Ogden Committee (Department of the Environment 1973).

How this internal separation of roles will work in the long term is not clear but progress should be assisted by two innovations. First, the full publication of quality test results under the Control of Pollution Act 1974 should, when implemented, ensure that the Water Authorities' pollution control function is entirely public. Secondly, since the local authority membership of Water Authorities comes from many more Counties than was the case with the old River Authorities individual members should therefore be less concerned with the rate burden on their own constituents since the costs of pollution prevention will be borne by the population of the whole Authority (Okun 1977). The former River Authorities rarely prosecuted local authorities as there were too many members in common. Public acceptance of higher charges to finance higher standards will, however, be forthcoming only if the Water Authorities are seen to be putting their own house in order by reducing pollution from their own works and maintaining scrupulous objectivity over pollution monitoring. The River Authorities' reputations as enforcement authorities became tarnished through the secrecy over consents and effluent analyses, compounded by the few prosecutions for abuses, and the enforcement reputation of the Water Authorities will be crucial to further standard raising, owing to social attitudes being a critical determinant of water pollution and other environmental standards, as well as finance, administration or technical constraints.

Interest and pressure groups

Perhaps the most obvious interest group in the water pollution control system is the Institute of Water Pollution Control. Such a group becomes most active at times of uncertainty when the roles of its members are threatened by administrative change and, given the extent that administrative arrangements affect policy, these groups do influence the evolution of policies and plans.

The Institute actively lobbied the Department of the Environment and other agencies in the lead-in to the Water Act 1973 and the reorganisation in 1974 in England and Wales (Okun 1977). Prior to that the Institute had advocated to the Royal Commission on Local Government in England that sewage treatment and disposal should be organised regionally rather than at local authority level. When regionalisation was proposed in the Water Act 1973 and particularly the multi-functional arrangement whereby headquarters of Water Authorities would not have Directorates organised on functional lines, giving a Directorate for Sewage, the Institute responded negatively, fearing for the representation of its members in senior positions. Similarly, given the decision to take Chief Executives from outside the existing water industry – outside the 'ring fence' – the Institute responded at its 1973 annual conference that 'The sewage and industrial waste water treatment function is the heart of the whole hydrological cycle, and should be treated as such' (Okun 1977, p. 124); whether such overt claims for special treatment and influential positions had any effect on administrative developments can never be known.

A major pressure on effluent disposal management comes from local authorities, and particularly District Councils in England and Wales. As sewerage agents for the Water Authority, Councils have to satisfy both the Water Authority's duty for financial self-sufficiency and their constituents' need for sewer replacement or first time sewerage for new development, over which the District has absolute power. These aims may well conflict and in any case considerable problems have also arisen over the apportionment of administration costs for the split arrangement, especially when District engineering departments are responsible for other local authority functions such as roads. The problem is compounded, first, by the absolute right of developers to connect to sewers irrespective of their condition and by the powers under Section 16 of the Water Act 1973 for developers and local authorities to requisition foul sewers, although this has advantages to Water Authorities in that sewerage provision is not provided unnecessarily in advance of developments and costs can be recovered in part from developers on a formula basis (Thomas 1976). Secondly, communication difficulties have arisen owing to insufficient representation of Districts on Water Authorities and thirdly by the numerous Districts with which the Authorities have to liaise.

Professional and local government organisations naturally have most interest in the administration of the water planning system but in addition many conservation and amenity groups – and particularly the anglers' organisations – seek to influence the water pollution control system. Also industrialists and farmers both have a keen interest in this field, and their role is emphasised because a policy of persuasion and cooperation is being practised by Purification Boards and Water Authorities as being slow but more efficient in the long term. Industrialists successfully lobbied the Conservative government to include the secrecy clauses in the Rivers (Prevention of Pollution) Act 1961 as they had in 1937 to exempt pre-1936 discharges from control by the setting of consent conditions. The current attitude of the Confederation of British Industry is to accept but guide the process of change to higher standards and consequently higher treatment or direct discharge charges, but individual industrialists may be harder to convince. The strength of the farming lobby is demonstrated by the general exemption of agriculture from the Control of Pollution 1974 Act since the National Farmers' Union argued that good agricultural practices inevitably lead to pollution. Some industrialists might well argue the same for industry but then what are 'good practices' for the industrialist – or farmer – and his profitability may not be good for our rivers and their wildlife.

Effluent disposal and pollution control policies, plans and schemes

Policy alternatives

Numerous alternative strategies exist for effluent disposal and pollution control. Fundamentally contrasting are approaches based on attempting to regulate and thereby diminish the volume of potential pollutants for which to provide disposal facilities and those based on accepting those volumes created and disposing of or treating these. The latter *laissez-faire* approach has characterised past effluent disposal practice and, with insufficient treatment capacity, considerable river, estuarine and coastal pollution has resulted. Emphasis is shifting, albeit slowly, towards attempted regulation, particularly of industrial effluent loads either through legislative powers backed up by penalties for illegal pollution or through charges for all or part of polluting discharges following the 'polluter pays' principle. Alternatively incentives in the form of grants for industrial pollution pre-treatment plant can be given or industrialists can be encouraged to reduce discharges direct to rivers and estuaries. Regulation has not been tried in the domestic sector and indeed this must involve curbing water consumption which, as yet, has not been attempted on any scale so that policies here focus on raising treatment capacity and standards, particularly where they are likely to yield best environmental value for each unit of capital investment.

Each approach to regulating or charging pollution volumes may be unsatisfactory on its own (McIntosh and Wilcox 1978). Financial encouragement may be insufficient to stop profit-conscious industrialists passing on effluent disposal problems to the environment. Low disposal or treatment charges may encourage industrialists to 'purchase' environmental absorption capacity, rather than investing more on pollution abatement plant to reduce discharge levels, particularly at times of expensive capital. Charges set too high may unfairly discriminate against industries with necessarily large volumes of effluent such as food processing. Furthermore any charging scheme must be complemented by toxic chemical emission control and may infringe common law riparian rights to receive unpolluted water. Grants for pollution abatement plant in effect reward industrialists for having been a polluter instead of imposing a penalty. Legislation may be unenforceable or only enforceable in public agencies, such as Water Authorities, and difficult to police in the case of private industry and farming.

Disposal alternatives include providing high quality treatment for all effluents at considerable cost or concentrating on coastal and estuarine disposal because these are not sources of potable supply – to the detriment of estuarine and coastal wildlife – selecting certain rivers for lower quality standards and channelling effluents there, perhaps through industrial location policy, thereby continuing to use these watercourses as open sewers to the sea.

Elements of all these policies exist today, either deliberately or by default, and considerable controversy surrounds the directions of future strategies concerning both 'ends' and the 'means'. For example, the final objectives of estuarine pollution control involving either complete restoration of some intermediate standard are still to be determined and the efficiency of different means of pollution abatement – principally persuasion, economic regulation or legislative enforcement – is subject to continuing debate.

Control of Pollution Act 1974: the future policy framework

Water pollution control is profoundly affected by the legislative and financial context of plans and schemes. The major developing policy framework in Britain is the Control of Pollution Act 1974 which in theory provides a significant step forward in environmental legislation. The Act tackles four main areas: the control of waste disposal on land (Part I), the prevention of water pollution (Part II), the control of pollution by noise (Part III) and the control of air pollution principally from vehicle exhausts (Part IV). Although complete implementation has been slow, when fully operational the Act should have a major influence on cleaning-up and protecting British rivers, groundwater, estuaries and coastal waters. For the first time water pollution control legislation will cover both Scotland and England and Wales together. The legislation's impact, however, will be greatest in England and Wales since the long-term programmes for sewerage and sewage treatment improvement agreed between Regional Councils and Purification Boards already incorporate most of the unsatisfactory sewage effluent discharges to Scottish rivers and tidal waters.

Water pollution control powers.   Part II of the Act extends existing controls to all discharges to inland and coastal waters, including underground supplies as necessary and also discharges to land, since these frequently find their way to watercourses (Lester 1977). Control will also be exercised over piping pollution into tidal waters and discharges from working mines. All discharges of trade or sewage effluent will be subject to control through imposing consent conditions, including those pre-1937 discharges previously uncontrolled, and penalties including imprisonment may be imposed for causing 'entries' of wastes into a river, such as from a tanker spillage. Dischargers will have to advertise details of their effluents, covering the nature, volume, composition and temperature, and regional water authorities as polluters through their own sewage works will have to follow a similar procedure and maintain public water registers of consents, conditions and results of sample analyses (Department of the Environment 1976).

To improve inland waterways from an amenity point of view the Act provides that boats with sanitary appliances designed to discharge sewage directly into the water will no longer be allowed on British waterways unless the appliance is sealed. In addition the Secretary of State for the Environment can confer powers on Water Authorities and Regional Councils to charge for direct discharges of effluents to rivers, estuaries and the sea and also can call in all and modify consent conditions issued by Water Authorities for their own effluents from sewage treatment works if the effluent may have an 'appreciable effect' on the quality of the receiving stream (Lester 1977). This provision retains ultimate central government power to monitor overall standards and ensure equity between conditions imposed on industry and those imposed on themselves by the Water Authorities (McLoughlin 1975).

As well as removing the pre-existing secrecy on consent conditions and discharge analyses the Act gives members of the public the right to prosecute Regional Councils, Water Authorities or industry if the quality of discharges into streams, rivers and the sea fails to meet the standards prescribed in the published consent conditions. This provision restores some common law rights lost in the 1951 and 1961/5 river pollution legislation, since when only water authorities or a member of the public with prior permission of the Attorney General or the Lord Advocate could take proceedings for pollution. Given that information on the discharges was not publicly available prosecutions by members of the public were most unlikely.

Broadly the only exceptions under the Act are for agriculture. So long as farmers pursue 'good agricultural practices' as recommended by the Ministry of Agriculture, Fisheries and Food they are protected from prosecution under some parts of the Act.

Implementation delays.   Recurring national economic difficulties delayed the full implementation of the Act with both government and industrialists arguing that they could not afford to make the necessary investment in treatment plant to raise effluent discharge standards to meet existing and new consents. The Act contains powers for government to implement sections as and when possible to take account of political and administrative considerations and the time needed to make the necessary statutory elaborations on the bare statements of powers in the Act.

The sections of the Act bringing pre-1937 discharges in England and Wales into control and sections relating to clearing debris from river beds causing pollution by sediments in both Scotland and England and Wales were implemented by 1978. In England and Wales implementation of the provisions concerning consents not covered by previous legislation such as the Rivers (Prevention of Pollution) Acts 1951 and 1961 was intended to follow in 1979. The 'offence' sections specifying the offences and penalties would have been implemented some six months later, to allow time for dischargers to make the necessary applications for consents for their discharges not covered by previous legislation before these provisions come into force. The only area where further delay was envisaged concerns sanitary equipment in vessels where the necessary pumping stations to remove sewage from the sealed equipment were delayed. However, further delay has occurred with the election of the Conservative government in 1979. The 'offence' and public disclosure of information clauses are likely now not to be implemented at all. By 1980 no date had been set in Scotland for full implementation, despite pressure from the Purification Boards, with the Convention of Scottish Local Authorities advocating a three-year delay owing to restrictions on public expenditure.

The review of consents: progress or pragmatism?   With impending full implementation of the Control of Pollution Act 1974 the National Water Council (1977d) initiated consultations aimed at reviewing existing consents to discharge pollutants to rivers and estuaries, both by industry and by Water Authority sewage treatment works. No such review has taken place in Scotland where, despite serious local problems, the scale of the pollution control problem is less daunting than that in England and Wales.

The stated objective of this review was to reduce consents considered too stringent and to raise those considered too low, in the interest of giving best environmental value for money by linking consents to quality objectives set for each river related to its existing and potential uses. The Council's view was that some consents inherited by Water Authorities showed undue emphasis on the Royal Commission standard and could result in wasteful allocation of resources in maintaining or up-rating sewage treatment capacity and standards to meet consents where high quality effluent was not strictly required by use of the receiving watercourse (Kinnersley 1976). Some of the new consents are to be short term where existing treatment facilities cannot yet meet the desired quality objectives.

Consultation with interested parties revealed considerable opposition to the review (National Anglers' Council 1978). This opposition was, first, to the concept of quality objectives, especially those to be set by Water Authority officials, which were seen as accepting low quality where existing uses did not demand the highest standards of river water. Secondly, the opposition was to the review of the consent conditions itself, which was seen to imply at best the continuation of existing pollution levels and at worst the lowering of discharge standards. Notwithstanding this opposition the National Water Council (1978b) has proceeded with the policy and Water Authorities are designating river quality objectives and reviewing their consent conditions.

There is no doubt that this policy follows the appreciation of the impossibility of all Water Authority sewage treatment plants meeting their own consent conditions by the time of the full implementation of the Control of Pollution Act 1974. The review was undertaken out of fear of Water Authority prosecution by members of the public for not meeting their own consent conditions. Furthermore the National Water Council (1978b) indicated that the review implies that Water Authorities would not be expected to prosecute industrial discharges if occasional samples (controversially defined as 5%) exceed the consent conditions, provided they are not outside the range of variation to be expected from well-run treatment plant. Water Authorities are expected to adopt an 'even-handed' approach as between their own and industry's discharges and would not expect private prosecutions in these cases (ENDS 1979). In essence this means that a little illegality will be tolerated and this fundamental change in policy, prior to which discharges above consent conditions were illegal although prosecutions could be waived, will have to be tested in the courts.

The review of consents to discharge pollutants into rivers appears to be a softening of the goals and objectives set out in the Control of Pollution Act 1974. There appears to be no mechanism for appeal against revised consents, no sound basis for setting quality objectives other than existing use which may be constrained by pollution levels, no timetable for the conversion of the short-term consent conditions into permanent conditions and at least some acceptance of declining river quality standards in certain areas where existing uses permit. Given these 'problems' it would appear that not only common law rights to receive water undiminished in quality could be infringed but also the review may go against the statutory duty under the Water Act 1973 for Water Authorities to maintain, improve and develop fisheries and to restore and maintain the wholesomeness of rivers and other inland water. Clearly very careful public monitoring of Water Authority and Purification Board standards and water registers will be necessary (Macrory and Zaba 1978). Although these agencies are sensitive now to pollution problems, water quality improvement is a long-term concern and standards can easily fall in the face of cuts in government expenditure.

The regional pollution prevention plans

Given the overall policy framework of the Control of Pollution Act 1974, the task of the Regional Councils and River Purification Boards in Scotland and the Water Authorities in England and Wales is to increase their treatment capacity to provide discharges of higher quality where, in their judgement, this will have most environmental effect. Also they need to persuade or force industry to meet their new or existing consent conditions and pay more realistic charges for treatment or direct discharges. To this end these agencies are both increasing or have increased their sewage treatment and sewerage budgets, and have agreed with industry generally a level and method of charging for pollution treatment at sewage works. However, on the question of payment for direct discharges to rivers much heated debate continues and charges have yet to be introduced (Water Research Centre 1977, 1979).

The North West Water Authority (1977a) through its Water Quality Advisory Panel has determined a policy and plan for preventing deterioration of river water quality, while acknowledging that capital for improvement works

Table 4.3   North West Water Authority policy for river water quality.

Long-term aim
Restoration and protection of the Region's river water quality.

Short-term aim
First to prevent deterioration of the present situation and second, as far as capital is available and local needs exist, to improve river water quality.

Practical steps towards short-term aim
  (i) To protect, and, as far only as is necessary, to improve the rivers which provide, or are expected to provide in the foreseeable future, the high quality potable water supplies of the Region.
 (ii) To prevent deteriorioration of river water quality that would result in an unacceptable change of character of the river, although some local deterioration of water quality in individual river stretches might have to be accepted within this policy.
(iii) To prevent deterioration of river water quality at certain specified points in river basins which are of special significance.
 (iv) To reduce and, as far as practicable, to eliminate gross pollution of rivers that constitutes a nuisance.
  (v) Where there are pressing local needs, to take advantage of any opportunities that might arise for improving river water quality.

The relative priorities of the steps should be treated as being generally in accordance with the order in which they appear above.

Source: North West Water Authority 1977a.

is not unlimited. The policy will be used to guide development control decisions by local authority planning departments and set priorities within the Authority's capital works programme. The plan (Table 4.3) is couched in excessively general terms indeed but does list priorities, the highest being the protection of potable supplies and the lowest being *ad hoc* local improvements 'where there are pressing ... needs'. Pollution prevention is given the highest priority of all water planning problems by the Northumbrian Water Authority (1978a) but so far most Authorities, constrained by capital expenditure ceilings, have allocated higher priority in their Annual Plans to inland pollution treatment rather than estuarine problems or the renewal of sea discharge systems despite the very strict European Economic Community directives on the quality of bathing water which certain British beaches do not meet. This priority reflects the low direct public health threat from sea pollution (Pullin 1975).

Such overall regional policies are translated into increases in capital budgets for sewage treatment plants and revenue for river pollution monitoring. The main period of greater capital expenditure in England and Wales was immediately after 1974 but before subsequent government spending restrictions, when, in recognition of the unsatisfactory legacy of neglect, the Wessex Water Authority allocated 86% of its total capital works budget to sewerage and sewage treatment, relaxing this to 58% by 1978 reflecting substantial government cuts in total available capital (National Water Council 1978a). Each Water Authority Annual Report at this time gives details of sewage treatment plants upgraded or newly installed.

Standards of sewerage effluent discharges are being raised by these improvements, but the process is slow and likely to get slower once the easier or cheaper schemes are installed. In the Thames Water Authority area during 1976/7 the percentage of sewage works for which consent conditions were met for over 90% of samples taken increased from 31% to 42%. For the Northumbrian Water Authority the percentage of sewage treatment works' samples complying with consent conditions rose in the same year from 56% to 62% and for consented trade effluent discharges the compliances rose from 59% to 64%. These figures show the scale of improvement still needed and illustrate the temptation to modify consent conditions to ensure compliance. The role of the Water Quality Advisory Panels can be seen in the Welsh Water Authority where the Panel responded to the 74 fish-kills reported by the Welsh Rivers Divisions in 1976/77 by requesting a review across the whole Authority of the facilities for controlling discharges from sewage and water treatment plant.

Similarly in Scotland the River Purification Boards respond both on this day-to-day level of recommendations about particular pollution incidents and in formulating plans with the Regional Councils to set priorities for capital expenditure programmes. Being independent, the Purification Boards have greater freedom to take appropriate counter measures in cases of persistent pollution from sewage treatment works. For example, the

Highland River Purification Board successfully prosecuted the Highland Regional Council in 1977 for continued pollution of the Dalchalm Burn in Sutherland from a sewage pumping station. Such prosecutions, or their threat, can have considerably greater influence on the effluent disposal agent than mere persuasion. Indeed central government departments face considerable embarrassment from these cases, which may well become considerably more numerous when public prosecutions under the Control of Pollution Act 1974 are possible.

Some of the financial resources for quality improvements may come from housing and industrial plant developers, who can contribute to treatment facilities if the Water Authority is unwilling or cannot afford the necessary expenditure. However, this can lead to lower standards if isolated works installed by the developer are poorly maintained. Several Water Authorities are now insisting that such private expenditure is used to provide the necessary extra capacity at existing works.

Revised charging schemes: treatment at sewage works.   In addition to increased expenditure on sewage treatment capacity, increased charges for industrial waste water treatment are being implemented. Currently these charges amount to only 1·5 per cent of Water Authority revenue and even less in Scotland.

Charging systems for industrial effluent treatment at sewage works should cover transmission, reception, treatment and disposal costs, based on the strength, volume and suspended solid content of the effluent and perhaps also special treatment costs. Until recently consent conditions and charges have been negotiated on a local or sub-regional basis by the river and local authorities and anomalies have occurred including many areas where no charges were levied at all. Since 1974 there has been movement towards more consistent trade effluent charging practices and three- or five-year phased programmes of charge increases to match true treatment costs.

The Water Authorities and the Confederation of British Industry have reached agreement on a formula for charging for treatment at sewage works but controversy still surrounds whether these charges should be fully equalised within regions (Dart 1977a). Such equalisation appears equitable at first sight, such that one factory should pay no more than another with the same volume and strength of trade effluent. The Wessex Water Authority has a regional charging scheme based on a formula incorporating the amount and strength of effluents and costed by dividing the total treatment bill by the total effluent quantity to obtain a unit cost. However, prior to 1980 equalisation was undertaken by the North West Water Authority across smaller geographical areas in recognition of the differential financial costs of effluent treatment. For example at old plants where construction cost debts are paid off treatment charges can be low but at new plant loan debt still adds substantially to unit costs. Alternatively, disposal at sea may require only primary treatment at lower cost. Therefore the penalty of complete equalisation, industry argues (Dart 1977a), is that established firms who have paid for treatment plant in the past in their locality through charges or rates to local authorities now have to contribute to new plant elsewhere where no such contributions were made and therefore no treatment capacity was installed.

In all areas the charges for trade effluent treatment at sewage works are rising towards those based on true costs, after many years of low or non-existent charges such that no industry in Birmingham paid for effluent treatment until the late 1950s (Freeman 1977) and in Scotland some Regional Councils still make no charge partly to encourage industrial development. The economic self sufficiency duty here is assisting Water Authorities in that they can point to the lack of government subsidies to pay for pollution treatment in contrast to the rate support grant to local authorities prior to 1974. But before full costs are met by these increases Regional Councils and Water Authorities are making losses on these services, thereby limiting the speed towards higher standards, and industrialists have an imperfect incentive to install their own treatment facilities or reduce pollution loads.

Charging schemes for direct discharges?   Similarly there are moves to levy charges on direct discharges to watercourses. Until now no such charge has been made, although the industrialist may incur expenditure on pre-treatment to meet the negotiated consent condition. The principle behind a direct discharge charging system is to set the charge so that partial 'in house' pre-treatment or pollution abatement is undertaken by industry, the amount being determined by its cost, which will be different for all firms. If the charge level is set based on both average abatement costs and a total effluent discharge level for a river reach based on river quality objectives, then firms should install pollution abatement plant so as to minimise their total pollution costs by paying a charge for some pollution discharged to the river and some for abatement. Since the last increment of pollution from industrial processing is the most costly to prevent, some pollution would always be discharged, but no more than is cost-effective for the firm or would exceed the levels needed to maintain the river quality objectives. This, it is argued, produces a solution to controlling discharges and hence pollution which is less wasteful since all firms are competing for the finite river pollution assimilation capacity and, in theory, only exactly that amount of pollution abatement investment will take place to meet the river quality objectives rather than one firm spending 'too much' to bring their discharge down to some artificial consent condition or fixed emission standard such as those advocated by the European Economic Community.

However, the theoretical effects may not occur in practice. There may be insufficient firms discharging to a river catchment or reach for perfect competition which, in any case, may itself be wasteful since it may encourage investment in abatement capacity which is later not needed as market fluctuations occur. Also the system only works with common organic pollutants where one firm's pollution is a substitute for another's and there can be a real market. In addition a system of over-riding consent conditions or standards for toxic substances is still required, as is the case in all the European Economic Community countries where direct discharge charges exist, so that a charging system adds to rather than reduces administration costs.

The possibility of direct discharge charges has aroused opposition in Britain, partly because charges *seem* to give industrialists the right to pollute rivers so long as they pay, although a payment conveys no more rights than a consent. Also such charges appear both difficult to set, in that either the external diseconomies caused by environmental pollution cannot easily be quantified (Kinnersley 1976) or because average pollution abatement costs are unknown (McIntosh and Wilcox 1978). Charges may also be difficult to enforce when discharges are not permanently monitored. Some criticisms probably just hide an industrial opposition to such charges which if properly set could, first, provide revenue for the Water Authority and River Purification Board pollution control programmes, and be used thereby to 'compensate the environment' for having to bear the cost of industrial pollution. Secondly, they could provide an incentive to the industrialist to reduce polluting effluents. Nevertheless the charges do add to the costs of industrial production – although so would a properly enforced consent condition system – which may have implications for competition between otherwise similar concerns in different countries, hence the European Economic Community's desire to introduce and standardise charging systems.

While the powers to impose direct discharge charges are available in the Control of Pollution Act 1974, the Secretary of State for the Environment has shown no move to implement this section. Some pressure in favour of the charges may come from industrialists seeing competitors paying nothing for direct discharges while themselves paying substantial true-cost treatment charges for trade effluent disposal at sewage treatment works. However, Water Authority and Regional Council plans to introduce such a charging scheme are not well advanced and much consultation would be necessary before full implementation. Perhaps some experiment in tackling the difficulties of establishing an economically sensitive charging scheme and of measuring the costs and benefits of the scheme itself is warranted although, as in so many water planning fields, such experimentation is shunned. However, since in Britain so much trade effluent is discharged to sewers, any benefits of adopting a direct discharge charging system might well not be worth the administrative costs.

The 'underground crisis': financing sewerage replacement.   The network of public sewers in Britain is very extensive at over 200 000 km and has grown piecemeal over many years; many of the sewers built in the nineteenth century are still in good condition thanks to the excellence of Victorian design standards. Others, however, are in advanced stages of dilapidation particularly in inner city areas where they have been disturbed by the laying of other services and also in coalfield areas where subsidence has taken its toll. While most sewers last 100 years or more there is a growing replacement problem, although the exact state and future life of many systems is unknown (Lambert 1977).

Annually expenditure on sewer replacement in England and Wales is substantial (£150millions at 1975 prices) but there is evidence that twice as much should be spent to halt decline and undertake proper maintenance (National Water Council 1977c). Prior to 1974 sewer replacement was improperly coordinated owing to the large number of relevant authorities and it was subsidised by the rate support grant so that true costs were poorly appreciated. The public appeared indifferent to expenditure on maintenance until bursts appeared, by which time it was too late. In the North West Water Authority area there is a 20-year backlog of maintenance and current expenditure of £15millions is thought to need multiplying six-fold to clear this backlog and initiate a properly coordinated programme of replacement before sewers collapse (North West Water Authority 1978b).

The annual plans of Water Authorities show an increasing awareness of the sewer replacement problem and part of the increase in capital requested by the North West Water Authority has been granted by the government. However, current government policy, such as it is, and consequent expenditure levels are almost certainly still insufficient to keep pace with dilapidation. The difficulties and costs are greater than with water mains, since sewers are generally larger and deeper, although some technical innovations such as re-lining existing sewers have been developed to reduce costs. Problems concern the standard of replacement: to replace at the highest technical standard would probably make sense in the long run, but at an unacceptable current cost. Similar difficulties occur with storm water sewers where historical standards have been very high and indeed higher than would be considered strictly cost-effective today. Yet to reduce standards means lower sewer capacities and consequently periodic flooding which also appears socially unacceptable.

The planning of sewerage replacement encapsulates many of the most problematic aspects of water authority planning: massive capital sums are required; it is difficult to fix future standards of provision; a substantial legacy of neglect has been inherited from former agents; and data on which to base plans is patchy. The scale of the problem would appear to be beyond that of regional or local government authorities. Further capital borrowing by the North West Water Authority will only increase loan debt to be paid by the regional community. Here is a case where central government must relax the financial self sufficiency duty of Water Authorities and give grants not loans to tackle what is in essence a national problem.

Narrowing the focus of our examination of water pollution control policy, plans and schemes we analyse below, first, the installation of the sewage works of a New Town. This scheme illustrates the typical concern of most water engineers with detailed design of sewage treatment works and their day-to-day operational efficiency rather than with the overall economic policies for pollution control. The second example concerns intractable pollution problems on the river Clyde in Scotland and the difficulties of sustaining a rational investment plan given a fluctuating national economy. The two examples together provide some opportunity to examine the different administrative systems for pollution control in Scotland and England and Wales.

Washington New Town sewage treatment works

Washington New Town is located at the tidal limit of the river Wear, a few kilometres from both Sunderland and Newcastle-upon-Tyne. It was designated in 1964 in response to a government initiative for regional development in the North East which included plans for a new town with a population of some 80 000. The existing population of Washington was approximately 20 000, which has risen to some 49 000 in 1978. Sewage treatment in 1964 was 'nominal', discharging direct to the Wear although passing through a dilapidated settlement tank supposedly providing some treatment. Industrial discharges direct to the river were virtually uncontrolled which as a result was listed as grade 3: 'requiring improvement as a matter of some urgency'. The population and industrial growth in Washington since 1964 necessitated installing a modern sewage works to treat the increasing volumes of domestic and industrial waste water (Eno and Pollington 1975).

The administrative context. The efficiency of the Washington sewage works today is a function of the Washington Development Corporation's desire for a large up-to-date works to cater for an increasing domestic sewage load and which also would provide no constraint to the attraction of diverse industrial developments to sustain the New Town. In addition, the particular skills of the Development Corporation's own staff ensured a successfully designed plant with both innovative features and a close regard for operational efficiency.

In 1966 the Development Corporation took over the main drainage function of the Washington Urban District Council. This drainage responsibility does not always fall to New Town Development Corporations but in this case the designated New Town area covered more than the existing District Council area. This take-over was important in securing national economic resources for sewage treatment, rather than relying on local finance, through the Development Corporation's links with the Ministry of Housing and Local Government. This resulted in an integrated view of the works' design, rather than the piecemeal addition of extra capacity as and when needed, which is often the case with expanding towns elsewhere.

Design objectives. A 30/20 effluent standard was the objective of the scheme but this could not be met in the first phase of construction which, when commissioned in 1969, only provided primary treatment. Interim consent conditions were imposed by the Northumbrian River Authority of 150 mg/l suspended solids, 0·2 mg/l cyanide and 1·0 mg/l toxic metals. The first stage was designed to treat sewage from the eventual projected population equivalent of 140 000, industrial effluent contributing some 50 000 equivalent to this total. To this end large primary settlement tanks were installed, together with grit extraction plant and emergency sludge storage lagoons, all designed to cope with the eventual flow of 31 000 m^3 per day, which would not be achieved until AD 2000.

The need for a secondary biological treatment stage became apparent as early as 1970, since the growing volume of sewage from a rising population receiving only primary treatment indicated that pollution levels in the Wear were in danger of rising as a result of the works' effluent. In addition, without the biological treatment the concentration of cyanide in the effluent would have increased substantially with the impending establishment of metal processing industries which the Development Corporation was eager to attract to provide employment.

For the design of the secondary plant the Development Corporation decided to use the expertise of their Assistant Chief Engineer and specially appointed Sewage Works Manager/Chemist rather than consultants, an uncommon decision for a relatively small authority. Several constraints led to the adoption of a surface aeration system rather than treatment by filtration. The site was too small to allow sufficient filtration tank capacity and also the possibility of fly nuisance with the filtration system affecting the planned riverside park and wildfowl reserve nearby pointed to surface aeration. The aeration tanks were designed so that the biological processes could withstand the shock loading of pollutants possible from industrial plant and detailed arrangements of treatment equipment followed patterns only then existing in Germany and Austria (Eno and Pollington 1975). An important feature of the design was the provision of ample pipework interconnecting both aeration tanks to promote maximum operational efficiency.

The Development Corporation, eager to foster an image of the New Town as progressive and imaginative, also encouraged the designers to allow for maximum automation of the plant, partly to reduce operational costs through equalising the use of parallel capacity at the works, but also to enable closer monitoring of possible sudden polluting discharges from the industrial premises. The installation of an on-site mini-computer was considered which would have monitored levels, flows and treatment results and adjusted treatment processes accordingly. These plans, however, were overtaken by the 1974 reorganisation and deferred. With the Northumbrian Water Authority's regional view of capital investment the further development of the already sophisticated Washington works came some way down a list of priorities including many works which at reorganisation were quite inadequate.

Sludge disposal problems.   The disposal of sludge from the primary and secondary settlement tanks has been a continuing problem at Washington. Many alternative methods have been reviewed and again the image of the Development Corporation was important in the eventual choice. The cheapest alternative was simply pumping the sludge to lagoons on the site, to accumulate without further treatment. This old fashioned 'disposal' method was considered to be 'incompatible with the image of a progressive New Town' (Eno and Pollington 1975, p. 576) and, along with pumping to waste land and ploughing in, it was quickly discarded. Perhaps with the current recycling consciousness the disposal of sludge on agricultural land would have been adopted thereby using the sludge as an agricultural resource, although the necessary 1200 hectares would not have been easy to find and cost analysis at the time favoured tankering the sludge some 10 km to a sea outfall at Ryhope near Sunderland. This sea disposal has continued since although, following reorganisation, the Northumbrian Water Authority is commissioning a sludge vessel for sea disposal from the Tyne to which the Washington works will contribute. The broader analysis of water planning problems possible with the regional authorities seeking economies of scale has resulted in the review of new alternatives.

Operational results.   The Washington works have easily met the design requirements in producing an effluent better than the 30/20 standard. However the predicted build-up of sewage flows has not been fully realised. This amounts to a shortfall in industrial wastes since the firms the town has attracted have in the main comprised 'dry' plants. This has meant that the primary stage, designed for the predicted large ultimate flows, is well in excess of current requirements although good management has turned one of the large tanks into storm storage as this is not otherwise provided.

The innovatory secondary treatment plant has performed well, although partly as a result of the low loadings the energy consumption has been some-what high per m^3 treated. The plant is still operating below capacity and the overall design is such that additional secondary capacity can be added easily as needs arise. The Development Corporation, for example, hopes to attract a large brewery to the town and the basic design could cope with effluents from such a plant. Also, such is the modern design of the works, resembling more a laboratory than the popular view of a sewage works as being dirty and unpleasant, that staffing has not proved difficult as elsewhere, although this is an area of traditionally high unemployment.

Uncertainty concerning future predictions still presents operational problems. Initially the works were plagued by massive suspended solid loadings from waste waters from the nearby Glebe colliery. Being a pre-1937 discharge the Development Corporation and River Authority could not impose consent conditions. Protracted negotiations with the National Coal Board had little effect and eventually an industrial direction was issued, but before it could be implemented the colliery closed. Rapid growth of a watch manufacturer in the town has caused problems of dealing with a variety of wastes including cyanide, and strict control has been needed to safeguard both the secondary biological treatment processes and the quality of the final effluent, particularly as part of this passes through the wildfowl reserve on its way to the Wear.

Effluent disposal has also provided difficulties for the manufacturers. The watch manufacturer has had to face constantly changing consent conditions imposed by the River and Water Authority in response to changing watch production technology and consequent changing waste characteristics. One manufacturer of glass fibre, which yields waste water containing phenol, chooses to bypass the sewage works and take the effluent by tanker direct to a sea outfall. This must be an unsatisfactory solution in the long term, simply transferring pollution from the Wear into coastal waters, but the firm complains that the charges for treatment at the sewage works are higher than the cost of sea disposal. This illustrates so clearly the problems Water Authorities have in managing true-cost charging policies while cheap and nasty disposal alternatives are still permitted. Until the Control of Pollution Act 1974 is fully implemented, and thereby coastal discharges are controlled, this type of loophole will continue.

Assessment. The installation and operation of the Washington New Town works has been a pollution prevention success, largely because the Development Corporation was determined to promote an image of progressiveness and technical efficiency and the coincidence of two key designers facilitated the planning process. The scheme re-emphasises the lack of technical impediments to pollution prevention and, since the installation of the secondary treatment plant at Washington, pollution in the tidal reaches of the Wear has improved sufficiently to raise them from grade 3 to grade 2 (Northumbrian Water Authority 1976). This improvement is directly linked to the improved sewage works' effluent with full biological treatment and also to reduced direct industrial effluent discharges, particularly from chemical and metal plating industries.

The North and South Calder Waters – Glasgow

The river Clyde flows 120 km north-westwards across the central lowlands where the bulk of Scottish water pollution occurs (Fig. 4.1; Fig. 4.2). Industrialisation in the Strathclyde region dates back to the industrial revolution. The constant discharge of trade and sewage effluents from this industrial expansion and the parallel population growth made the Clyde and its tributaries, including the North and South Calder Waters, some of the most seriously polluted rivers in Britain (Clyde River Purification Board 1976b). Policies and plans for raising river water quality against an historical background of local authority neglect of sewage treatment, show both significant successes and continual implementation problems through recent economic constraints.

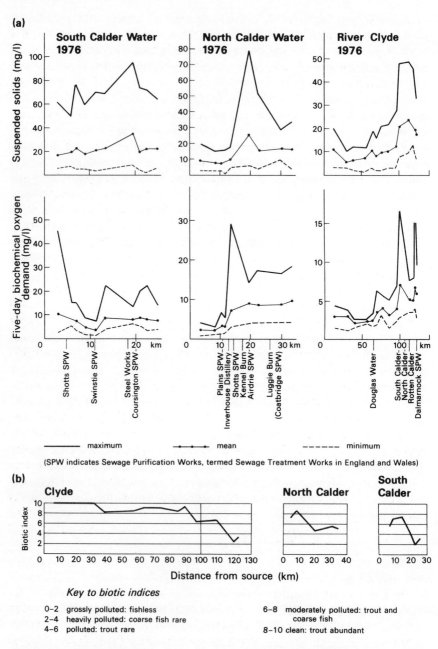

Figure 4.2   Polluting effects of the North and South Calder Waters and the River Clyde.

The regional context.   In the upper reaches the Clyde is clean with only over-loaded sewage works at small isolated villages giving localised problems. At Lanark, however, the river receives the effluent from the town's borderline-

standard sewage treatment works and in the next 15 km effluents are discharged from a further eight works, three of which are unsatisfactory. The
Ashgill works, for example, serves a population of 1350 and has consent
conditions stipulating 30 and 40 mg/l BOD and SS respectively. The means of
effluent samples in 1975 were 34 and 42 mg/l with extremes of 90 and 79 mg/l
representing serious pollution when the works are overloaded.

Just south of Glasgow the Clyde, still relatively clean, meets the North and
South Calder Waters which are both heavily polluted by sewage treatment
and industrial effluents. Downstream pollution levels are further increased
with the very unsatisfactory effluent discharging to the estuary from the
Shieldhall and Dalmuir works, serving some 650 000 people. Here only
primary screening and settlement treatment is given to over 400 million litres
of sewage per day. The works' effluents comply with the statutory consent
conditions but these are set very high, reflecting the old and inadequate works
from which only a poor effluent can be expected. For example at Dalmuir,
built in 1894, the consent for suspended solids is 150 mg/l. The mean of eight
samples in 1975 showed a discharge within the consent of 72 mg/l, yet this is
over twice the Royal Commission standard. The works are unlikely to be
reconstructed until 1984 at the earliest since priority is being given to the even
more unsatisfactory Shieldhall plant. In addition to sewage effluent dozens
of industrial plants discharge directly to the Clyde, its tributaries, and
the upper estuary where, until 1973, no fish had been seen for over 100
years.

The responsibility for the pollution and its treatment lies with the Strathclyde Regional Council, as owner of the sewage works, as well as with the
polluting industrial plants scattered throughout the area. The responsibility
for pollution control lies with the Clyde River Purification Board, established in 1975 to cover an area almost coinciding with the Strathclyde region.
The Board employs 13 inspectors, backed up by a team of 27 chemists and
biologists to analyse river and estuarine samples and has the statutory duty to
promote the cleanliness of rivers, other inland waters and specified tidal areas
within the region. The Rivers (Prevention of Pollution) (Scotland) Acts of
1951 and 1965, together with the Clyde River Purification Board Act 1972
which covers the former Clyde Board area, are used to set and enforce
consent conditions for all discharges to the river and controlled tidal
areas.

The Clyde River Purification Board policy is for improvement in all effluent discharges to at least the Royal Commission 30/20 standard and to
enforce, and where possible tighten, consent conditions to effect this
improvement. In addition the Board encourages better industrial practices to
halt the area's long history of accidental polluting spillages. The Strathclyde
Regional Council Sewage Treatment Division has essentially the same goal of
cleaner rivers but owing to central government pressure to reduce public
expenditure, plans to complete new and reconstruct old works have in many
cases been pushed back in time, for example at Lanark.

Table 4.4   Details of sewage treatment works discharging to the North (N) and South (S) Calder Waters, Glasgow.

Works	Population served	Dry weather flow Ml/d		BOD	SS	Clyde RPB designation
Stevenston Wood (N)	8 500	2·3	consent	30	40	passable
			mean	21	27	
			range	9–34	16–32	
			samples	10	10	
Coatbridge (N)	50 700	22·8	consent	20	30	satisfactory
			mean	31	44	
			range	6–84	5–116	
			samples	14	14	
Chapelhall (Kennelburn) (N)	1 700	1·5	consent	150	100	unsatisfactory
			mean	92	92	
			range	24–190	47–308	
			samples	10	10	
Chapelhall (Burnbrae) (N)	900	0·6	consent	–	150	unsatisfactory
			mean	–	67	
			range	–	40–98	
			samples	–	10	
Swinstie (S)	15 000	3·4	consent	20	20	passable
			mean	30	36	(biological
			range	15–45	18–70	filtration
			samples	9	9	plant)
Motherwell (Coursington) (S)	8 130	5·6	consent	20	30	satisfactory
			mean	10	9	(modern
			range	1·5–35	3–21	activated
			samples	12	12	sludge plant)

Source: Clyde River Purification Board 1976b.
Ml/d = Megalitres per day.

Continuing pollution problems in the North and South Calder Waters.   The North and South Calder Waters are tributaries of the Clyde which show contrasting pollution control problems resulting from different effluent types. The pollution problems continue owing to a legacy of under-investment in treatment plant. Therefore expected standards are low since interim consent conditions are set somewhat arbitrarily with regard to anticipated works performance rather than to desired river quality standards.

Pollution in the North Calder is mainly from the Regional Council's sewage works, particularly Burnbrae, Kennelburn and Stevenston Wood (Table 4.4) where effluents are seriously polluting. Extreme samples fall well outside the consent conditions set by the Purification Board, which are themselves lenient reflecting the outdated treatment facilities. The Kennelburn works, perhaps the worst of all, are due to be connected to the Daldowie works which provides modern treatment and discharges direct to the Clyde. However, the necessary North Calder trunk sewer has been delayed owing to limits on capital spending by the Strathclyde Regional Council, to the dissatisfaction of the Purification Board. The Stevenston Wood and

Glenmavis Works are less problematic. The former is also to be connected to Daldowie, but at the overloaded Glenmavis works the important final effluent settlement is not provided, causing localised pollution although effluent from Glenmavis will eventually be connected to Airdrie works. Modernisation of these small works comes some way down the list of priorities of the Regional Council which is concentrating resources on the large works discharging to the Clyde estuary, spending for example some £40millions on Shieldhall. One unfortunate problem is that when the Coatbridge works was being reconstructed in 1973 insufficient storm retention capacity was installed owing to lack of land. This results in polluting discharges to the North Calder in flood conditions, although normal dry weather flows come within the standard Royal Commission consent condition (Table 4.4).

The industrial effluents discharging into the North Calder Water are less serious. Waste from the Inver House distillery is potentially very polluting but the effluent is now mainly pre-treated and sent to the Airdrie sewage works. However, accidental spillages occurred three years running between 1975 and 1978, some of which have resulted in serious pollution. For example, in November 1976, 1 300 000 litres of highly polluting distillery mash waste were discharged from a tank which collapsed at night, discharging into the cooling water pond which overflowed causing pollution serious enough to kill fish in the river. With the consent of the Purification Board further discharges were disposed of down a disused mine shaft without harmful results, although close monitoring of such short-term solutions is essential as a similar discharge from a distillery to a mine shaft in the North Calder in 1971 broke out into the river from underground causing intense pollution for 10 km downstream.

The River Purification Board favours pollution control through cooperation and persuasion rather than resorting to judicial processes. For example, pollution from a ditch tributary of the North Calder at a large intensive dairy farm near Baillieston resulted from inadequate provision for sludge clearance when installing a settlement tank as part of a modernisation plan to deal with yard drainage. Following unsatisfactory effluent samples from illegally polluting discharges the farmer agreed to cooperate with the Board by cleaning out the tank more regularly and no further pollution has occurred.

In contrast to its neighbour, pollution in the South Calder Water comes mainly from industrial effluents (Tables 4.4 and 4.5). The effluent from the Coursington sewage treatment works is good by any standard, but that from Swinstie is only 'passable'. Reconstruction of this and the Shotts works has been postponed indefinitely by the Strathclyde Regional Council (Pullin 1977). The main culprit, however, is the British Steel Corporation. Effluents from both the Ravenscraig and Clydesdale steel works have been grossly polluting in the past, with massive suspended solid loadings as well as harmful metal contaminants such as zinc. At Ravenscraig British Steel is spending £7millions to deal with these wastes, including a 6 km pipeline to take coke

Table 4.5   Polluting industrial effluent discharges to the North (N) and South (S) Calder Waters.

Name	Volume Ml/d	Selected quality parameters				Remarks
British Steel	Not	parameter	pH	BOD	SS	
Corporation	known	consent	6−8	20	30	effluent
Ravenscraig		mean	7·8	19	38	from iron
Works (S)		range	7·3−8·3	4−22	13−106	works
		samples	12	12	12	sections
		parameter	NH₃/N	zinc	lead	
		consent	1	0·5	0·5	
		mean	4·8	0·9	0·2	
		range	0·2−10·2	0·6−1·5	0·1−0·3	
		samples	12	7	7	
British Steel	Not	parameter	pH	BOD	SS	
Corporation	known	consent	6−8	20	30	discharge
Clydesdale		mean	7·4	35	80	from steel
Works (S)		range	7·3−7·5	11−84	36−132	and tube
		samples	5	5	5	works
Cairneyhill	Not	parameter	SS	oil		
Quarry (N)	known	consent	60	Nil		contaminated
		mean	112	−		surface
		range	12−380	25		water
		samples	15	1		
Inverhouse	11·4	parameter	BOD	SS	temp (°C)	
Distillery		consent	20	50	22	cooling water
Ltd (N)		mean	31	62	23	effluent
		range	2−280	8−572	11−32	
		samples	17	18	7	
Organon	Not	parameter	BOD	SS	pH	
Laboratories	known	consent	20	30	6−8	
Ltd (N)		mean	−	−	−	
		range	44	32	5·9	
		samples	1	1	1	

Source: Clyde River Purification Board 1976b.
Ml/d = Megalitres per day.

oven effluents to the Regional Council's Carbarns works where biological treatment capacity is available, rather than discharging them to a borehole. In the meantime consents to use further boreholes are being given by the Purification Board as the existing hole has become choked, but these consents have time limits so that this short-term method of pollution disposal can be carefully controlled.

The random nature of accidental or otherwise unforeseen pollution discharges makes monitoring and control very difficult. It is not practicable to sample all discharges all the time and unfortunately the enforcement work of the Board usually follows a serious pollution incident as they cannot be anticipated and preventative schemes implemented in advance. Since one serious incident may harm a stream's self-purification processes for perhaps six months, the problems of sustaining a pollution control programme can be severe. For example in 1975 a small spillage of very strong liquor from the Ravenscraig works drained to the South Calder via a surface water sewer. Even after dilution in the river more than 100 mg/l of ammonia was recorded 5 km downstream. However by the time formal samples had been taken for analysis the concentrations were negligible. Fish in the river were killed, however, as well as other organisms which sustain the self-purification process. Oil has been discharged accidentally from the Clydesdale works from an outdated drainage system. A new plant has been installed to crack the oil and water emulsion discharge and was initially designed also to give biological treatment to the separated water. The effluent treatment plant has proved satisfactory but spasmodic pollution is still caused by the inadequate drainage system.

The pressing need for a cleaner South Calder Water comes from the newly created Strathclyde Regional Park, located just where the South Calder meets the Clyde. The park was opened in 1976 and facilities for yachting, fishing and other water-based sports are provided. Pollution levels in the park's large lake are crucial to the success of the whole park as a regional recreational centre. When the scheme was initiated the lake could have been designed to fill from either the relatively clean Clyde or from the South Calder. The latter was chosen because the Clyde's sediment load at times of flood would have led to rapid silting. However at a time of economic difficulties many of the plans to reconstruct sewage treatment works on the South Calder and for industrialists to provide pre-treatment of their direct discharges or for the Regional Council to install greater trade effluent sewer capacity were initially postponed, for example the Swinstie works. As a result the water quality of the lake has at times only just been satisfactory, and accidental spillages have caused serious problems. In December 1975 coke oven rinse oil found its way into the river and lake, killing fish and temporarily restricting recreational use. The oil came from a choked borehole discharge and formal samples were on this occasion taken for analysis. In a subsequent prosecution the British Steel Corporation pleaded guilty and was fined a mere £50.

Assessment. Pressure on industrialists and sewage treatment divisions to raise river quality in the Clyde region and on the North and South Calder Waters is relatively recent. Only since 1965 have the River Purification Boards had satisfactory legal powers to enforce pollution control. This is a relatively short time in which to modify industrial practices and to design, build and operate new treatment works or reconstruct old ones, yet significant advances have been made, particularly on the Clyde.

The speed of improvement, however, is dictated by the economic environment since truly massive expenditure is needed to reach the agreed goal of cleaner water. Yet towards the end of the period has come financial stringency and both industrialists and the Strathclyde Regional Council plead insufficient funds for expanding waste treatment facilities. Prosecutions, however, are rare since the Purification Board, perhaps with some justification, sees them as not wholly effective without the resources to provide the treatment to effect the legally backed consent conditions, hence the Board's dual programme of persuasion and enforcement. Nevertheless a series of prosecutions of the Regional Council and industrialists by the Purification Board might release the necessary funds for a properly planned river improvement investment programme, although public and government support might well not be forthcoming especially if industrial profitability were threatened in a region of high unemployment.

More fundamentally one might question the value of raising industrial production costs to provide cleaner water for free recreational use. However the current combination of the relaxed consent conditions and absence of direct discharge charges must encourage complacency in dischargers when these conditions are met yet pollution is still serious. Finance is badly needed to install new treatment plant and revenue from a direct discharge charging system could make a contribution. However this would involve one set of industrialists (the direct dischargers) subsidising the pollution treatment costs of another (those using the treatment plant) since revenue from direct discharge charges cannot be paid to the environment to compensate it for damage from pollution!

The separation of pollution control and sewage treatment administration appears to be successful, and a useful contrast to the situation in England and Wales, in that the Clyde Purification Board continues pressuring publicly the Regional Council to increase effluent treatment expenditure. However, perhaps given a sustained period of investment difficulties the Board may find itself no more effective in forcing increased expenditure than the equivalent pollution control sections of the Water Authorities across the border.

Evaluation

Most interested parties in the water pollution control field would agree that the system is not perfect but each would have, in this criticism, a different viewpoint. The water planners are clearly under pressure to raise standards, the industrialist is concerned with losing rights to discharge wastes into watercourses yet the conservationist is unhappy to see any such discharges while the ordinary member of the public may be alarmed at rising water rates to pay for sewage treatment and sewerage investment.

Any evaluation, then, must attempt to examine this water resource planning field from the viewpoint of the national good, difficult though this may be, to establish whether current developments are along the right lines.

Does society provide water planners with an adequate framework of legislation, institutions and financial provision?

Financial provision is currently inadequate for the massive task of sewerage replacement and of pollution reduction in areas of dense population, in estuaries and at the coast. Ahead of implementation of the Control of Pollution Act 1974 its effectiveness cannot be judged; while it appears to remove all pre-existing legislative constraints to pollution reduction, previous legislation has proved partially unenforceable and interpretations of the Act and the revised consent conditions may modify its intended effects. Inherent contradictions between pollution prevention and sewage treatment mean that institutional arrangements in this field can never be perfect within multi-functional organisations; the separation of functions in Scotland cannot yet be said to have realised its theoretical advantages.

To what extent do public attitudes and preferences towards water and associated land resources affect policies, plans and schemes?

Public attitudes towards pollution are ambivalent: while cleaner rivers and beaches are demanded the necessary financial allocations to produce improvements are denied the Water Authorities and Regional Councils. In times of recession economic forces dominate and expenditure is reduced thereby revealing the lower social priority of environmental care compared with living standards. The review of consent conditions to allow Water Authorities to meet the Control of Pollution Act 1974 requirements reflects a dilution of the aims of that Act in the face of insufficient public expenditure: to criticise the Authorities is misguided when they can only operate with resources voted to them, although the review has received little public debate from which increased resources might flow.

How do the inherent characteristics of water in Britain influence the choice of alternative policies, plans and schemes?

The density of population and the small size of British rivers reduces the alternatives in sewage and pollution abatement to intensive treatment at sewage works whereas in other countries effluent dispersal in rivers or lakes might be less unsatisfactory. The nearness of coastal areas allows the potential for sea disposal, both of sewage and sludge, from which no serious environmental deterioration has been observed. Sluggish lowland rivers in certain areas, such as the Norfolk Broads, bring problems of eutrophication from fertilisers in runoff.

To what extent are resource management principles incorporated into water policies, plans and schemes?

The concepts of river quality objectives, discharge consent conditions and other standards in theory recognise the need to reduce pollution to levels where the self-purifying life-support mechanism in water bodies is not destroyed. Similarly, recycling water through treatment works for re-use enables sustained yield of water resources at lower costs than otherwise. Water pollution control institutions in both Scotland and England and Wales are catchment-based to link management structure with the resource base.

How well is water planning integrated with other forms of public planning?
In the water pollution control field integration with land use planning is adequate, partly thanks to the sewerage agency arrangement allowing coordination with local authorities. Polluting industrial development in areas of high unemployment causes greater integration problems, as on the Clyde, when such development might be deterred by pollution abatement costs. Nevertheless the integration of pollution prevention with public health maintenance through safeguarding water supplies is as strong as could be hoped for.

Is water planning comprehensive and systematic and are all interests adequately involved?
Perhaps the main strength of the water planning system in the pollution prevention field is the long tradition of technical excellence, of which the Washington New Town sewage works is just one example. Perhaps the main inefficiency is the system of annual government expenditure allocation which makes long-term planning of effective pollution prevention very difficult. The multi-functional organisation of Water Authorities assists pollution prevention, being large and catchment-based and where the need for clean water supplies and water space for recreation encourages high standards. Decision making in the past has been incremental as illustrated by legislation but now appears systematic: priorities are set, objectives demarcated and monitoring is regular through river pollution surveys although targets are certainly not always met. Charging structures are still sub-optimal and uncharged direct discharge remain anomalous reflecting the strength of industrial lobbies in the pollution field today, as in the past, in contrast to environmental interest and pressure groups which, although involved in decision making, have less economic power to support their cases for raising standards.

Selected further reading (for full bibliography see pp. 254-66)

For basic material on pollution, sewage treatment and scheme design see:

Fish, H. 1973. *Principles of water quality management.* London: Thunderbird Enterprises.

The results of river and estuarine pollution surveys are in the reports below and their successors:

Department of the Environment and Welsh Office 1971. *Report of a river pollution survey of England and Wales*, Vol. 1. London: HMSO.
Scottish Development Department 1976. *Towards Cleaner Water 1975*. Edinburgh:HMSO.

The problem of replacing aging sewers is chronicled in:

North West Water Authority 1978b. *Underground dereliction in the North West*. Warrington: NWWA.

Charging for pollution treatment and disposal is analysed in the following papers:

Dart, M. C. 1977b. 'Industrial effluent control and charges.' *Water Pollution Control* **76**(2), 192–204.
McIntosh, P., and J. Wilcox 1978. 'Water pollution charging systems and the EEC'. *Water* **23**, 2–6.

The National Water Council position on the review of consent conditions is to be found in:

National Water Council 1978a. *Water Industry Review 1978*. London: NWC.

For an excellent analysis of the Control of Pollution Act 1974 see:

Macrory, R., and B. Zaba 1978. *Polluters pay: the Control of Pollution Act explained*. London: Friends of the Earth.

5 Planning water for recreation and amenity

Including water recreation and amenity planning in Water Authority responsibilities is a recognition of the multi-purpose potential of water resources.
However, while in some cases the public can be given access to existing water
space with few consequences, major extension of water recreation facilities
and amenities is not without its costs. The effluent disposal load in rivers may
have to be reduced to improve angling facilities. Water treatment plants at
existing water supply reservoirs may need upgrading to gain full recreational
use and landscaping river engineering works and replacing trees to protect
amenity all add to scheme costs. Finally, water recreation developments may
endanger wildlife and reduce the scientific value of rare habitats.

The pursuit of policies to satisfy social goals for improved water recreation
and amenity services creates dilemmas concerning other social goals within
and beyond the water field. Society's preferences for pure and wholesome
water supplies, for relatively cheap effluent disposal or even for a better
health service may be compromised if even limited financial resources are
diverted from them to water recreation and amenity.

Planning the recreation and amenity use of water is a relatively new role of
the water industry and in expenditure terms recreation and amenity provision
definitely has a minor role compared with water supply sewerage and sewage
disposal. In 1977–78 the Water Authorities spent £4·24millions from their
revenue and capital accounts together on water recreation and amenity, and
£4·19millions on protecting fisheries including both sport and commercial
ones. Together these amounted to about 1% of the total Water Authority
expenditure. In Scotland the Regional, Island and District Councils are
responsible for water recreation and amenity services and their annual expenditure on such services is also a small fraction of their total budgets. For the
British Waterways Board amenity services are of major importance. Total
expenditure on waterways used for pleasure cruising was £7·74millions in
1977, or about 50% of the Board's total budget.

The problems of planning water space are considerable, principally
because of the pressure on the resource base – the available water space – and
the fragmentation of responsibilities. Additional problems are the low
financial priority given to this area of water planning and the difficulty of
deciding which interests should benefit from public funds.

Water for recreation and amenity

One difficulty of resource planning in the water recreation and amenity field is that the techniques for resource appraisal are largely beyond the traditional areas of professional competence of Water Authority staff. Conventional hydrological and water engineering appraisals of water resources include consideration of rainfall, evaporation, river flow, groundwater levels, dissolved oxygen, suspended solids and other similar variables. As demands on water recreation and amenity facilities have increased a need to broaden evaluations of water resources has become apparent. Although variables such as river flow and water quality are important, others like surface water area, area of waterside lands, steepness of slope at the water's edge, the recreational carrying capacity of water space and the amenity value of the water, must now be included. However, evaluation of our water resources in these new terms is deficient and the measurement of attributes such as amenity value is problematic.

The characteristics and use of water space and associated land

Land associated with water space is just as important in recreation and amenity planning as the water space itself. This is because of the need for access and because activity beside the water is likely to be greater in volume than activity on and in the water, and certainly no less creative.

An accurate picture of the amount and types of water space and associated land resources, their distributional characteristics and their present use is a fundamental planning requirement which has led to recent surveys (Water Space Amenity Commission 1977a, 1977b, 1977c, 1977d). These surveys only cover England and Wales and systematic inventories are not yet available for Scotland. At present, estimates of water space and land vary in accuracy and the degree to which they are up to date, making appraisal difficult (Table 5.1).

In 1976 there were 537 reservoirs of two hectares or more in size, owned or managed by Water Authorities in England and Wales (Fig. 5.1). Three Water Authorities, the North West, Yorkshire and the Welsh, embrace about 70% of the reservoirs in England and Wales. In 1976 some form of recreation was carried out at nearly two-thirds of the reservoirs in England and Wales. The water industry's land ownership is comparable to that of the National Trust with about 131 953 hectares of land associated with the reservoirs owned by the Water Authorities. Many of the gathering grounds are large tracts of land in uplands of high amenity value and within National Park boundaries.

The total area of wet mineral workings in England and Wales expands each year as mineral extraction proceeds. Clusters of gravel workings such as at the Cotswold Water Park in the Thames valley are being actively developed for their recreational potential. Organised water sports such as sailing, water-skiing, power-boating and angling benefit, as well as some informal

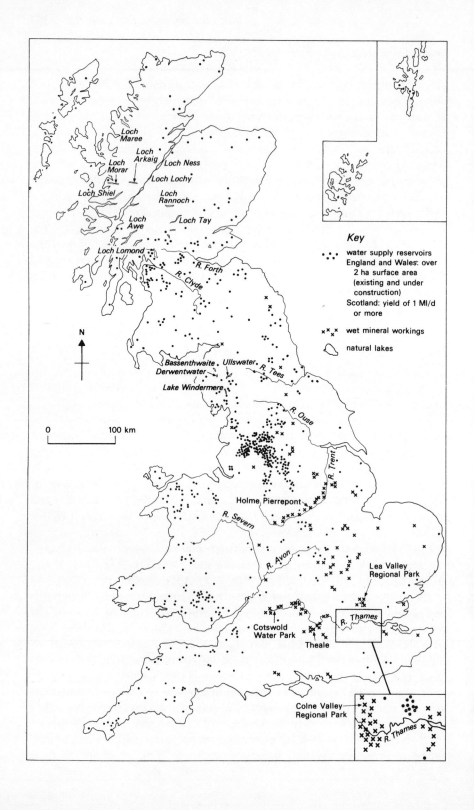

Key

••• water supply reservoirs
England and Wales: over
2 ha surface area
(existing and under
construction)
Scotland: yield of 1 Ml/d
or more

×·× wet mineral workings

natural lakes

Loch Maree
Loch Arkaig
Loch Ness
Loch Morar
Loch Lochy
Loch Shiel
Loch Rannoch
Loch Awe
Loch Tay
Loch Lomond

R. Forth
R. Clyde

N

0   100 km

Bassenthwaite
Ullswater
R. Tees
Derwentwater
Lake Windermere

R. Ouse

R. Trent

Holme Pierrepont

R. Severn

R. Avon

Lea Valley
Regional Park

R. Thames

Cotswold
Water Park
Theale

Colne Valley
Regional Park

R. Thames

Table 5.1   An inventory of water space in Britain.

Category of water space	Kilometres	Hectares
England and Wales		
non-tidal river (with a dry weather flow of 1 million gallons or more)	36 016[1]	
tidal rivers	2 712[1]	80 800[4]
state-owned canals	2 928[1, 3]	
− commercial waterways	483[†1]	unknown
− cruising waterways	1 770[†1]	
− remainder waterways	632[†1]	
water supply reservoirs	N.A.	22 884[5]
state-owned canal feeder reservoirs	N.A.	1 339[2] – 1 600[4]
natural lakes	N.A.	5 300[4]*
		2 753[6 x]
wet mineral workings	N.A.	2 800[4]**
coasts	4 422[1]	N.A.
Scotland		
state-owned canals	298[3]	unknown
coasts	10 185[3]	N.A.

Key:	N.A.	− not applicable
	*	− natural lakes in the Lake District only
	**	− figures for 1969
	†	− includes figures for Scotland
	x	− figure for natural lakes of over 10 hectares in the planning area of the Welsh Water Authority
Sources:	1	− Tanner 1976
	2	− Tanner 1973a
	3	− Huxley 1976
	4	− Seeley 1973
	5	− Water Space Amenity Commission 1977b
	6	− Welsh Water Authority 1978b

pursuits. There are also 43 country parks in England and Wales which provide water recreation opportunities usually of an informal nature.

Scotland's water space exceeds by far the demands placed upon it. There are about 3800 lochs of over four hectares and the North of Scotland Hydro-Electric Board alone controls 32 840 hectares of reservoirs (Coppock and Duffield 1975). Whilst loch shores close to large urban centres may be heavily used (Tivy 1974, Potter 1978), a large proportion of Scotland's coastal and inland water space is remote and scarcely used.

The importance of Britain's coastal resources for every form of recreation and amenity must not be overlooked, especially as inland water space is comparatively scarce. The coastline differs markedly in its development and attractiveness for different uses. Boat moorings show a distinct affinity for sheltered waters and are noticeably concentrated around the Solent, the

Figure 5.1   Principal areas of enclosed water space in Britain.

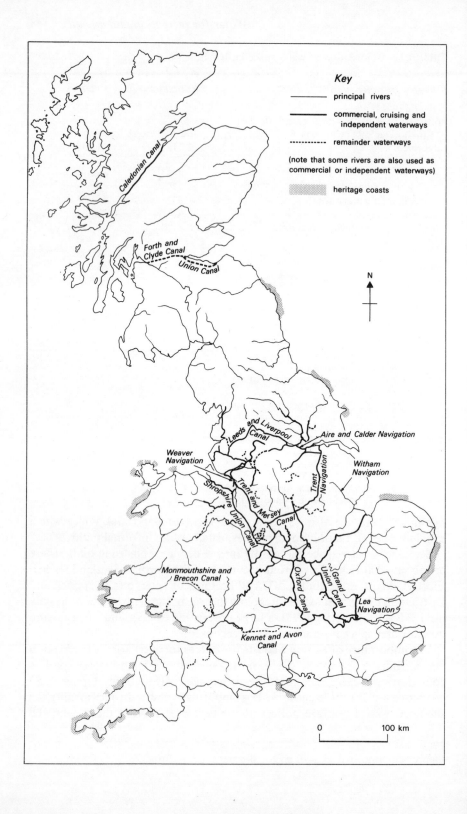

Key

—— principal rivers

━━ commercial, cruising and
    independent waterways

---------- remainder waterways

(note that some rivers are also used as
commercial or independent waterways)

▨ heritage coasts

N

Caledonian Canal

Forth and
Clyde Canal

Union Canal

Leeds and Liverpool Canal

Aire and Calder Navigation

Weaver
Navigation

Witham
Navigation

Trent Navigation

Shropshire Union Canal

Trent and Mersey Canal

Monmouthshire and
Brecon Canal

Oxford Canal

Grand
Union Canal

Lea
Navigation

Kennet and Avon
Canal

0   100 km

Thames estuary and the Menai Straits. Nevertheless the coastline offers enormous potential for the development of water recreation facilities and preservation of natural beauty through heritage coast policies (Fig. 5.2).

The complexity of the types of water space is well illustrated by an inventory of enclosed water space in the Severn Trent Water Authority area (Tanner 1976). This revealed 390 water bodies of two hectares or more in size including 46 natural lakes, 39 water supply reservoirs, 26 canal feeder reservoirs, 108 wet mineral workings and 122 ornamental lakes.

Britain's navigable rivers are used intensively for the full range of water recreation, while un-navigable rivers are used almost exclusively for angling. The state-owned inland waterways were categorised under the Transport Act 1968 into commercial, cruising and remainder waterways (Fig. 5.2). Independent inland waterways are also used for a variety of purposes including recreation. The cruising waterways, which are mainly narrow canals, are now by far the most important lengths. On these angling and pleasure cruising have become the most important activities with about 4000 km of tow paths being used by anglers, walkers and picnickers. Scotland has no cruising waterways but the commercial Caledonian canal and the remainder Forth and Clyde canals are, despite their categorisation, important for recreation. Government policy is to treat remainder waterways in the most economic manner possible and the British Waterways Board is left to consider whether or not they can be incorporated into the cruising network. Many of these canals have cruising potential but are in need of costly restoration. Although the use of Britain's canals for recreation and amenity is growing, the British Waterways Board remain convinced that there is still a brighter future for the waterways in freight carrying as well as in amenity services than the government is prepared to recognise.

Water space, however, is not only limited simply by its extent, but also by its distribution vis-a-vis centres of demand and by the multiplicity of other roles with which it serves society. Distance between these recreation and amenity resources and demand centres has a marked impact upon their use (Central Water Planning Unit 1976e). Problems of accessibility to suitable water space beset many water sports especially where exclusive use is required or where particular types of water are needed.

Conflict between resource roles

Multiple use of water space sometimes gives rise to conflicts. Policies often reflect assumptions about conflicts but there is little conclusive scientific evidence on the extent to which uses actually conflict and the effects of such conflicts. Here further research is required and as with the techniques of resource appraisal most Water Authority staff are not well-equipped

Figure 5.2 Principal linear water resources in Britain. The principal rivers are named in Figure 4.1.

professionally to evaluate potential clashes between uses and how best to avoid them.

Effluent disposal and recreation.   The extent to which effluent disposal and pollution limits the potential of water space for recreation is controversial and may be less than expected (Turner 1978, Kooyoomjian and Clesceri 1974). River water quality improvement benefits may be high where explicit and gross pollution clearly degrades recreation experience. For example, where reaches of rivers such as the Trent and Tame are totally fishless, the angling benefits of water quality improvement can be substantial. Benefits may also be important if water quality endangers public health. However, some pollutants such as toxic substances may not be perceived by recreationalists whose preferences for water bodies are often related more strongly to the perceived attractiveness of the surrounding area than to perceived water quality (Coughlin 1975). For example, water quality may well not be relevant to the angler for whom the quality of the total experience and the opportunity to escape daily routine may be more important (Driver and Knopf 1976). Results of research on the relationship between water quality measured by conventional parameters and recreational use of water are mixed varying between weak and strong relationships, although research also shows that recreationalists, particularly swimmers and anglers, can be quite sensitive to water quality, particularly with experience (Scherer and Coughlin 1971, Ditton 1969).

Water supplies and recreation.   Many of the country's direct-supply reservoirs have old water treatment plants which are designed only to treat high quality water from protected catchments. Recreation can lead to pollution of reservoir water and traditionally recreation has been regarded as incompatible with wholesome water supplies. Water industry conservatism about the recreational use of reservoirs has in the past been more related to traditional agency policy than to specific research findings (Baumann 1969). Investigations of recreationalists' impact on water supplies have proved inconclusive with findings ranging from little or no water quality impact to a moderate risk of pollution in heavily used areas (Ditton 1969). Provided money for adequate water treatment is available there is little reason for water supply authorities to continue their traditional opposition to recreational use.

Regulating and compensating reservoirs, to maintain stream flow and to preserve fishing and other rights of landowners, are not affected in the same way: there is little point in ensuring purity if water is to be released into rivers which may receive effluents. Since the mid-1960s new regulating and storage reservoirs, such as Clywedog in the Upper Severn catchment and Datchet in the Thames catchment near Windsor, have been specifically designed to include water recreation facilities.

Nature conservation and recreation.   Water Authorities have a statutory responsiblity to promote both water recreation and nature conservation and the conflict between these life-supporting and the basically materialistic resource roles presents some serious problems (Harding 1977). Most of the ecological effects of water recreation are thought to be adverse and whilst angling, wildlife study and research interests can work to preserve unspoilt waters and create an awareness of their value they may also have detrimental impacts. Angling may disturb breeding birds and the ecological balance of waters may be upset by stocking or removal of fish species. Walking often leads to trampling and erosion of waterside vegetation. Water recreation can itself be a source of pollution with damaging ecological effects. The net result of recreation pressure in wetlands is impoverishment of aquatic flora and fauna through the disappearance of species. Eutrophication occurs naturally over time but is often accelerated by human interference. The role of water recreation in the process is imperfectly understood but boating probably exacerbates the effects of eutrophication partly by increasing turbidity through stirring up muddy deposits and partly by accelerating bank erosion which increases organic matter in the water.

The clash between nature conservation and recreation is heightened by growth of recreation at a time when natural wetlands, which are important for wildfowl survival especially, are disappearing because of agricultural reclamation, afforestation and land drainage (Tanner 1973a). However wildlife can be protected by seizing the opportunities inherent in change. The imaginative use of artificial wetlands, such as the Royal Society for the Protection of Birds' reserve at Rye Meads which is based around tertiary treatment lagoons, is an example.

Incompatibility between water recreations. The principal water recreation activities in Britain are now swimming, angling, rowing, canoeing, sailing, power-boating, pleasure cruising, other forms of boating, water-skiing and sub-aqua (Tanner 1973a, 1973b). The wide variety of water recreation and greatly differing needs means that given limited water space, coexistence is sometimes difficult. The 'noisy' water sports, such as power-boating and water-skiing often clash with the 'quiet' ones such as angling and wildlife study. Anglers may be disturbed by boating and vice versa. However, there is little evidence of deep rooted conflict between anglers and boaters, possibly because they both develop psychological buffering devices enabling them to ignore the worst nuisances. Although some anglers fish from boats there is evidence that some plan their fishing day to avoid boats (O'Riordan and Paget 1978). Conflicts can successfully be reduced by zoning use in time and space and by setting limits on use so as to avoid overcrowding water space.

The social context of water recreation and amenity planning

Since the mid-1950s British society has become increasingly recreation orientated, generating until relatively recently a remarkable and sustained growth in demand for water recreation and amenity facilities. During this period Britain's water industry has been preoccupied with the traditional major tasks of water supply and effluent disposal, responding cautiously and sometimes slowly to the new recreation demands. This response reflected not only a genuine desire to ensure that new facilities were worthwhile and did not jeopardise the quality of existing services, but also the antipathy of water engineers and scientists to recreation planning as the newcomer amongst water industry responsibilities. This antipathy was magnified by difficulties over the availability of finance for facilities especially during the 1970s economic recession.

Changing social expectations and the explosion of demand

Society now views the leisure and recreation opportunities which an area offers as an important quality of living indicator which influences decisions about work and homes (Coppock and Duffield 1975). British society's increased orientation towards recreation is related in a complex way to increases in income and mobility, changes in education and fashion, a gradual shortening of the working week, longer paid holidays and recognition of the value of recreation to personal health and as a social activity (Dower 1965, Patmore 1972). The result has been greater participation in sport and outdoor recreation and, partly as cause and partly as an effect, higher expectations of facilities. Sport and outdoor recreation has grown faster than leisure activity as a whole, whilst water-based activities have shown some of the fastest growth rates of all. For instance, the number of sailing clubs affiliated to the Royal Yachting Association increased from about 400 to over 1600 between 1945 and 1973, and the number of canoe clubs increased from 12 to 350 over a similar period (Select Committee of the House of Lords 1973). Sailing and canoeing have become increasingly part of school activity and the trend away from team to individual pursuits favours water sports. Angling is also growing at an annual rate of about 7%. New and relatively expensive water sports such as water-skiing, power-boating and sub-aqua activity have also become popular. Membership of the British Sub-Aqua Club increased from 2097 in 1950 to 20 725 in 1975 and the number of water-skiers increased more than three-fold over the same time period (Gilg 1978).

Technical innovation has attracted more people to water sports and encouraged new ones. The rapid growth of dinghy sailing in the 1950s was largely due to innovatory use of fibreglass in dinghy construction which reduced costs and made the sport accessible to a wider market.

The use of inland waterways, especially for pleasure cruising, has grown continuously since 1967 and in a one-day count in 1974 23 061 pleasure boats were recorded compared to 12 724 in 1967 (British Waterways Board 1978). The popularity of passive informal recreation has grown, including pleasure motoring which is probably one of the most common forms of recreation of all placing enormous pressure upon water space in the countryside and particularly at the urban fringe. Leisure and recreation has become important commercially because of the growth of demand for specialised equipment, from which manufacturers and retailers have made high profits, and because of the important contribution made by recreation and tourism to local economies.

Lower real disposable incomes following the mid-1970s recession have led to a decline in the rate of increase in demand for facilities and some substitution of expensive sports by inexpensive ones. Some reservoir sailing clubs in England experienced a fall of up to 30% in membership but demand for angling remains unaffected. The energy 'crisis' and the rising cost of petrol may also affect patterns of car-based informal recreation.

Matching increased expectations and participation in sport and recreation with facilities in short supply is a task which many water sporting interests believe should fall upon the public sector. However, whilst the case for providing informal recreation facilities from public funds is strong, the same cannot be said for recreation activities catering only for minority pursuits.

Legislation and changes in government and water industry attitudes

Prior to the late 1960s the water industry in England and Wales was only peripherally involved in recreation. Responsibility for fisheries and angling was, however, an exception. Fisheries responsibilities go back to the inception of the Board of Conservators following the Salmon and Freshwater Fisheries Act 1861. The distinction between the protection of fisheries, which are the habitat of salmon and fresh water fish, and the activity of fishing, which is the occupation or recreation of those who fish, is important. The statutory duties of Water Authorities are mainly concerned with the ecological well-being of fisheries but they also take action against pollution harmful to fish, issue fishing licences, restock and enforce methods of legal fishing (National Water Council 1978a). Under the Water Act 1973 and the Salmon and Freshwater Fisheries Act 1975 the Water Authorities have a positive duty to maintain, improve and develop salmon, trout, freshwater and eel fisheries (Hunt 1977).

Planning for water recreation and amenity facilities is also a recent phenomenon in Scotland. Prior to the 1975 reorganisation neither the water industry nor the local authorities were significantly involved and in the fisheries area private salmon fisheries organisations remain (see p. 27).

Early history. The water companies were pioneers in providing water recreation facilities in Britain especially for angling, but the more widespread public exclusion policies inhibited recreational use of water supply reservoirs and gathering grounds. The variation in attitudes of water supply undertakings to public access to gathering grounds was noted in John Dower's report on National Parks in 1945, suggesting that some undertakings were prejudiced against recreation and amenity use (Water Space Amenity Commission 1977b). The Heneage Committee on Gathering Grounds concluded in 1948 that sailing might be extended on reservoirs if rigorously controlled (Ministry of Housing and Local Government 1948). The Committee also recommended against access to reservoir banks and bathing but, subject to adequate safeguards, the public should not be excluded from gathering grounds. Subsequently sailing was introduced during the 1950s at further reservoirs.

The 1960s: relaxation of attitudes. Growing recreation and amenity pressures were reflected in a relaxation of government and water industry attitudes during the 1960s, although the role of the water industry in recreation and amenity provision remained largely restrictive.

Under the Water Resources Act 1963 the River Authorities were given a slightly expanded but still limited role in providing recreation facilities. They could 'if it appears to them reasonable to do so' (Water Resources Act 1963 Section 80) permit reservoirs and inland waters to be used by members of the public for any form of recreation considered appropriate. They were also required to assess the effect of water resource proposals upon the preservation of public access to areas of natural beauty. This clause of the Act went some way to recognising that such areas were important for informal recreation. The 1963 Act, however, still left recreation and amenity provision as a highly peripheral River Authority function being classified in the Act only as one of a large number of 'additional functions' and 'miscellaneous provisions'. During the 1960s greater public access to water bodies was allowed by both the River Authorities and the Water Companies but restrictions on permitted uses were sometimes severe and investment in facilities extremely modest. Recreation and amenity provision was not planned in anything but a piecemeal fashion.

In 1963 The Institution of Water Engineers recommended that angling was an acceptable use of reservoirs whilst sailing might be permitted where it could be controlled and managed by a club (Institution of Water Engineers 1963). It also suggested that rowing might be permitted although there were severe doubts about canoeing involving human water contact in capsize drills. Public access to many reservoirs was still restricted without adequate reason (Ministry of Land and Natural Resources 1966) and a government circular called for reconsideration of restrictive policies. The government issued in 1967 a 'Report on safeguards to be adopted in the operation and management of waterworks' (Ministry of Housing and Local Government 1967) which recognised that public access to, and recreation on, direct supply reservoirs would increase the pollution risks to public health. However the report recommended that angling, rowing and sailing might be allowed and that canoeing might now be acceptable if training in the reservoirs were prohibited. The report distinguished clearly between river regulating and direct-supply reservoirs and suggested that on the former all forms of recreation including swimming should be allowed. Relaxation of attitudes was reflected in the Countryside Act 1968. Section 22 echoed the Water Resources Act 1963 by stating that water undertakings could 'if it appears reasonable to do so' permit recreation on their reservoirs. Similar provisions were made in the 1968 Act for public access to gathering grounds and other waterside lands.

The 1970s: the water industry's new role.   The Water Act 1973 marks a further shift in government recognition of the importance of satisfying demands for water space. The Act explicitly committed the government for the first time in water legislation to using the nation's water resources as public recreation and amenity assets and gave the Water Authorities a positive development role. Other government policy in the 1970s in the field of sport and recreation also had important implications for the Water Authorities. In the 1975 White Paper on 'Sport and Recreation' the government accepted that recreation should be regarded as 'one of the community's everyday needs' and the facilities for it as 'part of the general fabric of the social services' (Department of the Environment 1977b).

Inland waterways as recreation and amenity assets.   During the late 1960s the government also committed itself to the use of much of Britain's inland waterways for recreation and amenity purposes. While the canals did not pay for themselves they did perform a number of vital services, including industrial water supply and drainage, and therefore they could not be subjected to wholesale closure (British Waterways Board 1965). Even if the canals were to be kept just as water channels and closed to navigation there would still be a continuing maintenance cost of about £600 000 per year. The British Waterways Board concluded that the additional cost of keeping the canals open for recreational use was a further £340 000 per year. Realising that some social benefits could be gained to offset a financial loss the government accepted the logic of the Board's advice that the non-commercial waterways were a valuable recreational asset which should be kept open. This was recognised in the Transport Act 1968 in which the government committed itself to retaining 2253 km of the 3219 km of waterways. The cruising waterways were to be maintained primarily for powered pleasure craft and would be subsidised by central government.

The fundamental issues: investment and equity

Investment is central to improving water recreation and amenity provision in Britain and shortage of money is a major impediment to progress. The main issues are, first, whether facilities should be paid for out of public or user funds and secondly, if public funds are to be used, how the money should be distributed amongst the various demands.

The distinction between public and user funds is central to this debate which concerns whether or not society is willing to provide water recreation facilities as a social service paid for by public funds. For many forms of recreation, including to a minor extent water recreation, this question has already been answered. Large exchequer grants are available for facilities of many types under the Countryside Acts and the National Parks and Access to the Countryside Act 1949. Also local government has provided some facilities for sport and recreation since the last century. The question is, therefore, by how *much* public funds should finance recreation facilities. Resolving this question is difficult since it involves competing and changing social preferences and is influenced by national economic performance. Although inland water facilities generally lag behind demand in England and Wales, the mid-1970s recession emphasised that not all areas of demand may continue to grow rapidly.

The Select Committee of the House of Lords (1973) reporting on sport and leisure concluded 'that water recreation is incapable of being self-financing' – a statement which raises doubts about the ability of the Water Authorities, with their self-financing obligations, to provide water recreation facilities. For most forms of water recreation and amenity reasonable user charges will not create enough revenue to finance the capital costs of facilities. Alternatively, truly economic charges are likely to prevent many people from taking part in water recreation, discriminate against the less well-off and invite widespread charge evasion. Boaters and anglers may be charged for what they use but it is difficult to see how bankside walking and picnicking, which may involve pollution control costs, can be charged for on any satisfactory basis. On the other hand, overcharging domestic and industrial water consumers to finance water recreation and amenity may also be regarded as inequitable. The planning of water recreation and amenity may well have to be based upon setting user charges to cover maintenance, and public funds for the capital costs of facilities.

Allocating public funds amongst various demands raises problems of equity. Provision of facilities tends to be a consequence of pressure group activity with the most heavily pressed demands being satisfied most. Some sectional recreational interests are well organised to articulate their demands while carefully avoiding the image of a small minority acting in their own narrow interests, yet others may be poorly organised. An uneven distribution of facilities may, therefore, result and unless the distributional consequences of allocating public funds are properly analysed and inequities avoided, public funds will be provided to support the sectional and elitist interests which are most vocal at the expense of poorly articulated demands for more broad-based facilities.

On the other hand the scope for private enterprise in water recreation and amenity provision appears to be limited. Many amenities have a seasonal demand and tend to be commercially non-viable. With the exception of waterside developments on inland waterways, the involvement of private enterprise has been small.

Legal complexities and limitations

The legal rights of recreationalists relating to water and associated land resources are extraordinarily complex. Although the letter of the law differs between Scotland and England and Wales the problems are similar. The law as a whole is designed mainly to protect private property rather than to promote recreation. It creates severe problems for some sports thereby encouraging the formulation of clubs to promote collective interests and help solve problems. Because the Water Authorities often do not own the rights to the use of rivers, natural lakes or coastal areas, they cannot control recreational use here except through agreement with riparian and other owners. However, the Water Authorities do control gathering grounds and the water supply reservoirs thereon and can open them to the public and lease water space to clubs.

The problems of using rivers without permission where there are no established rights of way are twofold. Both passage along the water and the use of the river banks, which are often in multiple riparian ownership, are trespass. In law fishing rights can be bought and sold, being the only recreational rights subject to market conditions in this way. Fishing rights can be leased or purchased – a system which protects some sportsmen but excludes others who may be unable to meet the costs (Tanner 1973a). Natural lakes are often in single ownership and recreational use can usually be negotiated with the owner by water sports clubs, again resulting in exclusive use.

The law relating to towpaths is equally complex (Water Space Amenity Commission 1977c). On some towpaths, such as 119 out of 200 km alongside the navigable Thames, there are established rights of way. However, there is no common law right for the public to use towpaths along the British Waterways Board canals although on 606 km of canals such rights have been established. Otherwise towpaths are generally in private ownership.

The legal difficulties of canoeists are an illustration of the way in which the law hinders some water recreations and some groups while protecting others. There are about 100 000 canoeists in Britain and touring and long distance canoeing is popular. As canoeing has grown so have legal problems. Riparian owners have often not allowed permission for access, passage or exit along stretches of rivers. Sometimes this is related to the objections of anglers where riparian owners lease rights to angling clubs. Here the law protects landowners and their angling club tenants. Obtaining permission for canoeing is often difficult because of the large number of owners involved. The British Canoe Union has campaigned for recognition of its problems and the Sports Council has helped by negotiating agreement along rivers like the Tyne. This agreement is subject to payment and restrictions relating to use and access points. The difficulties of the canoeists are exacerbated since not all canoeists belong to the Union and those not belonging can transgress the agreements to the detriment of all. Similar conflicts between angling and canoeing have occurred on the River Spey in Scotland.

The water recreation and amenity planning system

The central problems of responsibility and finance

The provision of water recreation and amenity facilities to match growing demands requires coordination. This may be achieved by giving comprehensive powers to one or a few authorities for which such programmes are a major responsibility and for which there is adequate finance. However, in Britain responsibilities are divided; the Water Authorities cannot regard water recreation and amenity provision as a top priority.

The Water Space Amenity Commission has no powers to implement its recommendations and cannot like the Sports Council grant-aid recreation schemes; its effectiveness relies almost entirely upon its powers of persuasion. It is not an independent advisory agency. Water Authority chief executives sit on the Commission making it impossible for a truly independent perspective to emerge on the policies which Water Authorities *ought* to follow. In view of the water industry's antipathy towards recreation and amenity planning the Commission acts as a useful, yet limited, counter balance within the industry promoting arguments for recreation and amenity provision (Water Space Amenity Commission 1978). The Commission has also persuaded Water Authorities to cooperate in basic data collection exercises designed to provide essential information for planning and has produced some much needed guidelines on conservation and land drainage policy (see p. 220).

The problem of grant-aid.   With their wide-ranging statutory responsibilities and the comparative urgency of investment to meet other responsibilities, both the Water Authorities and Regional Councils have often been unable to find the finance necessary for water recreation and amenity. Although both sets of authorities do receive grant-aid from central government agencies, patterns of grant-aid are complicated, the sums involved are generally small and availability depends upon the differing emphases of the grant-aiding agencies.

The Scottish Tourist Board, for example, provided £352 115 for water related projects between 1971 and 1978 and none of this assistance was given to the water industry: the money being spent largely upon private marina, yacht charter and sea angling developments. Its English counterpart can finance projects with local authorities, but only in assisted areas, and cannot assist the Water Authorities. The Countryside Commissions in both Scotland and England and Wales can grant-aid regional water authorities as well as private landowners, associations and clubs for example for projects which improve access to the countryside. The Sports Council grant-aids Water Authorities in England, but this is controversial in Wales (see p.175). With so many different grant-aiding agencies involved, executive authorities have sometimes been uncertain about the financial support available to them.

Divided responsibility. Fragmentation of responsibility has grown with the expansion, rather than the reformation, of the institutional framework. It is also encouraged by the nature of recreation and amenity resources, being as they often are, by-products of some primary function such as water supply or forestry. Multiple ownership of resources also complicates planning. The Water Authorities are not only responsible for putting their own rights to the use of water space to the best recreational use but also, by gaining the consent of owners, for securing the use of waters owned by local authorities, private companies or individuals.

In England and Wales a major division of responsibility occurs between the local planning authorities and the water industry. This division of responsibility is less in Scotland because the Regional and Island Councils are multipurpose planning authorities. The most important of the many agencies outside of the water industry with statutory duties for water recreation and amenity planning are the Countryside Commissions and the Sports Councils (one each for Scotland and England and Wales), the National Park Authorities and the English and Welsh County and District Councils. The latter are important executive authorities, planning and supplying recreation and amenity schemes in the context of their structure and local plans. Here the Greater London Council's responsibilities are exceptional because the recreation and amenity function of the Thames Water Authority is fulfilled by the Council in its area. The Countryside Commissions are mainly advisory and grant-aiding bodies responsible for promoting the enjoyment of the countryside, the conservation of its natural beauty and the securing of public access for informal recreation. Formal and active sport in both town and country is the responsibility of the Sports Council and through the regional sports councils several regional water recreation plans have been developed (South Western Council for Sport and Recreation 1976). The Tourist Boards attract holiday-makers to Britain and therefore have strong interests in promoting facilities for water recreation and the Nature Conservancy Council provides conservation advice to the water industry. National Park Authorities have strong interests in ensuring that the use of water space in the parks is compatible with their park plans (Parton 1978).

Apart from the Water Authorities none of the above authorities are organised on a catchment basis, and therefore the Water Authorities add jurisdictional complexity to the administrative framework. Divisions of responsibility also occur at the central government level. Although the Department of the Environment holds a central position, the Departments of Trade and Industry, the Department of Education and Science, the Welsh Office and the Scottish Development Department, all have direct financial and monitoring responsibilities for one or more agency in the water recreation and amenity field.

The precise consequences of divided responsibility are multifarious and include duplicated and overlapping effort leading to a wastage of financial resources and individual authorities having insufficient power to act effectively. Slowness in decision making and the provision of facilities also occurs because of the complicated patterns of consultation involving extensive inter-agency liaison and numerous committees. For example, at the national level in England and Wales consultations are needed between the Countryside Commission, the Sports Council, the Department of the Environment, the Nature Conservancy Council and the water industry in the preparation of policies and plans. At the regional level the consultative machinery is particularly extensive involving the Water Authorities, the Regional Councils for Sport and Recreation, the National Park Authorities and the local authorities.

Consultative difficulties at the local level are exacerbated because local views are insufficiently represented. These problems are illustrated in the East Anglian Broadlands where a unique approach to increasing local representation has arisen. The lack of forum for exchanging views between interested parties led in 1974 to the establishment of the Broads Consultative Committee which included representatives from eight local planning authorities, the Anglian Water Authority, the River Commissioners and the Nature Conservancy Council. However, the Committee was criticised by the Nature Conservancy Council for lack of success in providing a forum for discussion about the future of Broadland. Now under much local pressure, the Anglian Water Authority has established an executive committee, called the Broads Authority, to manage Broadland. This Authority brings together those responsible for Broadland use and planning, increases local control over Broadland management and appears to be well positioned to take some of the actions necessary to protect the fragile Broadland environment.

The signs of difficulties caused by divided responsibility are clear. The Secretary of State for the Environment has found it necessary to establish a consultation group which met for the first time in 1975. This group consists of Chairmen of the Directors of government agencies in the sport and recreation area only, and includes Water Authority representation. Also the newly formed Regional Councils for Sport and Recreation have been given an important coordinating role in the recreation field.

The limitations of the Water Authorities

There is no doubt that water recreation and amenity planning is the poor relation amongst the duties of the Water Authorities leading to questioning of their suitability for the task (Williams A. 1977). The Water Authorities rightly regard their primary duty as the conservation and supply of water for domestic and industrial purposes, a duty which involves massive expenditure upon both water supply and waste disposal systems. Access to water space for recreation and provision of facilities is viewed as important but not if it jeopardises the quality of water supplies and is not at least partly self-financing.

These priorities are clearly reflected in Water Authority budgets where recreation and amenity programmes are often given a low status because they compete for funds with other programmes considered more essential. For example, the huge capital requirements of both urgently needed sewage plant modernisation programmes and schemes to safeguard adequate water supplies for the future provide the strongest competition. Delays in implementing recreation programmes have been caused by temporary problems. The water supply emergency created by the 1975–76 drought diverted money away from other programmes including recreation and sluggish national economic performance in the mid-1970s led to delays in implementing recreation programmes as finance suddenly became scarcer.

The weakness of the professional standing of water recreation and amenity planning within the Water Authorities is also problematic. Apart from recreational fisheries, on creation the Water Authorities did not have an established professional expertise in the field and although some have employed experienced recreation officers the number of non-fisheries professionals remains very small. For example, out of a total employment of 5600 in 1978 the Welsh Water Authority employed 99 fisheries staff, most of whom were bailiffs. Only a further 14 full-time staff were employed on other recreation and amenity duties. The scarcity of money for recreation and amenity is related to the professional composition and internal politics of the Water Authorities, biased as they are towards engineering schemes. For example, the British Waterworks Association objected strongly to the creation of the Water Space Amenity Commission because it viewed recreation as a threat to the main duties of the Water Authorities (Okun 1977).

Local planning authorities have an established professional expertise in recreation and amenity planning and are, arguably, more sensitive to the needs of the public in the recreation and amenity field. They do not, however, have the professional expertise to cope with some water management problems related to the recreational use of water. Although in theory the Water Authorities must take structure and local plans into account in their planning there is a danger that their policy decisions will be incompatible with these plans. Greater liaison between authorities can reduce problems but there have been instances where Water Authority recreation development plans have included proposals conflicting with local authority policies (Williams A. 1977).

The frustrations of the British Waterways Board

The development of the recreational and amenity role of Britain's inland waterways is frustrated by severe financial limitations and by continued uncertainty about future patterns of organisation. The Board has become a basic management authority with little opportunity to fulfill a true developmental role. Despite an annual government subsidy the backlog of maintenance on the commercial and cruising waterways amounted to £60millions in 1977 and the picture of the waterways is one of years of neglect. In 1978

£3millions of repairs were required just to maintain the waterways in a safe condition.

The Board has little option but to put maintenance first so that very little money is available for recreation and amenity planning. The Board reacts to problems as they arise rather than planning to meet the demands of the future. Nevertheless it is preparing long-term plans for boating and waterway amenities. Private enterprise, particularly small businesses, are important in providing facilities adjacent to the waterways and here the waterways differ from other types of water space. Marina developments, private moorings, chandlers and water-side housing and public houses are common. The future of the cruising waterways depends upon whether or not they can achieve a greater degree of self-financing through appropriate user charges.

Splitting the management of the waterways amongst the Water Authorities, as suggested in the 1973 Water Bill but later dropped, would have created problems. Being based upon watershed boundaries Water Authorities are basically unsound for waterways management. This is because waterways operations are related to high rather than to low points: the highest points together with their reservoirs and sources of feed, being of greatest operational importance (Inland Waterways Amenity Advisory Council 1977). Incorporating the British Waterways Board with the proposed National Water Authority was also suggested. However given that a National Water Authority has been abandoned the difficulties and frustrations of the British Waterways Board are likely to continue.

Competition and consultation: interest and pressure groups

Competition for recognition and funds has grown with increased public participation in water recreation and the development of new water sports. Most water recreation and amenity interests have also become more organised. For example, because of the difficulty of gaining adequate government recognition for its commercial as well as its recreation and amenity functions, the British Waterways Board has itself become an active pressure group aiming to rally public support for more funds. The Board is supported by organised, publicity-conscious pressure groups such as the Inland Waterways Association which rarely misses an opportunity to publicise the freight-carrying and amenity potential of the canals (Richardson and Kimber 1974, Ingham 1975).

The means by which interest and pressure groups participate in policy making vary and inequities arise because some pressure groups are legitimised by legislation which requires consultation while others are not and some are barely represented at all. An important and arguably under-represented set of interests, which also may be the greatest number of people, are those of passive recreationalists. Theoretically they are represented by the members of the Water Authority Boards, the Countryside Commission and the National Park Authorities, but at a time when much water space is let exclusively to clubs in order to recoup costs, the extent to which passive recreational interests are catered for is arguably inadequate.

In the past the water industry, acting through its professional institutions and associations, influenced decisions about reservoir recreation. Today the anglers' pressure groups are also extremely powerful. The long established statutory duty for fisheries in the water industry and fisheries legislation provides angling interests with a powerful position from which to influence policy; 55% of the Water Authorities' total expenditure in 1976–77 on recreation, amenity and fisheries went on fisheries although by no means all of this went on angling facilities. Anglers are well represented on the statutory fisheries advisory committees of Water Authorities and the strength of angling consultative bodies ensures provision of angling facilities. However, angling consultative bodies are apparently often dissatisfied by policy decisions. Given their powerful position relative to other recreational interests and their sometimes parochial views, it is doubtful whether all the interests of angling bodies should be satisfied. Although anglers should contribute to recreation planning, if Water Authorities bow too readily to their demands then other water interests including recreational ones unaffiliated to consultative bodies will suffer.

Although practice varies the Water Authorities are not obliged to have recreation and amenity advisory committees. For example the Welsh Water Authority does have a Regional Fishing, Recreation and Amenity Advisory Committee whereas the Thames Water Authority does not, whilst some Authorities have user consultative panels. The interests of the many formal and informal water sport and recreation groups are often quite singular, narrow and therefore competing. Groups such as the British Canoe Union, the British Water Ski Federation, the Royal Yachting Association and the Ramblers' Association all pursue their own particular interests. These often also favour minority rather than general interests. These groups are also to some extent represented by the Sports Council and Countryside Commission with which the Water Authorities must consult. Such groups have rights to object to proposals at public inquiries and to petition against Parliamentary Bills although relatively few proposals are subjected to such processes.

Planning techniques

Rational water recreation planning should be based upon measurement techniques to determine socially and environmentally acceptable levels of provision. These techniques, each with substantial short-comings necessitating further research, are relevant to assessing, first, the social benefits of water recreation facilities, secondly the carrying capacity of water space and thirdly the environmental impact of recreation. These techniques, particularly the first, are often distrusted by water engineers because of imprecision but they are no less imprecise than certain accepted techniques in other fields, such as the calculation of the return periods of flood events.

Investment in water recreation facilities should depend upon demonstrating that expenditure is worthwhile. This involves measuring social benefits usually in monetary terms. Measurement attempts have included equating benefits with total participant expenditures, time spent and willingness to pay for recreation. The 'Clawson technique', based upon willingness to pay, is the most influential work in this field (Clawson 1959, Clawson and Knetsch 1966) from which other applications and refinements have flowed (Smith and Kavanagh 1969, Smith 1970, Osborne 1974). First, existing patterns of participation are observed to establish individuals' willingness to pay for the recreation experience, including travel to and from the site. From this analysis the relationship between the total cost of a site visit and the rate of participation can be determined. Next, for an individual site, a demand curve is derived from this general participation function. From the distribution of population around the site, and hence travel costs, the relationship between total costs and participation is used to determine the number of site visits expected as a function of the cost of site admission. Thus for any particular admission cost the number of visitors per year can be calculated and the revenue yielded is one measure of benefits.

This technique can be a useful practical tool for benefit assessment but it suffers several shortcomings. Modifications have incorporated the effects of population socio-economic characteristics on recreation benefits but the technique allows inadequately for the effect of supply on demand, particularly the effect of competing facilities and activities which is important as the level of recreation provision improves. The technique also depends upon valuing travel costs which is controversial. Furthermore it uses aggregate social behaviour without understanding the motivations which explain individual participation and its rationale and it is difficult in practice to express the impact of crowding as a cost to the user (Local Government Operational Research Unit 1977, 1978a).

If water space becomes overcrowded the benefits of recreation experiences may decline. The level of recreation use an area can sustain without an unacceptable deterioration in its character and quality or in the recreation experience – its carrying capacity – is, therefore, a vital input to water recreation planning as the Llangorse Lake example later in this Chapter illustrates. Crude carrying capacity values are now sometimes used in the management of water space. The most common technique calculates the physical space requirements for particular activities and subsequently derives capacity values by using unit space requirements for particular uses, such as three sailing boats per hectare of water space (Dartington Amenity Research Trust 1975, Broads Consortium Committee 1971). However, evaluation is more complex than physical capacity calculations. Ecological capacity, economic capacity – the intensities of different land uses at which maximum economic benefit is gained – and perceptual or social capacity must also be accounted for (Gilg 1978, Mitchell 1979). Multi-faceted carrying capacity techniques are required, perhaps to include individuals' tolerance of crowding to allow sensitive management of potentially overcrowded water space.

A better understanding of the environmental impact of recreation development should lead to improved carrying capacity evaluations. Relatively sophisticated impact assessment techniques are developing as a result of American environmental legislation, to include predictions of the nature, magnitude and significance of the environmental effects of schemes (O'Riordan and Hey 1976), yet comprehensive impact evaluation for water recreation developments and other water schemes is rare in Britain despite pressing need.

Water Authority policies, plans and schemes for water space

Since the 1974 reorganisation Water Authorities have actively developed recreation and amenity facilities. However, recreation and amenity policies which embrace plans and schemes have only emerged slowly.

The recreation and amenity programme of the North West Water Authority for 1974–79 provides an example of a pragmatic approach to planning in which schemes have been implemented in the absence of complete policies. Nineteen schemes costing £193 000 were completed by November 1978. A further 24 schemes costing twice as much were authorised but not completed, and 16 additional schemes were awaiting authorisation. Amongst these were tree planting and landscaping schemes, nature conservation projects and schemes to provide car parks and urban fringe picnic sites – all typical of Water Authority recreation and amenity developments during this period.

Water Authority Section 24 plans contain only broad, but nevertheless important, statements of policy on recreation and amenity. For example, the South West Water Authority's plan ranks recreation and amenity as twelfth out of 14 objectives (South West Water Authority 1978). Apart from setting priorities some of the plans also make broad recreation and amenity statements. For example, the Northumbrian Water Authority's plan states an intention 'to develop within operational constraints, and subject to users' willingness to pay for facilities, the use of waters and associated land under the Authority's direct control for appropriate active and passive recreational purposes and to encourage the use of other waters where practicable' (Northumbrian Water Authority 1978a).

The Welsh Water Authority's strategic plan for water space is the first of the Water Authorities' recreation and amenity plans. It therefore provides an indication of future trends since other Water Authorities are also developing similar overall recreation and amenity policies. For example, the North West Water Authority has formulated one element of a policy for the conversion and upgrading of old single-purpose water supply reservoirs to multi-purpose use including recreation and amenity. This is discussed after the broader Welsh strategy.

Table 5.2   Goals and objectives of the Welsh Water Authority's (WWA) strategic plan for water space recreation and amenity.

GOALS

The basic goals of the WWA for recreation and amenity are:

(a)   To carry out resource surveys and prepare strategic and tactical plans.
(b)   To secure the use of water space in the Area for the purpose of recreation.
(c)   To have regard for nature conservation, amenity, food and timber production.
(d)   To identify possible conflicts so that the best solutions can be found.
(e)   To obtain a proper financial return for expenditure on facilities.

OBJECTIVES RELATED TO GOALS ABOVE

Goal (a)

  (i)   To complete surveys and prepare a strategic recreation and amenity plan for water space in the WWA region, and the area of the Severn Trent Water Authority in Wales, having regard to structure and local plans prepared by local authorities.
 (ii)   To prepare tactical plans and programmes for individual resources and subjects as a continuing process.
(iii)   To consult with the Severn Trent Water Authority, local authorities and other interested bodies.
 (iv)   To include the strategic recreation and amenity plan as part of the statutory Corporate Plan for all the functions of the Authorities and to present it to Ministers for adoption.

Goal (b)

  (i)   To achieve the best possible social and economic use, so far as is practicable, of water space owned by the Authorities for recreational purposes.
 (ii)   To take steps to secure the use of other water space, with the consent of the owners and other interests.
(iii)   To provide, or otherwise make available, facilities or services for people using the water or land for recreation either by providing new facilities or by improving existing facilities.
 (iv)   To maintain, improve and develop game and coarse fisheries.
  (v)   To make byelaws, where necessary to preserve order, prevent damage, or to regulate behaviour for the benefit of the whole community.

Goal (c)

  (i)   To have regard for the desirability of preserving natural beauty, of conserving flora, fauna and geological or physiographical features of special interest and their positive management.
 (ii)   To have regard for the protection of buildings and other features of architectural, archaeological or historic interest.
(iii)   To take into account the effect which proposals for any activity of the Authorities would have upon the beauty of, or amenities in, rural or urban areas or on the flora, fauna, features, buildings or objects of special interest.
 (iv)   To have regard for the desirability of preserving and improving public rights of access to water and associated land and the countryside in general.
  (v)   To have due regard for the status of certain areas designated because of their international, national or local importance.

Goal (d)

        To identify areas that are of the highest value for conservation and amenity, most suitable for a particular recreation, of highest value for agriculture, and those where there is room for compromise.

Table 5.2 (cont.)

Goal (e)
    To make adequate and realistic charges, where appropriate, for the
    recreational use of resources and facilities.

Source: Welsh Water Authority 1978b.

The Welsh Water Authority strategy

The Welsh Water Authority's strategy contains policies embracing water space in its area and the part of Wales in the Severn Trent Water Authority area. It is a framework for tactical plans such as the Lyn Brenig Management Plan and specific schemes, and it outlines the Authority's goals, objectives and priorities for water recreation and amenity given its overall low priority status (Welsh Water Authority 1978b).

The goals and objectives reflect the Water Act 1973 and the Countryside Act 1968 (Table 5.2). For example, objective (ii) of goal (b) is derived directly from the Water Act 1973 and objective (iv) of goal (c) from the Countryside Act 1968. In the sense that goals are basically ends while objectives are the means by which ends are achieved, the goals and objectives in the strategy are sometimes unclear. For example, goal (a) is to carry out surveys and prepare plans but represents a statement of means rather than ends. Goal (c) is more a consideration than either a goal or objective. Some objectives are also arguably too vague to be of real value. For example, goal (e) is to be achieved by making 'realistic' charges although the meaning of the term is unclear.

The strategy recognises some of the basic needs and issues of water space recreation and amenity planning. For example water owned or managed by the Authority will receive prior attention and facilities will be provided close to concentrations of population or in areas under pressure from holiday-makers. The fullest use of existing facilities is preferred to expenditure upon new ones, subject to the prevention of overloading. The Authority will provide more coarse fisheries in the areas of greatest need, will try to solve conflicts between river canoeing and angling and will actively protect wildlife of special interest. The plan is, however, sometimes inexplicit about which user groups will be given priority over others in the provision of facilities from limited funds.

The availability of finance is crucial and the Authority has opted for self-financing projects where possible and to make maximum use of grant-aid. However, in 1978 the Sports Council for Wales refused to make grants to the Authority arguing that its funds were limited in comparison to the Welsh Water Authority, despite the policy of its English counterpart to grant-aid other Water Authorities. For 1977–78 the Authority calculates that recreation, amenity and fisheries functions operated at a deficit of £835 000, and the plan places emphasis on the need to provide low cost basic facilities for general public enjoyment.

Policy development: the West Pennine moors reservoirs

The North West Water Authority's 'Policy for Reconciling the Authority's Responsibilities for Water Supply and Recreation in Particular Cases' is a statement of policy about what the Authority sees as the conflicting duties in water supply and recreation in an area containing an unusually large number of reservoirs (North West Water Authority 1977b, Liddell 1978). The policy is best explained by looking at one sub-area – the West Pennine moors.

The West Pennine moors comprise 233 km^2 of moorland, valley and reservoir landscape in the Ribble and Mersey catchments. They have been an important source of water for Lancashire towns for over 100 years and now supply Merseyside, Chorley, Bolton and Blackburn from a series of old, originally single-purpose reservoirs. The moors are also used for farming and outdoor recreation. The main landowner is the Water Authority which has many tenant farmers. Following a history of restrictive use to protect water supplies, a West Pennine Moors Plan, which is a local plan for recreation, is now being developed by the Lancashire and Greater Manchester County Councils in cooperation with the Water Authority and six District Councils and includes promotion of further recreation on reservoirs and gathering grounds (Lancashire County Council 1976a, 1976b, 1978). A number of interrelated planning problems have been highlighted including the conflict between different types of recreation activity, conflicts between recreation and the conservation value of the reservoirs, the problem of controlling existing levels of largely unmanaged recreation, the considerable backlog of environmental neglect, and strong local opposition to further recreation as well as the technical problems of using reservoirs and gathering grounds, developed primarily for public water supply, for recreation.

Although not an area of outstanding agricultural potential it does support a significant livestock economy and the upland pasture could be much more productive. The farming community is opposed to further recreation development because of existing trespass, vandalism and litter; pasture improvements are likely to increase their resistance. Prejudice against the Water Authority and its plans is to be expected from farming families who have long-standing grievances dating back to the wholesale clearances of farms from the moors during the last century to protect gathering grounds and the later restrictions on the use of fertilisers which led to a decline in pasture quality.

Public participation exercises show that other local residents are broadly opposed to further recreation although there was some support for using reservoirs for quiet water sports. However, the planning authorities must balance the needs of the local area with those of the North West region as a whole. The Lake District and Peak District National Parks, both important for water-based recreation, are already heavily pressurised and require relief. The promotion of outdoor recreation in the West Pennine moors is one possible solution.

The future of the moors is undecided. In the meantime the Water Authority is concentrating on controlling informal recreation and pursuing improvements such as installing car parks, footpaths, wardens' accommodation, extensive tree planting and landscaping and the reinstatement of eroded hillsides.

Limits imposed by water treatment facilities. Unfortunately the majority of the moors' reservoirs are of direct-supply variety, although some are compensating reservoirs. Because reservoirs are linked together more than one is serviced by one water treatment plant. The recreational capacity of the direct-supply reservoirs and their gathering grounds is largely determined by the efficiency of their water treatment plants, which is generally low. Plants have been rated on a scale from A to F by the Water Authority according to how many of six desirable treatment features such as disinfection, clarification and chlorination are incorporated. Generally, plants with an A rating have the most satisfactory combination of treatment facilities whilst those with an F rating have the least satisfactory combination. Although some are already being substantially upgraded, none has better than a C rating and many have the lowest F rating. This reflects the lack of investment in water treatment facilities in the past.

Minimum water treatment plant requirements for the future have been fixed by the Water Authority. The quality of treatment needed has been determined by the characteristics of the water source, such as the extent of potentially polluting habitation and agriculture in the catchment, the likelihood of pollution and the extent to which the Authority has ownership control of gathering grounds. A comparison of existing and required treatment plant ratings shows that some reservoirs already have adequate facilities but others require substantial improvement (Table 5.3).

If water treatment plants are upgraded recreational use in the future could be far greater than at present. Not all water treatment plants are considered to require an A rating. This reflects the rating criteria which relate to general catchment characteristics rather than to specific recreational requirements. As a result, even if the required treatment upgradings are made, facilities will still constrain recreational possibilities.

The extent to which other improvements can be made in the short term depends on cost (Table 5.3), although it is likely that complete upgrading will be achieved in the medium term. In some cases, inexpensive improvements can substantially raise the rating. For other plants the cost of improvements is higher, ranging from low (up to £5 000) to moderate (up to £15 000), while £50 000 would be considered to be a high cost. Fortunately most improvements can be made at a low to moderate cost but nevertheless in the short term the Water Authority places them some way down its list of priorities. The quality of water treatment plants alone does not determine the recreational use to which a reservoir and its gathering grounds can be put. Much also depends on the environmental policy which the local planning

Table 5.3 Reservoirs, water treatment plants and recreation possibilities in the West Pennine moors.

Reservoir	Treatment plant	Existing rating	Required rating	Potential rating at: low cost	mod. cost	Existing recreation	Permissible recreation with reqd. rating	Comments
Calf Hey	Crane	C	C	B		angling	reser.-limited land-selected	
Ogden	Crane	C	C	B		angling		
Holden	Compensation reservoir	–	–	–	–	angling	no constraint	sporting rights reserved by previous landowners
Entwistle	Sweetloves	F	C	C	B	angling & rambling	reser.-limited land-selected	
Wayoh	Wayoh	C	B	See comments		rambling & angling	land-selected	current extensions will give A rating by 1980
Jumbles	Compensation reservoir	–	–	–	–	Country Pk. rambling, sailing & angling	no constraint	
Belmont	Compensation reservoir	–	–	–	–	sailing	no constraint	
Springs	Springs	F	C	C		none	reser.-limited	
Dingle	Springs	F	C	C		angling	land-selected	
Delph	Sweetloves & Ferns	F	C	C	B	sailing	reser.-limited	
Earnsdale	Sunnyhurst	C	C	–	–	angling	land-selected	
Sunnyhurst Hey	Sunnyhurst	C	C	–	–	angling	reser.-limited land-selected	

Pickup	Fishmoor	F	C	C	B	none	none practical	reservoirs might be phased out as part of modernisation programme
Cocker	Cocker	F	C	D	—	angling	none	
Jackhouse	Cocker	F	C	D	—	angling	none	
Upper Roddlesworth	Rivington	F	C	See comments		angling, considerable public access	no constraint after approx. 1980	
Lower Roddlesworth	Rivington	F	C	"			"	
Rake Wood	Rivington	F	C	"		over	"	
High Bullough	Rivington	F	C	"		gathering grounds	"	
Anglezarke	Rivington	F	C	"		"	"	some water from Anglezarke and High Bullough goes to Chorley T.P. but this will be phased out in 1980
Yarrow	Rivington	F	B	"		"	"	
Upper Rivington	Rivington	F	B	"		"	"	
Lower Rivington	Rivington	F	B	"		"	"	

Source: North West Water Authority

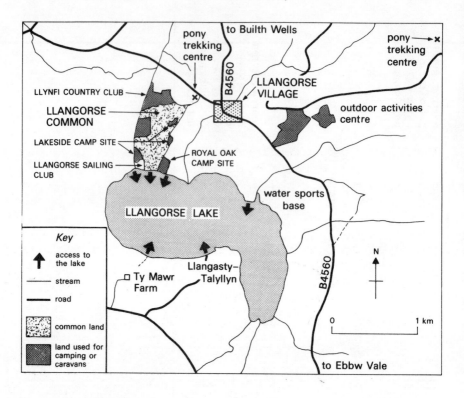

Figure 5.3   Recreational facilities at Llangorse Lake.

authorities choose to adopt. This may range from severe restriction of further recreation to vigorous promotion of additional and more intensive recreation: much depending upon the policies developed in the Moors Plan. In addition, the physical characteristics of the reservoirs themselves may constrain their eventual use. For instance, steep-sided reservoir shorelines present many difficulties for access to the water.

Assessment. Both the Welsh strategy and the policy for the West Pennine moors reservoirs are basically concerned with resolving conflict between resource roles and developing multi-purpose resource use. However, the legacy of the past is a major problem. Single-purpose reservoir design and underinvestment in water treatment plant is a common problem in Britain. Improving water treatment facilities presents no major technical difficulties and the costs of modernisation are small compared with those of sewage treatment plants. However, opening up reservoirs is not straightforward because of conflicts with farming, landowning and nature conservation interests. Furthermore the need for facilities must be clear. In the West Pennine moors, with few exceptions, the response from water sports organisations to public participation exercises was surprisingly disappointing, perhaps indicating a lower level of demand than expected. How Water Authorities will tackle such problems and set their financing and user group priorities will only become clear as overall recreation and amenity strategies, like the Welsh strategy, are implemented.

Other policies, plans and schemes for water space

Local planning authorities influence the recreation and amenity use of water space through development control decisions undertaken in the context of structure and development plans such as local plans or National Park plans. The role of local planning authorities can be illustrated by three contrasting examples. Llangorse Lake is a strictly finite resource under extreme pressure whilst the Forth and Clyde and Union Canals are a derelict resource with limited recreational potential and the Cotswold Water Park is an example of expanding water space with an enormous recreational future. Each case illustrates how local planning authorities intervene in the use of water space to help maximise social benefits, how water space planning is closely linked to other local authority responsibilities and why public intervention is limited and often needs to be combined with private initiative.

Llangorse Lake: a case for public intervention

Llangorse Lake is a natural lake which covers 145 hectares of the Brecon

Beacons National Park. Surrounding privately-owned farmland restricts public shore access which is possible mainly at Llangorse Common (Fig. 5.3). The lake has been popular for angling and casual recreation for years with a greater diversity of water sports becoming common during the 1950s. The lake is well situated for regional recreational demands and is designated as of regional significance by the Sports Council for Wales. Water recreation here has increased in recent years and pressure upon the lake and common is now severe.

Llangorse Lake is now used for a wide variety of water sports including angling, sailing, canoeing, rowing, motorboating, speed-boating and water-skiing as well as by naturalists and research agencies (Dartington Amenity Research Trust 1973). Associated with these activities are recreational facilities including caravan sites, jetties and an outdoor activities centre with its own water sports base.

Limited space: user conflict.   The level of use which Llangorse Lake can sustain without a significant deterioration in the nature and quality of the recreation experience is limited by the size of the lake itself – a small area considering the wide range of water sports and their popularity. The lake can become very crowded and the quality of the recreation experience declines especially at peak periods, but also at other times depending upon the mix of activities.

Speed-boating and water-skiing adversely affect sailing and vice versa and there is insufficient water space for safety. Also while speed-boating can add visual interest for the casual observer, the boats create a noise problem. These conflicts are lessened by the daily and weekly patterns of use: sailing and canoeing occur throughout the week when speed-boating and water-skiing activities are least but both 'peak' on Sundays.

Two responses to these conflicts have arisen. First in 1970 Breconshire County Council, after complaints about recreation pressure on the lake, consulted interests and sought to impose byelaws to control the use of power-boats. The lake users most closely involved opposed the byelaws at a public inquiry, arguing for reasonable voluntary limits and stressing the lack of alternative waters. The byelaws were subsequently rejected by the Secretary of State for Wales.

The second response is a cooperative venture since 1972 by the Lake Users' Committee, advised by the Sports Council for Wales. This consists of rules for power-boats on the lake, restrictions on their use at peak periods and advises an anticlockwise circulation of craft. The rules work reasonably well for most of the time but have no official status and cannot therefore be enforced. Partly as a result of the voluntary code not being followed a serious accident involving a water-skier occurred in 1976.

Ecological instability.   The ecological capacity of the resource base to support present uses is also in considerable doubt. Llangorse is internationally significant as a nutrient-rich lake, being designated a Site of Special

Scientific Interest in 1954 by the Nature Conservancy. The flora is rich and diverse and the lake edge vegetation shows classical zonation of marshland communities including reedbeds, sedge and rush. The fauna includes important wintering wildfowl and summer breeding birds. A combination of factors may seriously accelerate the natural eutrophication process. Apart from the nutrients in runoff from surrounding farmland, an important nutrient source is the Llangorse sewage treatment works which are now the responsibility of the Welsh Water Authority. These works, designed for a population of 360, now receive sewage from the outdoor activities camp-site which has planning permission for 200 people and which has accommodated up to 500 people. The works can become overloaded when sewage discharge into the lake occurs. Also some minor but illegal sewage discharges from various recreational facilities have occurred. A further possible source of nutrients is the mud on the lake bed which is disturbed particularly by speed-boating. Chemical tests by the Water Authority do not show any clear deterioration in the lake since 1972 despite sewage discharges on many occasions. Botanical studies however have shown a definite change in the composition of the lake's aquatic community. This may be natural or could point to accelerated eutrophication from recreation pressure. The National Park Authority, local landowners and the Nature Conservancy Council in particular are concerned about a sudden acceleration in eutrophication especially after experience on the Norfolk Broads. Unfortunately until more research on causes of eutrophication at Llangorse Lake is undertaken a convincing argument for change in the lake's use cannot be made. Water sports also disturb ecological stability in other ways: wash from motorboats damages lakeside reed vegetation and any boating can disturb wildfowl.

In the meantime two responses have been made. The Water Authority has plans for a larger sewage works although implementation has been delayed by financial constraints. Secondly, the National Park Authority whose members are drawn mainly from local councils has proposed a Local Nature Reserve at the lake, an idea first considered in 1948. Such a nature reserve to safeguard wildlife would not necessarily imply discontinuation of water sports although further limitations may become necessary. Many different types of recreational use could still be accommodated with minimal effect on the lake's ecological stability.

Political differences. Planning the use of Llangorse Lake has always been a difficult political exercise. The ownership of the lake itself, disputed for 20 years and an obstacle to public intervention, was only recently settled in favour of a local landowner. The number and variety of interest groups produces a complex situation in which opposite viewpoints and distrust have been rife and agreement is difficult. The owner of the lake is not opposed to its use for water sports but other riparian owners fearing restrictions on their farming activities have expressed concern about a nature reserve, while also wishing to protect the local environment. The commercial operators, the lake users excluding the naturalists, and the Sports Council wish to see as few restrictions as possible, consistent with adequate safety levels. The local inhabitants benefit from the trade which recreation brings but suffer from the congestion, noise and eyesores it also creates. The Park Authority strongly favours establishing, by agreement if such can be obtained, the Local Nature Reserve which obviously worries the commercial operators and many lake users, although the naturalists and the Nature Conservancy Council are in favour. The Water Authority remains peripheral, although construction of a larger sewage works is significant, but has interests in seeing the coarse fisheries of the lake developed to their full potential.

Following a public meeting in 1975 the Park Authority, anxious to involve all interests in decisions about the lake's future, proposed a working group as a forum for declaring interests and for producing plans with the widest measure of agreement. The Llangorse Working Group with over 30 members from all the groups involved, and technical advisers from agencies such as the Sports Council and the Nature Conservancy Council, has so far led to increased understanding of opposing viewpoints, declaration of interests and discussion of possible management measures such as zoning of the water space and the establishing of a nature reserve. Initially the role of the Working Group is to work out goals and objectives for the future management of the lake and through this process it may mark the start of public intervention into the future use of the lake.

Assessment.   Current use of Llangorse Lake has evolved more by private initiative than by public decision. However, as pressure on the lake grows with lake uses including recreation expanding without regard for ecological stability, public intervention becomes necessary and more likely, particularly now that the ownership issue – which complicated and prevented attempts to plan the use of the lake – is now resolved. The Working Group is an imaginative attempt to coordinate and plan the use of the lake by involving local interests. The problems of Llangorse Lake are similar to those of Broadland and by involving local interests in a Working Group a form of local management similar to that developing in Broadland is being adopted. While the Working Group includes all interests in a situation where there are few alternative courses of action, its size and composition make it somewhat unwieldy. Success in reaching agreement over vital issues will only follow if all interests wish the Working Group to succeed. If successful the idea of the Working Group might well be emulated elsewhere. The planning of the lake also depends upon the solution of two data constraints. Detailed evidence is required on the sources, significance and effects of nutrients on the lake's aquatic communities. The determination of the physical capacity and perceptual capacity according to different user groups is also required.

The Forth and Clyde and Union Canals: local amenity enhancement or restoration?

The Forth and Clyde and Union Canals were originally built to transport industrial goods. Statutory closure to navigation occurred in the 1960s after years of neglect and decline. Being remainder waterways, expenditure on maintenance has been minimised with the canals being at the mercy of local expediency. Both are now severed at numerous points either through complete infilling or by obstructions, such as road crossings disregarding the prior need to maintain navigable headroom. Parts are vandalised, derelict and silted up. In 1974 there were 65 obstructions on the Forth and Clyde Canal, some reducing headroom to one metre, and the Union Canal is obstructed in 10 places.

In 1971 the Inland Waterways Amenity Advisory Council recommended against restoration and promotion of the canals to cruising status judging them to be of local amenity value only. However in 1974 it suggested partial restoration and a new regional study by statutory authorities of the canals' recreation potential including the possibility of complete coast to coast restoration (Inland Waterways Amenity Advisory Council 1971, 1974). The change in approach followed the successful fostering of local interest in the canals by active canal and amenity societies and local radio stations. Although the British Waterways Board's remainder waterways powers are statutorily limited, it combined with the Regional and District Councils to form working parties to study each canal. In 1977 recommendations were produced for the Union Canal and proposals for the Forth and Clyde Canal will follow (British Waterways Board 1978).

Recommendations for the Union Canal range from improving public towpath access to promotion of increased canal use, developing canalside facilities, environmental improvement and dredging and removal of obstacles. The removal of all obstacles on the Union Canal alone is a formidable task estimated to cost about £1million. Despite the high cost the policy of pressure groups such as the Scottish Inland Waterways Association is to work towards total coast to coast restoration to provide a trans-Scotland waterway.

Given local authority financial involvement and the possibility of attracting Countryside Commission and other grants, the central issue concerns the amount of public money which should be spent on canal improvements and the type of facilities to be provided. Without doubt individual canal stretches have considerable local amenity value, especially close to urban areas, and these can be enhanced at relatively low public cost by small-scale access, safety, recreation and environmental improvements including tree screening, landscaping, towpath surfacing, life belt provision, industrial archaeology information boards, lunch hour leisure spaces and light boat-hire facilities.

The future of the canals is one of imaginative, low cost, local amenity and small-scale recreational use and the statutory authorities should encourage canal user societies to continue to invest their own time and money in pursuit of their own particular goals. Informal facilities for walkers, picnickers and for educational study are likely to benefit a wide cross-section of local society at low cost and may also enhance tourist appeal in tourist centres. On the other hand, expensive clearance and restoration of coast to coast navigation is likely to benefit a smaller section of society represented by the canal, boating and seagoing yacht enthusiasts. It is extremely doubtful whether public money should be made available for this purpose especially as there is no real shortage of water space for recreation in Central Scotland.

The Cotswold Water Park: local planning authority initiative

The Cotswold Water Park was designated in 1967 by Upper Thames Valley local planning authorities. It lies to the north of Swindon between South Cerney and Lechlade where extensive gravel extraction, begun in the 1920s, is still creating dozens of wet gravel pits. Within the 5700 hectare park there are about 800 hectares of water space, already equivalent to the amount of open water in the Norfolk Broads.

Worked out pits have been leased from landowners largely on the initiative of private water sports clubs and separate lakes are already used for sailing, angling, canoeing, rowing, water-skiing and power-boating. Naturalists and casual recreationalists also use the park and a private enterprise marina catering for family entertainment on and by the water has been developed. The park lies outside the Cotswolds Area of Outstanding Natural Beauty and the landscape is ordinary and with few viewpoints. Gravel extraction changes the natural scenery creating raw landscape intrusions as well as generating heavy gravel lorry traffic. Aggregate stockpiles and gravel washing plant can remain next to a pit long after use. The Nature Conservancy Council regards the lakes as being of outstanding biological significance because the pits are colonised by a rich variety of aquatic flora and fauna soon after extraction ceases (Collins 1975).

The Park master plan, approved in 1970, is being integrated with the Upper Thames District Plan and the county structure plans for the area. Being close to the M4 and M5 motorways the park is regionally well located with two million people living within one hour's travel time. Through development control and planning initiatives, such as road and landscape improvements, the master plan aims to resolve the conflicts between gravel extraction, the environment of existing villages and recreation and nature conservation. For example, heavy gravel traffic needs routing around villages and away from recreational traffic. An important object of development control is to enhance the after-use of pits for recreation. Without the imposition of conditions in planning permissions worked pits are rarely directly suitable for recreational use. Recent planning permissions include conditions requiring gravel extractors to grade shore lines, to retain trees and to landscape the pits. Spoil heaps can make useful viewpoints and trees and hedgerows soften the landscape and reduce wind exposure. However, even with these after-use conditions the creation of the water park is hindered by the legacy of planning permissions granted decades ago without conditions for future extraction (Cotswold Water Park Joint Committee 1970).

A further major initiative made by the local planning authorities and the Countryside Commission is the designation of two publicly-funded Country Parks within the water park. For example Keynes Park has been developed for sailing, angling and other quiet pursuits such as birdwatching. Planning the after-use of the pits allows the future availability of water space to be anticipated, allows the maximum use of lakes to segregate conflicting pursuits and has also allowed selection of a suitable site for an aquatic nature reserve.

However, the maturation of the water park will be gradual. Local planning authority involvement in developing facilities is limited by financial constraints and because public funding is inappropriate for some activities. This is particularly so where water space is plentiful and private enterprise and clubs are able to fund their own facilities without prejudicing the recreational opportunities of a wider public.

Assessment. The cases of the Forth and Clyde and Union Canals and the Cotswold Water Park, although in many ways dissimilar, both show how local planning authorities can promote water space use using sources of finance or powers such as development control not directly available to water industry agencies. Both cases also indicate the inseparability of water amenity and recreation developments from wider local authority planning responsibilities. The opportunities provided by the Forth and Clyde and Union Canals for local amenity improvement are probably best viewed in the wider context of enhancing housing, transport, other recreational and tourist development for individual communities. At the same time the potential provided by gravel working in the Upper Thames is also probably best realised by strict development control and as part of village improvement schemes and traffic planning. All three studies demonstrate the case for limiting publicly-funded plans and schemes to those which benefit large cross sections of society and for encouraging private group initiative and private enterprise in other circumstances.

Evaluation

Underlying any evaluation of water space planning are two basic issues. The first concerns the extent to which Water Authorities are suited to plan water space. The second concerns the distributional consequences of water space policies when benefits are difficult to measure and where facilities are allocated roughly in proportion to pressures exerted on regional water authorities by groups pursuing their own ends.

Does society provide water planners with an adequate framework of legislation, institutions and financial provision?
Incremental growth of the planning system and resource ownership patterns produce institutional complexity in water space planning. By virtue of the multi-purpose Regional Councils, Scotland is in theory slightly less complex than England and Wales. Division of responsibility hinders policy making and grant-aiding is confusing and sometimes anomalous. Water Authorities cannot treat water space planning as a top priority and considering their broad water space duties, their professional composition is inappropriate. Their self-financing obligations may conflict with treatment of recreation and amenity more as a social service. The common law also hinders water recreation where it protects exclusive use which may be against the public interest. Some areas of water space planning may be under-financed but public funds should be used discriminatingly and only where substantial social benefits accrue.

To what extent do public attitudes and preferences towards water and associated land resources affect policies, plans and schemes?
Public preferences have led to the identification of water space as a national asset to be developed for the maximum social benefit. From a low level of provision, growing recreation pressures have led gradually to policies favouring multiple use of water supply reservoirs focussing attention on water treatment improvements, as at West Pennine moors, and 'designed in' recreational facilities at new reservoirs. Recognition of demands for formal water sport facilities is now being matched by recognition of less well articulated informal recreation and amenity needs leading to a more appropriate emphasis upon informal water-side opportunities, especially in the urban fringe, and upon landscaping land close to water.

How do the inherent characteristics of water in Britain influence the choice of alternative policies, plans and schemes?
Water space shortages occur in England and Wales, particularly close to conurbations. However, scarcity is not really an issue in Scotland. Shortages are emphasised because uplands of rare natural beauty and extensive water space, like the Peak District, are already heavily used for recreation and are subject to conservation policies. As water space is used more intensively so its life-supporting qualities are endangered, as at Llangorse Lake and on the East Anglian Broads, making public intervention necessary.

To what extent are resource management principles incorporated into water policies, plans and schemes?
Because other recreation and amenity planning agencies are not based upon river basins, catchment-based planning by Water Authorities is perhaps less clearly advantageous for water space than for other fields of water planning. On the other hand, regional scale allocation of water space provides the best

approach to conflicts between recreations due to growing multiple-use of space. As pressure on water space grows more attention is paid to carrying capacities in order to preserve the resource, although pressures leading to overuse are strong and are proving difficult to control.

How well is water planning integrated with other forms of public planning?
In an area of fragmented responsibility the unified Scottish management structure is advantageous for liaison between water space and other areas of public planning. Nowhere is the need for liaison between local planning authorities and Water Authorities more obvious than in the water space planning field where both sets of authorities have unique experience and access to different planning tools, as demonstrated by development control in the Cotswold Water Park. Yet integration is less strong than could be hoped for and reliance must be placed upon *ad hoc* liaison arrangements which are of growing importance.

Is water planning comprehensive and systematic and are all interests adequately involved?
In terms of identifying goals, objectives and priorities the new generation of water space strategies now emerging from Water Authorities and exemplified by the Welsh strategy, indicate that policies are being derived more systematically than in the past. However the quality of decision making is constrained by gaps in knowledge, for example in assessing the effects of recreation and other uses of water upon each other, and in estimating the social benefits of recreation. In most of the case examples examined participation and consultation was a strong feature but nevertheless the water industry tends to be a recalcitrant partner in water space development and responds largely only when pushed. Given this, there is some danger of unplanned inequities in publicly-funded facilities reflecting the powerful position of some pressure groups like angling consultative bodies compared with others.

More importantly, regionalised water management may well be ill-suited to reconcile many essentially local recreation and amenity problems. What may be necessary are complementary locally accountable groups such as those which have emerged in Broadland and at Llangorse lake.

Selected further reading (for full bibliography see pp. 254-66)

For the fullest analysis of Britain's water space and its use see:

Tanner M. F. 1973a *Water resources and recreation*. Sports Council Water Recreation Series Study 3. London: Sports Council.

For a discussion of the social context of recreation including Scottish recreation resources see:

Coppock, J. T., and B. S. Duffield 1975. *Recreation in the countryside*. London: Macmillan.

For an understanding of the problems of joint use of water space by water sportsmen see:

O'Riordan, T., and G. Paget 1978. *Sharing rivers and canals.* A study of the views of coarse anglers and boat users on selected waterways, Sports Council Study No. 16. London: Sports Council.

For an appreciation of the ecological and institutional problems associated with heavily used ecologically sensitive water space see:

Nature Conservancy Council 1977. *The future of Broadland.* London: NCC.

For the first Water Authority water space recreation and amenity strategy see:

Welsh Water Authority 1978b. *A strategic plan for water-space recreation and amenity.* Consultation Edition. Brecon: WWA.

6 *Land drainage and flood alleviation*

Floods, drought and water-related disease are hazards facing our society for which the British water industry has responsibilities. Such risks are often imperfectly understood by the public and, indeed, are not easily assessed by scientists, thus making policy formulation and scheme implementation far from straightforward.

Risk reduction is the rationale of urban flood alleviation policies and schemes but these form only one part of regional water authority 'land drainage' responsibilities, which also include draining agricultural land to increase its productivity. The physical interlinking of agricultural drainage with river management and flood control has led to integrated management, which at first sight appears anomalous. Therefore we are concerned in this Chapter with surplus water and counteracting policies, in the interests of both food production and flood damage reduction.

Compared with other water planning areas capital expenditure on land drainage is small, amounting in England and Wales to just £39millions or less than 10% of total capital expenditure in 1978; the ratio of agricultural to urban land drainage expenditure is approximately 40:60. In Scotland the sums involved are almost insignificant in relation to other water budgets, totalling in 1978 only £0·6million. In both areas revenue expenditure is small but within multi-functional planning agencies revenue expenditure, including staffing, cannot be allocated accurately to functional areas.

Land drainage and flood alleviation directly affect a far smaller section of our society than water supply or sewage disposal. Those most directly affected are the farmers whose land requires drainage, people unfortunate enough to live in flood prone areas and those who need urban storm drainage for their housing or factory developments. While appearing to concern just sectional interests, land drainage however has important wider implications. These concern not only food production to support a large population but also the amenity value of rivers, the scientific value of wetland sites and the wildlife interest of both, which all in society can study and enjoy.

Significant characteristics of the land drainage and flood alleviation field include the complexity of the planning system, which directly involves all levels of policy-making and executive agencies from local committees to central government. This system is dominated by powerful agricultural interests. The complexity is mainly a result of the strength of this agricultural lobby, which has maintained stable institutional structures for land drainage through many reorganisations of other parts of the water planning system. A further characteristic is a newly attempted rigour of economic appraisal within the planning process for land drainage schemes, where 'rule-of-thumb' methods existed before. The reason for rigorous economic appraisal lies partly in the difficulty of intuitive assessments of the cost-effectiveness of plans and schemes, which in turn is related to problems inherent in predicting the likelihood and magnitude of future flood events. Rigorous appraisal is also required for decisions whereby national funds are allocated to benefit directly only a few members of society. Greater reliance on more systematic evaluative methods has therefore evolved in the land drainage area than in other areas of water planning and these methods have developed as schemes have become economically more marginal. However this does not necessarily mean that decisions concerning land drainage schemes are either simple or always correct or that similar rigour should not be attempted elsewhere.

The nature of flooding and land drainage problems

The prime natural function of river systems is to drain land but sometimes rivers overflow their banks. Also rainstorms can be sufficiently intense to cause surcharged drains. The result is flooding, which can cause damage to crops and buildings or loss of life. In certain agricultural areas natural soil drainage is very slow, causing limitations on land use which can only be removed with proper agricultural land drainage. Flooding from the sea can both cause damage and impede agricultural use.

Inland floods occur when runoff exceeds drainage capacity. Precipitation from depressions or thunderstorms exceeds infiltration rates and river channel or storm sewer capacity, especially where impervious urban surfaces increase runoff (Ward 1978). The larger the flood the rarer its occurrence, but flood events comprise a series of random events so making the timing of individual floods unpredictable. In agricultural areas soils become saturated, covered in water and unsuitable for grazing or arable cultivation. Such water-logging remains for some time after a storm or flood event. Low-lying and clay soil areas are predictably affected in this way virtually every winter. Coastal and estuarine floods generally result when high tides and storms coincide. Coastal embankments are either insufficiently high and are over-topped or are washed away and sea water encroaches on to agricultural land or invades properties and floods roads. In all these cases economic damage results, either owing to the contact of flood waters with damageable property or because the use of both urban and agricultural flood prone land is restricted.

The resource with which we are primarily concerned, then, is not the water itself but the land affected by flooding or poor drainage and its value to the community, although flood water is stored for later use in all storage and river regulation schemes. The interdependencies of land and water resources are central to this field. The use and productivity of flood prone or poorly drained land is limited but can be increased in the agricultural case by flood protection and field under-drainage and in the urban case by flood alleviation measures such as flood control schemes or flood proofing. Given flood alleviation, existing use can be intensified, such that recreation areas can be used throughout the year instead of just in summer when flood risk is less, or the use of the land may be changed. Full protection is generally impossible, since theoretically there is no maximum flood event. However, when reduced risk is provided by flood alleviation schemes industrial or other intensive urban development may become possible, perhaps on waste land previously showing no economic return. Houses may be built where previously only poor agricultural use was possible. In all cases the fundamental gain is in land and property values, as a reflection either of increased return from their use or of flood damages averted.

However, flood prone land in both urban and agricultural areas may itself be a valuable resource. Wildlife is attracted to where surface waters periodically accumulate. Specialised and rare flora and fauna congregate in wetlands subject to winter flooding where only low intensity agricultural use is possible. Pesticides and fertilisers are generally uncommon in these areas, partly because they would be leached away by floodwater, so that species endangered by such chemicals can thrive. Similarly, areas subject to periodic sea flooding attract rare wildlife which need such conditions to obtain food when similar habitats further north are frozen.

The draining of all agricultural land and the protection of all flood plains – even if that were possible – may therefore result in one type of resource being lost in favour of gaining another: the reduced flood damage or the increased crop potential of free-draining agricultural land may be gained at the expense of the intangible value of rich and diverse wildlife. Nevertheless there are many instances where this intangible wildlife and conservation value is absent and where land drainage and flood alleviation is necessary both to ensure the safety of human life and to protect from damage society's investments in the form of houses and factories. There are also many areas where land drainage schemes are essential to create or maintain agricultural viability. The fenland areas of East Anglia and Somerset are examples where agricultural use would be impossible without drainage schemes designed to regulate the water table and prevent surface flooding.

One of the major difficulties in planning the drainage of agricultural land and the protection of urban and coastal areas from flooding is the sparseness of information about the precise extent of the problem. In England and Wales this is currently the subject of surveys being carried out under Section 24(5) of the Water Act 1973 but until these surveys are complete full information is not available with which to prepare rational plans for future expenditure.

The nature and extent of urban flood damage

Urban flood prone land suffers several fundamentally different types of flood damage which have recently been the subject of extensive and detailed research (Penning-Rowsell and Chatterton 1977). It is usual to differentiate between tangible and intangible damages, based on whether or not monetary values can be assigned to the effects of flooding. Intangible damages include anxiety during or in anticipation of a flood event, ill-health following floods and inconvenience when communication links are broken and shops and offices are flooded. These intangible damages may be of great significance. Following extensive flooding in Bristol in 1968 the number of deaths among those whose homes had been flooded increased by 50% (Bennet 1970). Surgery attendances rose by 53% and hospital referrals and admissions more than doubled. Loss of life during floods – perhaps the prime intangible damage although insurance companies do quantify the value of life – is rare in Britain compared with floods in the United States and developing countries. Notable exceptions include the disastrous Lynmouth flood of 1952 (Ward 1978). However, the social costs of floods leading to increased ill-health and anxiety of the old and infirm cannot be ignored.

Tangible flood damages are either direct or indirect. Direct damages are caused by the physical contact of flood water with damageable property. The extent of damage can be quantified as the cost of restoring the property to its pre-flood value or its loss in market value if restoration is not worthwhile. Direct damages are a function of many variables, such as the land use of the flood prone area and its susceptibility to damage: damage to shops is generally greater than to parks and other open spaces. Other important variables concern the flood event itself, principally its depth but also the velocity of flood waters, their sediment and pollution content and the length of warning during which damage-reducing action can be taken (Penning-Rowsell, Chatterton and Parker 1978).

Indirect damages are losses caused by disruption of economic and physical linkages, for example when roads are blocked by flood waters necessitating expensive detours and time wastage. Telephone networks may be damaged as may be power and gas supplies to houses and factories. Inconvenience is caused and industrial production may be affected, not only as a result of direct flooding of the factory or offices concerned but as an indirect result of floods elsewhere. As with all natural disasters, conditions during a flood event are confused. Damage and inconvenience may spread far beyond the actual area affected and may, if the event is large such as the 1953 east coast floods (Cole 1976), affect the economy of a whole region. If London were flooded as much as is predicted (Ward 1978, Hollis 1978) the national economy would be seriously affected.

The likelihood or probability of a flood occurring in a given year varies with location. The magnitude of a flood needed to overtop the sizable embankments of the Thames at London is such that it is unlikely to occur on average more than once in perhaps 50 years. However, in other locations rivers overflow their banks or storm sewers become surcharged every year. This concept of probability, or the return period of a flood of a given magnitude (Sutcliffe 1978), is central to decisions concerning levels of expenditure on preventing damage. Clearly it is worthwhile spending more on preventing the same amount of flood damage occurring every year (the annual flood) than if it occurs only every 50 years (the 50-year flood).

Much damage caused in current British floods is the result of urban encroachment on to flood plains. This encroachment occurred principally during the nineteenth century, but also in the twentieth century before 1947 when planning legislation led to greater control of urban development (Penning-Rowsell and Parker 1974). Riverside locations for urban development were economically favourable, given the needs of navigation, water supply and effluent disposal. Such locations still attract urban development, either because inertia concentrates new development at the periphery of existing centres or because riverside locations are attractive for amenity reasons. While nowhere near the magnitude of problem in the United States, where development control has been virtually non-existent (White *et al.* 1958), nevertheless this continued urban development in flood risk areas is a nagging problem in Britain. In England and Wales it is caused by poor liaison between the local authority controlling the development and the Water Authorities responsible for drainage and flood alleviation.

A reliable measure of both actual and potential urban flood damage in Britain is not available. Research in the catchments of the Severn, Wye and the South Wales 'valleys' showed that nearly every urban settlement was flood prone and few settlements had full flood protection schemes (Parker and Harding 1978). On the other hand there is evidence of reducing flood frequency in many localities resulting from expenditure since the Land Drainage Act 1930 (Cole 1976). However, it may well be that the relative importance of different types of flood events is changing (Ward 1978); an increasing number of small floods is apparent, although this may be a consequence of increased media coverage of such events. These floods often result from blocked drains or inadequate culverts and cause little damage except road traffic interruptions. There may also be an increasing likelihood of extreme damaging events, when protective schemes are overtopped causing considerable damage.

Many damaging events occur each year, not always involving massive damage let alone loss of life but calamitous to those affected who may lose all their possessions or their means of livelihood. To take a single example, serious flooding occurred to the Meadows estate at Llandudno Junction during October 1976. Thirty new houses in a small flood basin were flooded to a depth of one metre by the Afon Wydden. The cause was the installation of an under-sized culvert by the developer; the estate and the A55 road were flooded again in February 1977 (Welsh National Water Development Authority 1977).

Caution is needed in defining flood damage before concluding that it is totally negative in effect. Repairing damaged property gives employment and therefore floods may create gains for some people which are losses to others. In addition, flood events can enhance social cohesion and generate 'community spirit' for some, to compensate for the anxiety of others. Viewed in this way flood alleviation schemes have broader implications than appear at first sight.

The need for agricultural drainage

On more than half the 11 million hectares of agricultural land in England and Wales field drainage is a fundamental requirement for efficient farming. On a further 3 million hectares the use of the land is limited by the absence of efficient drainage. To complete the improvement of this land the arterial drainage of 100 000 hectares is required and an unknown amount of agricultural land needs to be protected against river flooding (Johnson 1954, Cole 1976).

Much undrained agricultural land is by necessity only used for rough grazing. Draining this grassland will improve the soil and the grazing quality by increasing the growth of grass, permitting more effective use of fertilisers, and thereby allowing the duration and density of grazing to be increased. In addition the risk of disease, particularly from liver fluke, is reduced when cattle are grazed on drained as opposed to undrained grassland. Therefore the main reason for draining this and other land is to make it easier to farm and to yield a better return from crops and livestock.

Excessive soil water restricts the aeration of the soil, so denying soil micro-organisms the oxygen needed for respiration and growth. Waterlogging slows down the rise in soil temperature in spring – reducing the growing season – and lowers the bearing capacity of the soil for animals and machinery, aggravates the nitrogen deficiency in crops, damages seeds and seedlings and, finally, reduces the plants' resistance to summer drought by restricting root growth. Field drainage systems, and their associated arterial river works to carry away water from the field 'tile' drains, are designed to control the water regime to limits appropriate to the soil characteristics and the crop to be grown (Agricultural Development and Advisory Service 1974-7).

Surface flooding of agricultural land is simply an extension of water-logging and again reduces yields. In extreme cases the crop is a total loss, depending on crop type, the growth stage and the duration of the flood water on the land. Grass is generally killed if submerged for longer than three weeks owing to lack of oxygen. Potatoes and other root crops can be completely destroyed if flooded for only 24 hours. In addition, damage from flooding may not be limited to crops. When saturated for too long the structure of silty soils may suffer progressive deterioration in structure and thereby permanent damage (Miers 1967). However, floods on agricultural land in certain circumstances may be beneficial. Alluvial silt spread on sandy soils can increase fertility although flood plain soils generally have sufficient, and indeed often excessive, proportions of fine-grained silts and clays.

The threat of coastal flooding

In Britain the main threat from coastal flooding is on the east and south coast of England from the Humber to Kent (Ward 1978). In addition, however, localised parts of the west coast of England and areas of Scotland are at risk. Floods have occurred in the Severn estuary as a result of storms and the Severn bore, along the south coast such as at Bridport and Dawlish and on the Lancashire and Scottish coasts, notably at Fleetwood and Ayr.

In the disastrous east coast flood in 1953 over 300 lives were lost and property valued at £30millions was destroyed (1953 prices). The threat here is greatest with rare combinations of high tides, low pressure increasing the natural height of the North Sea, and strong northerly or northeasterly winds. In these circumstances a surge of water passes southwards down the North Sea which – being funnel shaped and shallowing towards the south – causes the surge to grow, particularly where it enters estuaries such as the Humber or the Thames. These surges can be as much as 1·8 m above tide levels in open sea and 2·3 m in the Thames estuary.

Unfortunately the effect of tides and surges is growing. Eastern England is falling very slowly relative to the sea so that mean sea level is rising at approximately 0·36 m per century, owing to isostatic readjustment and melting polar ice caps. If present trends continue the rise in maximum high tide levels relative to the sea will be 0·76 m over the next 100 years. Combined with the effect of embankments in the estuary raising water levels, tides are 1·22 m higher today at London Bridge than 100 years ago. The chances of flooding along the whole of the east coast have increased considerably (Horner 1978). As a result, in the 100 years before 1953 11 tides exceeded 4·6 m above Ordnance Datum in Hull. In the following 10 years this level was exceeded nine times.

The area considered at risk in London contains more than 250 000 houses, thousands of factories and hundreds of thousands of vehicles. Gas and electricity supplies would be dislocated by a flood thereby indirectly affecting hospitals, factories and residential property far beyond the flooded areas. More than 50 underground stations, 50 telephone exchanges, 35 hospitals, 4 major sewage works, 25 fire stations and 7 ambulance stations would be under water, many for several days.

Flooding from the sea is of three types. First, coastal defences can burst, as happened in Lincolnshire and East Anglia in 1953. Secondly, defences can be overtopped but not breached. This type of incident occurred on the north Norfolk coast both in 1953 and again in 1978. Thirdly, tidal rivers can overflow their banks because they are unable to outfall into the sea which is at a higher level. This occurred with the Great Ouse at King's Lynn in 1953 and in several subsequent years and also with the river Nene at Wisbech in 1978.

With the second of these categories property below sea defences will almost certainly suffer total destruction under severe conditions. In the other two cases damage will be considerable and exacerbated by large deposits of sand and mud which will hamper salvage and increase damage. Tidal rivers overflowing into urban areas will usually contain sewage contamination and, as with all flooding in storm situations, damage is further increased by wave action such that properties may suffer total loss. The salt in sea water also increases damage caused by flood waters by as much as 10–20% (Penning-Rowsell 1978b).

Agricultural land flooded from the sea will suffer much more than that affected by fresh water. Normal agricultural use will not be possible for approximately three years after the flooding. Special crops such as oats may be necessary in the early years of restoration to remove salt from the soil. These effects add to any damage caused by scour and silt or mud deposition which is common during the storm conditions when sea flooding occurs.

The social context of land drainage and flood alleviation

Compared with water supply and pollution prevention, agricultural land drainage is virtually unknown to the general public, perhaps because so few people are directly involved. In contrast society has definite ideas about protection from flooding, which appears to be a natural hazard for which there is general fear. To onlookers, those affected by floods appear to suffer considerably, although actual stress fails to match these apparent effects and indeed floods can become events promoting beneficial social interaction at times of mutual stress. However society has no clear view of the standard of flood protection to be given except that it should be virtually absolute. As well as being physically impossible, in that there is in theory no maximum possible flood, schemes based on such standards would be economically undesirable to say the least!

Land drainage and flood alleviation policies, plans and schemes reflect both these ambivalent public attitudes and changing government policy towards promoting the intensified use of a diminishing area of agricultural land. Although the two planning fields are closely linked, through the dual role of the administrative systems covering both agricultural drainage and flood alleviation, the two problems are naturally different and each has a different societal context.

Agriculture: myths and reality

Public attitudes towards agriculture are highly complex, which in turn fundamentally affects land drainage policy and practice. General attitudes, in contrast to strong government involvement with agriculture, have until recently reflected a romantic pastoral attachment if not indifference. It is uncertain whether recent antagonism towards the massive changes in nature and appearance of agriculture and its practices is more than just a passing phase.

The myth of naturalness. Agriculture is that part of British industrialised society which is closest to the forces of nature. The control of agricultural production by these forces, and the role of the physical characteristics of soils, weather and water in determining production and prosperity, has always been the backcloth to agricultural activity and attitudes.

Society sees agriculture as a 'natural' industry, caring for the countryside and performing a stewardship role in maintaining and improving the quality of the soil against the ravages of nature. Agriculture has been seen as a force for stabilising the traditional rural life style away from the degraded and alienating living conditions of urban areas (Blythe 1969). Such mythology has been exposed by Williams (1973) but a strong reverence and nostalgia for the 'traditional' rural and agricultural way of life remains. This continues to influence social attitudes to farming practice including land drainage.

Part of this reverence for the agricultural industry – to the extent that it is not seen as 'industrial' at all – is the myth that normal agricultural practices are the best means of preserving that unique natural beauty and value of the British countryside, with its diversity of flora and fauna, while simultaneously providing abundant cheap home-produced food. Why else should agriculture be exempt from most post-1947 town and country planning legislation, with its control over development, than because the agriculturalist has the best interests of the country at heart? Surely what is good for the farmer will naturally be good for the birds and the bees and of course for Britain?

The economic reality. The reality, of course, is of a highly capitalised intensive industry responding not to the call of nature but to the complexities of agricultural markets. Since 1945 successive British governments have sought to control the markets in agricultural produce and have thereby promoted dramatic changes in the pattern and practice of farming. The farm is no longer a place where a range of food products is grown to satisfy both the farm family and the town dweller. It is becoming a factory: factory-like in its processes and appearance and in the specialised nature of its production (Davidson and Wibberley 1977). Which crops are grown, and how they are grown, are less a function of inclinations of the individual farmer than of the changing patterns of subsidies, quotas and grants including those for land drainage.

Farming practice today is inextricably linked to the pattern of incentives arising from the post-war British policy developed from the Agriculture Act 1947. This and subsequent similar legislation established a system of annual support prices for farm produce related to the output required for those products and, in later years, to the costs incurred in producing them by efficient farmers (Munton 1974). Supporting the minimum price structure was a complex system of grants and subsidies geared to increasing the amount of land under cultivation and its productivity. Grants have been available for ploughing up uncultivated land, for fertilisers, water supply, new farm buildings and for drainage. These subsidies and grants have led inexorably to the intensification of agricultural production, with a strong emphasis on arable cultivation, especially wheat and barley. The corollary has been a reduction in the area of grassland, particularly in lowland England, partly as a consequence of drainage improvement allowing arable cultivation.

Since Britain joined the European Economic Community in 1972 the agricultural industry has experienced a change in the principles underlying government support, but a continuation of that support nevertheless. Instead of the minimum price structure, higher food prices for the consumer coupled with tariffs on foodstuff imported from countries outside the Community have encouraged increased output; many pre-existing grant schemes have continued. Encouraging further shifts to arable cropping, for which drainage is often essential, farmers have suffered from violently fluctuating livestock prices, and rising wage costs associated with livestock production, while prices for cereals have risen. Over-specialisation in certain livestock commodities has led to economic difficulty in some farming sectors and a realisation of the safety in diversification, but this is unlikely to recreate the old patterns of mixed farming (Davidson and Wibberley 1977). It is more likely that cereal land will be converted to intensive grass production for livestock reared indoors, and switched back to cereal production as markets dictate. Properly drained land will facilitate such flexibility and maintain profitability; reversion to less intensive general farming with a permanent balance of livestock and arable cultivation seems unlikely.

Land values and drainage costs.   The changes in agriculture since 1947 and even before have been changes in tenure, in productivity, and related to these and other economic factors, changes in the value of land. The yield of wheat, barley and potatoes has risen by a third since 1961, as a result of all aspects of more intensive farming and fuelled by rising land prices. These have encouraged farmers and landowners alike to seek higher output to maintain an acceptable return on land that may cost over £5000 per hectare.

While land values have generally risen ahead of the rate of inflation the cost of drainage works fell in real terms between 1954 and 1976 by some 50% owing to mechanisation (Cole 1976). Coupled with other technological changes in agricultural production, costs have fallen so tending to increase profitability. This in turn has contributed to the rising land prices. The net result is that drainage has become increasingly worthwhile but increasingly necessary to reap the returns required given the high price of agricultural land.

Who cares for the countryside?   The nineteenth century saw extensive drainage totalling 5 million hectares of the English lowlands. In the twentieth century drainage activity declined and existing drainage systems, which should last at least 100 years, became neglected. In 1945 only 12 000 hectares were field-drained in England and Wales but as a result of the Agriculture Act 1930 this annual total rose steadily throughout the next three decades. In 1974 the total reached 103 000 hectares and still was increasing at approximately 12% per annum. The bulk of this drainage continues to be in eastern England, particularly the fenland areas of East Anglia (Cole 1976). In Scotland drainage has always been less widespread but nevertheless the trend is for larger totals to be drained each year (Green 1976).

However, a generation of plouging-up grants, subsidised land drainage and increasing use of pesticides and fertilisers is beginning to dent and tarnish the nostalgic image of the peaceful rural countryside. Higher agricultural productivity is becoming associated with declining value of wildlife habitats and increasing landscape monotony. Public disquiet has centred most on the disappearance of woodland and hedgerows from the landscape (Council for the Protection of Rural England 1975) but criticism is developing of the effect of land drainage on the health and appearance of the countryside (Westmacott and Worthington 1974, Hill 1976).

In turn the agricultural industry has responded by emphasising its caring for the countryside (National Farmers' Union and Country Landowners' Association 1977). Only time will tell whether such caring can withstand the harsh economic pressures of Britain's declining economic fortunes in the last quarter of the twentieth century. Faced with increasing world food shortage and continuing balance of payments difficulties, recent government statements reaffirm agricultural support policies to improve and maintain the quality of agricultural land to promote greater self-sufficiency in food production. Indeed the prosperity of the national agricultural industry is a high government priority, and there appears to be no lessening in the political force of agriculture within the country. The result may be less rather than greater environmental care, and more emphasis on technical solutions to food production problems in which land drainage features as one small but significant part.

Legal and social aspects of urban flood alleviation

While the background to the land drainage policies and schemes is the complex of government policies for increasing agricultural production the social context of flood alleviation in urban areas embraces a series of public attitudes about the quality of urban environments. Floods can cause immense damage and distress. Our democratic society appears to demand that none of its members suffer in this way, almost regardless of cost. Such attitudes cause problems for rational flood alleviation planning.

The powers for institutional intervention. Once attracting their attention, floods are seen by the public as so unacceptable that state intervention is unquestionable. Central government allocates a steady annual sum of about £40millions to flood alleviation schemes. Legal powers are available under the Land Drainage Act 1976 and the Flood Prevention (Scotland) Act 1961 to permit Water Authorities and Regional Councils to finance flood protection schemes, to obtain access to river areas to carry out the works, and to repair, maintain and improve existing watercourses. Drainage authorities have powers to require individual riparian owners to carry out their obligations under common law to maintain their channels, bridges and other drainage installations. The Land Drainage Act 1976 for England and Wales, and the Agriculture Act 1970 for Scotland, both make provision for the installation of flood warning schemes. Local byelaws allow drainage authorities to regulate the use of flood banks and sluices and prevent the obstruction of watercourses. For example, legislation for London dating back to The Thames River (Prevention of Floods) Act 1879 gives the Greater London Council powers to control developments affecting flood defences. Additional legislation empowers the Council to construct the Thames Flood Barrier. All such powers complement those under the Public Health Act 1936, which allows the construction of sewers for both sewage disposal and land drainage by giving local authorities powers to execute works on watercourses in private ownership. For coastal flooding similar powers are available to Water Authorities and Regional Councils to construct new and maintain existing flood defences, again including the crucial right of access and the powers to require landowners to maintain defences and regulate the use of embankments.

The case for intervention. Over time it has been found that individuals cannot be left to protect themselves from flooding so it is the role of government and public bodies to protect the few affected from ignorance or their own poor memories.

There is often a public outcry during and immediately after a flood event but typically the problem may be forgotten soon after the flood waters have subsided. But flood alleviation is an indivisible commodity: the protection of one property cannot generally be provided in isolation since schemes usually necessitate river works which affect all riparian owners amongst others. Thus general agreement on flood alleviation plans is needed. Yet controversy often surrounds their implementation, particularly when this occurs many years after the flood event. Some who were affected may oppose the scheme through poor recall of the damage caused and others because their perceptions of future flood events are incorrect. Protection, however, can only be provided for all or for none.

Floods are discriminatory hazards and affect minorities within society. They harm most seriously the old and infirm who are unable to protect their homes and property (Penning-Rowsell, Chatterton and Parker 1978). As with many randomly occuring phenomena people appear to develop cognitive obstacles to proper understanding of risk (Parker and Harding 1979).

For example, people attribute regularity to flood occurrences, to reduce the unpleasant uncertainties in the timing of flood events. Others designate past floods as unrepeatable freaks: flood perception research in the United States and Britain indicates that flood victims often conclude that it will not happen to them again. They therefore do nothing to protect themselves from future floods (Penning-Rowsell and Parker 1974, Tobin 1979), happily ignoring the laws of probability which dictate that even high return period floods may recur the very next week or year. Those new to flood prone areas commonly feel that floods are phenomena of a past when people were not in control of nature. Others remember nostalgically the esprit-de-corps in past flood disasters and perhaps balance in their minds their fear of flood events with this benefit of social cohesion. Still others have not the resources with which to protect themselves, since evidence indicates that it is frequently the lower income groups which inhabit the lower priced property in flood prone areas (Harding and Parker 1974). Such groups also often fail to exploit democratic processes to obtain protection.

In the context of these multifarious public attitudes, plans to prevent flooding by the construction of flood defence works are often simply a reaction to disasters in the past. Consequently, protection standards are often set to prevent the recurrence of single, known events with little consideration, for example, of lower standards which might be more cost-effective yet would still cause some damage.

However, it is undoubtedly most problematic to decide what standards of flood protection are socially acceptable, given that absolute protection is not possible and that society provides no clear guides to water planners other than demands for total protection! Some contend that 'the reduction in capital losses and the protection of human life and health by flood protection would seem at least as comparable with the prevention of pollution and the provision of clean water supply' (Cole 1976, p. 347) and argue for comparable budgets. Certainly the level of total capital expenditure society should allocate to this aspect of water planning is ripe for debate but the public seems indifferent.

The flood alleviation and land drainage planning system

As with all water planning in Britain a different administrative system exists in Scotland than in England and Wales. Greater flood protection and land drainage problems occur in England and Wales and the planning system is correspondingly more active and, perhaps coincidentally, more complex. Nevertheless both systems are dominated by agricultural and landowning interests which have determined the evolution of institutions and influence their policies today.

England and Wales: local control and economic evaluation

Two principles govern the operation of the land drainage and flood protection planning system in England and Wales. First, the system is essentially more local than regional. In this respect special sub-regional institutions within the Water Authorities plan land drainage and flood alleviation schemes. Secondly, all expenditure on new works is subject to scheme-by-scheme cost-benefit analysis. This attempts to ensure that both capital and scheme-specific revenue costs are justified by the benefits of either reduced flood damage or increased land values in urban schemes, or by the economic value of increased agricultural production from agricultural schemes involving both arterial and field drainage.

The main institutions involved are the Land Drainage Committees of the Water Authorities, the Internal Drainage Boards and the County and District Councils. The Ministry of Agriculture, Fisheries and Food also has a central role in the planning process.

The organisation of land drainage planning therefore contrasts markedly with most other areas of water planning, because of the emphasis on cost-effectiveness, the availability of government grant-aid to subsidise drainage programmes and the consequent role of central government in decisions concerning each scheme. In other areas of water planning central government is only concerned with determining overall levels of capital expenditure which are then allocated to specific schemes by the Water Authorities with a degree of flexibility not present in the land drainage field. Here the presence of central government involvement guarantees expenditure directly in line with government aims.

An important statutory distinction exists in planning land drainage and flood alleviation protection schemes between 'main' and 'non-main' rivers. To carry out work under the Land Drainage Act 1976 watercourses may be designated as 'main river' by the Ministry of Agriculture, Fisheries and Food. On 'main rivers' the Water Authorities, through their Land Drainage Committees, have permissive power to carry out new land drainage and flood alleviation protection works and maintenance. On other watercourses, and these are usually more minor, Water Authorities have no such powers, which rest with either the riparian owner or the local District Council or an Internal Drainage Board.

Regional and local land drainage committees: the influence of agricultural interests.   The Land Drainage Act 1930 'put land drainage (including flood alleviation) in England and Wales on its feet' (Cole 1976, p. 345) by setting up Catchment Boards financed by precepts or statutory requisitions from County Council rates and responsible for the drainage of whole catchments. These Boards were the forerunners of the Water Authorities today, although they were only responsible for the single drainage function. They showed the early realisation of the importance of catchment-based water planning.

After 1948 these Boards, then as the River Boards, were exended to cover the whole country. They were given further powers in the fisheries and pollution field. The main subsequent water legislation, the Water Resources Act 1963 and the Water Act 1973, made no substantial change to the administration of land drainage. The direct descendants of the Catchment Boards are now the Land Drainage Committees established within each Water Authority under the Water Act 1973 (Section 19). The financial basis of the flood alleviation and land drainage work of these Committees is exactly the same as with the Catchment Boards. Through the Water Authority they raise precepts from the County Council covering their area. They also receive grants, from the Ministry of Agriculture, Fisheries and Food, towards capital spent on drainage work. Government policy (Department of the Environment *et al*. 1977) indicates that no reorganisation of this system is envisaged; it is seen as working efficiently and effectively.

These statutory Committees are a clear structural anomaly within the Water Authorities. They owe their existence to the 'community network' of mutually supporting interests which campaigned to retain a separate administrative system for land drainage while the Ministry of Housing and Local Government reviewed between 1969 and 1972 the organisation of the whole water industry (Richardson, Jordan and Kimber 1978). The Association of River Authorities, the Association of Drainage Authorities, the County Landowners' Association and other groups allied with senior civil servants in the Ministry of Agriculture, Fisheries and Food to keep land drainage separate from large multi-functional agencies – an alliance termed 'the MAFFia' by their opponents. Richardson, Jordan and Kimber (1978) conclude that only lack of parliamentary time led the Ministry of Housing and Local Government to concede the current statutory separatedness. Meanwhile the agricultural lobby had obtained major concessions in exchange for the incorporation of land drainage within the Water Authorities. These concessions included retaining both the grant-aid system and the Ministry of Agriculture, Fisheries and Food as the responsible Ministry. Two Ministry nominees were also included on Water Authorities to safeguard land drainage interests.

The Regional Land Drainage Committees consist of a paid chairman, who is a member of the parent Water Authority appointed by the Ministry of Agriculture, Fisheries and Food, together with other members appointed by the Ministry and two members from the Water Authority. The remainder are representatives from County Councils in the Water Authority area who have a majority on the Committees. District Councils are not represented and this caused criticism from the Association of District Councils of the lack of change foreseen here within the government Review (Department of the Environment *et al*. 1976). The government rejected change, both in the interests of limiting the size of the Committees and because the precepts are raised from County and not District rates (Department of the Environment *et al*. 1977).

Most Regional Land Drainage Committees have delegated their powers to Local Land Drainage Committees while the main Committee concerns itself with capital investment allocation, fixing land drainage precepts, general drainage charges as well as other financial matters concerning Internal Drainage Board contributions. The Local Committees often cover the pre-existing River Authority areas (Fig. 2.4), which in turn were also based on Catchment Board areas, and these Committees consist of representatives from the main committee and other County Council nominees. For example, in the Anglian Water Authority area the Regional Committee has established five Local Land Drainage Committees which are thereby responsible for the identification and execution of a rolling programme of land drainage work within their area. Similarly the Severn Trent Water Authority has established two local committees for the Severn and Trent catchments.

While the system of land drainage planning is local, the basis of much of the representation is national through the Minister of Agriculture. Membership of these committees is therefore dominated by farmers and landowners, partly because these are the people whom the Ministry of Agriculture, Fisheries and Food nominate to Water Authorities and also because nominations from County Councils are by default likely to be those with land ownership and farming interests. This dominance can result in anomalies such that within the Anglian Water Authority area the Norfolk and the Suffolk Local Land Drainage Committee, which has responsibility for the drainage of the Norfolk Broads, has had no representation from the crucial amenity and conservation organisations (George 1977).

The Greater London Council: a further structural anomaly.   For purposes of land drainage the Greater London Council is effectively the Regional Land Drainage Committee for the 'main metropolitan watercourses' within much of the Greater London area which, for other water planning functions, lies mainly within the Thames Water Authority area. In the case of non-main watercourses the GLC and the London Boroughs jointly operate the drainage function. The reason for this anomaly lies in the long tradition of efficient drainage works in London and the pressures put on government in 1973 to separate water responsibilities for London, and even create there an eleventh Water Authority (Okun 1977).

Of major significance is the Tidal Thames Flood Prevention Scheme started in 1971 and due for completion in 1982–83. It is the largest sea defence or land drainage scheme ever carried out in Britain. Under special legislation, constructing the flood barrier at Woolwich is the responsibility of the GLC while downstream embankment improvements are the responsibility of Thames, Anglian and Southern Water Authorities. The total scheme cost is approximately £500millions of which 75% comes as government grant-aid (Horner 1978).

The central role of the Ministry of Agriculture, Fisheries and Food.   The role of the Ministry in land drainage and flood protection planning is two-fold. First, the Ministry's Agricultural Development and Advisory Service advises farmers and Land Drainage Committees on the potential for land drainage works, both field drainage and main river schemes. This advice is part of the Service's general role of promoting agricultural productivity to obtain greater national self-sufficiency for food. Staff from the Service explain to farmers the benefits of drainage and the system of grants for field underdrainage which the farmer will have to install to capitalise upon arterial drainage improvements (Agricultural Development and Advisory Service 1974–7).

Secondly, all land drainage programmes and plans must be submitted to the Ministry which assesses the cost-benefit analysis undertaken by Water Authority staff to justify both land drainage and flood alleviation schemes. The regional offices of the Ministry also assist Authorities in assessing the agricultural benefits of land drainage schemes. The Ministry decision as to cost-effectiveness does not determine whether a scheme will go ahead and therefore is not analogous to planning permission given by local authorities. The decision only concerns whether the Ministry will give grant-aid on the scheme. However, since this grant-aid is generally more than half the capital costs of the scheme it is unlikely that Regional and Local Land Drainage Committees will proceed with a scheme if grant-aid is not forthcoming.

The level of grant-aid is fixed in relation to the Ministry's view of the flooding and land drainage problems in the areas of local land drainage committees. It is based on the level of capital expenditure on drainage in relation to the rate income of the relevant County Councils, to attempt equity of burden across the country. In 1977–78, for example, the level of grant was 40% in the Severn catchment, 64% for the Norfolk and Suffolk areas of the Anglian Water Authority and higher rates apply for coastal defence works. The Ministry works within a ceiling of capital expenditure, approved by the Treasury, above which the total grant-aid programme cannot rise. For the 1978–79 year this ceiling was £16·3millions and the Ministry in turn allocates ceilings to each Water Authority in proportion to amounts allocated in previous years.

The capital expenditure limits are an important restraint on the pace of land drainage and flood protection works, but the system of allocation dependent on capital sums spent in previous years is not entirely satisfactory. It does not allow the most cost-effective schemes to be given highest priority since they may not be in the same Water Authority area. However there is here a very real problem of financial management. Water Authorities and Regional Land Drainage Committees need to know how much grant-aid they can expect in the future to plan a programme of schemes yet until the schemes are presented to the Ministry for confirmation of cost-effectiveness and a decision about grant-aiding the Ministry has no firm idea of how much grant-aid will be requested. Therefore the Ministry resorts to indicating capital spending ceilings in advance of known need, which cannot be satisfactory, and waits for these amounts to be taken up by Water Authorities. The system suffers from all the faults of planning through budgetary control rather than defined need, but until a clearer picture of the national flooding and land drainage problems emerges from surveys currently in progress under Section 24(5) of the Water Act 1973, no better workable method presents itself.

In addition to grants from central government, organisations and individuals may apply for grants from the European Economic Community towards the capital cost of projects promoting Community objectives. In Britain the system is administered by the Ministry of Agriculture, Fisheries and Food and until recently grants were obtainable from the Agricultural Guidance and Guarantee Fund. The last such grants were awarded in 1978 when a total of £556 000 was approved for fifteen schemes. Since then grants for land drainage have continued but from the EEC Regional Development Fund and only for schemes in designated development areas.

The significance and autonomy of the Internal Drainage Boards.   There are 273 Internal Drainage Boards in England and Wales (Fig. 2.4) covering 1·2 million hectares and spending some £10millions annually (1975–76). They are virtually autonomous organisations covering most of lowland areas liable to flooding and poor drainage. Members are elected to the Boards from those owning at least 10 acres of land in the Internal Drainage District, the occupiers of at least 20 acres of such land, the owners or occupiers of land of an annual value of £30 or more or their nominees. Needless to say virtually all members are farmers or those with agricultural interests.

An Internal Drainage Board can undertake drainage work within its Drainage District, paid for by rates from its members. The Ministry of Agriculture, Fisheries and Food gives grants for 50% of capital costs. These Boards are responsible for works on field drainage and intermediate watercourses but not 'main rivers'. Their policies are strongly focussed on increasing agricultural productivity of land within their District. Owing to the dominance of agricultural members, seen as promoting their own interests by spending national grant-aid, the Boards have attracted criticism not only for ignoring important wildlife and conservation issues in their drainage work (Arvill 1976) but also for being 'a classic example of a private gravy train subsidised from public funds, hallowed by statute and institutionalised by a complacent bureaucracy' (Hall 1978).

Water Authorities have some powers to modify the extent of Internal Drainage Districts and could, through a highly complex process, petition the Ministry of Agriculture, Fisheries and Food to abolish a Board. These circumstances, however, are unknown although there is a steady process of voluntary amalgamation and rationalisation of Boards such that since 1930 more than 30 have had their responsibilities and powers taken over by the relevant Water Authority or its predecessor.

The development control functions of local authorities.   Central to any policy of reducing flood damage is the control of urban development on flood plains. Here the District Councils in England and Wales have an important function as regulators of development under the various Town and Country Planning Acts (Penning-Rowsell and Parker 1974).

This procedure of preventing or reducing development on flood plain land is far from perfect. Problems occur partly because of the permissive nature of legislation under which applications for development are referred from the local authority planning department to the Water Authority for comment. The procedure has been set out in a number of government circulars dating back to 1947. In 1962 and 1969 the Department of the Environment gave further clarification concerning development both on the flood plain itself and where development off the flood plain would create runoff liable to cause flooding downstream. Unwise development in flood risk areas continues, however, because the local planning authority may simply ignore the advice from the Water Authority, and as a superior power in planning terms the local authority is entitled to do this, or because on appeal to the Department of the Environment an application for development permission rejected by the local planning department may be allowed by the Secretary of State.

Many such cases occur but one example in Wales illustrates the problems involved. The Meadows estate at Llandudno Junction (p. 195) was developed in 1974 with drainage works inadequate for the eventual storm runoff. The Welsh Water Authority had no land use planning power to prevent this development, only to advise on the size of the culvert to remove surface water from the estate. In the Authority's opinion either permission for the development should have been refused, as on previous occasions, or the developer should have been obliged in return for obtaining planning permission to meet the cost of flood alleviation works adequate to deal with the anticipated runoff. However, planning permission was granted by the District Council on less exacting terms than these, so that two years later the estate suffered serious flooding. Now the Water Authority's Local Land Drainage Committee is having to install the necessary flood alleviation works at a cost of £160 000 to rectify the situation and, in effect, subsidise the development (Welsh Water Authority 1978a).

Many Water Authorities feel, as a result of similar experiences, that legislation is needed whereby they can demand contributions from developers towards drainage costs arising from development. In addition there could be a more positive requirement that planning authorities comply with advice given by Water Authorities in these cases. Alternatively, if Water Authority advice is ignored the District responsible for the development – or the developer – should pay the necessary land drainage costs rather than the Water Authority or the tax payer through the Ministry of Agriculture. Proposals for mandatory contributions from developers are envisaged (Department of the Environment *et al.* 1977), suggesting that the government, after less than total success with advisory circulars clarifying development control legislation, is considering more 'punitive' powers to forestall the consequences of unwise flood plain development.

Further fragmentation: the land drainage duties of local authorities.   Local authorities are responsible for land drainage works on non-main watercourses outside Internal Drainage Districts and also for coastal flood prevention schemes where Water Authorities do not undertake this work. This fragmentation does nothing to assist rational planning of land drainage and flood alleviation works.

District Councils have permissive powers to carry out improvement schemes on non-main rivers just as Water Authorities undertake work on 'main' arterial watercourses. Ministry of Agriculture, Fisheries and Food grant-aid is available for District Council schemes up to a maximum of 50% of capital costs. However, Water Authorities have often had difficulty in persuading small District Councils to improve watercourses with flood problems. The Districts have clear responsibilities for this work, but are reluctant to meet them in full owing to lack of funds for the local contributions, given higher District priorities for housing or education. In some cases the Water Authority has had to resort to converting the watercourses to 'main river' with Ministry designation, carrying out the works under its own powers, and then 'de-maining' the watercourse back to its previous status!

Some confusion was caused when the sewerage responsibilities passed from the local authorities to the Water Authorities with the Water Act 1973. Prior to 1974 District Councils often carried out channel improvements under the Public Health Act 1936, in effect considering the small watercourses as open sewers. The transfer of water responsibilities in 1974 was thought by some Districts to be complete. Yet the responsibility for land drainage works on non-main rivers continues, although some Districts have claimed that small urban watercourses are legally sewers and hence are financially the responsibility of Water Authorities. As a result of such misunderstandings in the highly complex administrative system some Districts have been slow to undertake necessary channel improvement and maintenance work.

County Councils can also carry out land drainage works at the request of riparian owners or land occupiers who would benefit from the scheme. Generally this activity has been small but County Councils have been more active in carrying out agricultural improvement schemes than District Councils, perhaps owing to greater agricultural and land ownership representation at County level. County Councils have additional powers to act at the request of or in default of District Councils, but here it is more likely that the Water Authority would undertake the necessary work which would be rechargeable to the District Council in question.

District Councils also have permissive powers wherever they have sea frontages to undertake coastal protection work under the Coast Protection Act 1949, which also applies to Scotland. These works may involve preventing erosion or flooding or both, and Water Authorities again can undertake the schemes on a rechargeable basis. For example, in Sussex, virtually all the coast where there is a flood risk is the responsibility of the Southern Water Authority, by agreement with the Districts, and the trend throughout the country is for Water Authorities to take an active part in this field.

The roles of owners and other land drainage and flood alleviation agencies.
Adding to the multiplicity of agencies with responsibilities for land drainage are highway authorities, navigation authorities and the riparian owners.

Riparian owners undertake a great deal of land drainage themselves and under the Land Drainage Act 1976 (Section 18) an owner may be obliged to carry out works. The indivisible nature of flood alleviation schemes becomes problematic in complex urban areas. With a multiplicity of riparian owners, implementing this Section is difficult yet without full cooperation a scheme may be impossible. In these cases the Water Authority may have to 'main' the section to allow a unified approach and then carry out improvement works in the normal way. However Authorities are rightly reluctant to assume responsibilities for sub-standard watercourses and thereby subsidise past neglect.

Highway authorities are responsible under the Highways Act 1959 for road drainage and for preventing highway flooding. The British Waterways Board has through its system of canals an important drainage function, having a duty to accept water draining into its canals which, when crossing natural drainage channels and slopes, receive considerable quantities of overland flow. The Board must ensure that canal overflow systems do not pass flooding problems on downstream and has powers to carry out flood alleviation works accordingly. Problems have occurred recently when insufficient funds have been available for even routine canal maintenance. Charges for receipt of water from upstream drainage authorities to finance the necessary works have only been made relatively recently. The situation is exacerbated where urban development, over which the Board has no control, generates increased runoff to cater for which the Board has no power to charge the developer for the necessary drainage works.

Land drainage and flood alleviation institutions in Scotland

Urban flood protection. Prior to reorganisation in 1975 flood prevention in Scotland was the responsibility of the many small burghs and Councils but these responsibilities were then transferred to the Regional Councils. Such is the lesser nature of flooding in Scotland that in some cases departmental responsibility within the Regional Council was not allocated until later when, for example, the Highland Region's Department of Water and Sewerage was given duties in this field. Given the recent acquisition of urban flood protection responsibilities Regional Council staff have lacked expertise in both engineering and economic aspects of this work, necessitating the re-training of sewage or water supply experts.

Regional Councils now identify, evaluate and design schemes for grant-aid by the Scottish Development Department under the Flood Prevention (Scotland) Act 1961. In 1978 such schemes were given grants totalling £0·3million. The Scottish Development Department has the power to confirm or reject schemes, which are not restricted to inland areas but can include estuaries, although not coastal areas covered by the Coast Protection Act 1949. This system covers urban schemes only and cost-benefit analyses of proposals have to be made to justify both the local expenditure and the central government grant which covers just capital costs, as in England and Wales.

Agricultural land drainage. In contrast to England and Wales it is the owner of land who is responsible for proposing schemes to drain agricultural land and the necessary arterial drainage improvement. Under the Land Drainage (Scotland) Act 1958 an owner or group of owners may apply to the Secretary of State for Scotland for an 'Improvement Order' for an area suffering from flooding, poor field drainage or land erosion by rivers. The Department of Agriculture and Fisheries for Scotland then issues the Order, if it considers the case warrants it, to specify the area to be improved, the works necessary to reflect the drainage improvement and their cost. In the case of land in multiple ownership the Improvement Order can set up a Committee to oversee the landowners' responsibilities, particularly with regard to maintenance. Four of the 45 Orders made under the Act before 1979 were thus arranged.

The Act provides for grant-aid for the capital costs involved – up to 50% but generally increased to 60% under the Farm Capital Grant Scheme – and requires the owner to maintain the completed work in good condition. The majority of schemes carried out under this legislation are large-scale arterial drainage projects undertaken jointly by several landowners, although the annual average total grant is only some £50 000.

Thus central government in Scotland, through the Department of Agriculture and Fisheries, has an even more important role than in England and Wales since both costing and design is carried out at central government level as the individual landowner cannot be expected to have these skills. The general public's involvement in this planning process is therefore even less direct than in England and Wales, where at least there is County Council representation on the Regional Land Drainage Committees, although in Scotland there is opportunity for the public to object within 28 days of a land drainage scheme being announced.

The key planning technique: assessing the benefits of flood alleviation and land drainage

Just as a single planning technique dominates water supply planning, namely demand forecasting, so in land drainage the key decision-making technique is cost-benefit analysis. Furthermore, given that costs can be estimated with reasonable accuracy, comprising as they do measurable quantities of material and labour, the main problematic and controversial area involves assessing the benefits of alleviating flooding, in terms of damages averted, and the benefits of agricultural drainage schemes as enhanced crop and live-stock production.

Recent research has contributed to both fields. Essential to assessing flood damages averted is gauging the probability of floods of a given magnitude and the Institute of Hydrology, funded by the Natural Environment Research Council (1975), has painstakingly systematised river gauging records and devised extrapolation techniques which allow estimation of flood discharges throughout Britain. Complementary research at Middlesex Polytechnic on standardising flood damage allows more comprehensive assessment of both direct and indirect potential flood losses (Penning-Rowsell and Chatterton 1977, 1980); this research has also systematised assessing the value of enhanced agricultural production following drainage works.

In the urban case the combination of height data for flood-prone proper-ties, the depth/damage characteristics of those properties and the return periods of floods of different extents and depths gives a height/damage or probability/damage relationship for the valley from which the annual average damage can be calculated. These future flood damages data are then discounted to give their present values. Such discounting is necessary because benefits accruing from future floods averted are worth less – irrespective of inflation – than those immediately available. The discounted benefits in total comprise the capital sum worth investing to prevent the future damages. In the agricultural case, the difference before and after installing a scheme in the gross return from crop and livestock enterprises, using flood plain or other-wise undrained land, less any costs such as for underdraining or increased mechanisation, gives the annual benefit from a scheme. This benefit is again discounted to give the present value of the amount worthwhile investing on the scheme to provide the increased agricultural productivity (Penning-Rowsell and Chatterton 1980).

Benefit assessment, however, is not without problems. First, there are major conceptual problems, including whether market-determined prices can measure real social value equally for all members of society. Secondly, there are major assumptions – including the discount rate – which pro-foundly affect calculated benefits. Yet these assumptions are often not technical but involve judgements, such as on the present value of future wealth. Thirdly, there are technical problems within the benefit assessment. The adequate counting of intangibles is problematic, whether wildlife loss from agricultural drainage or amenity loss when urban flood alleviation schemes leave canalised rivers. Also the precise measurement of benefits causes problems. With urban flood damages, for example, damage cannot be assessed as replacement costs since these overestimate the value of partly used household goods damaged during floods. Furthermore, while standardised damage costs for common house types are useful, they are nevertheless a simplification which may undervalue flood damage in particular cases. In the agricultural field problems occur with prices, taxes and subsidies. For example, land drainage works may allow a farmer to grow potatoes on hitherto useless land, for which he obtains at market £60 per ton. The benefits of the scheme are certainly not £60 per ton grown, because there are machinery, labour, and fertiliser costs to subtract. Moreover the £60 is an artificially high price maintained by a complex system of both quotas for potato growing and guaranteed market prices.

Furthermore, to arrive at the economically optimal flood alleviation or agricultural drainage scheme it is necessary to consider floods of all magnitudes and review schemes providing various levels of protection and drainage standards (Local Government Operational Research Unit 1973, 1978b). In theory, design standards should be raised until the benefits of the increased standards are less than the costs thereby sustained. In practice calculations can become intolerably complex. However, these can be facilitated by generalised initial trials followed by more detailed surveys, when cost-effectiveness appears satisfactory, to determine more accurately the optimal levels of capital investment (Fig. 6.1). Computer methods of calculation (Penning-Rowsell and Chatterton 1977) can speed the process and allow rapid reassessment of benefits with alternative economic assumptions and hydrological inputs, so that those making decisions can be fully aware of the sensitivity of the results to the assumptions made.

Land drainage and flood alleviation policies, plans and schemes

The main thrust of policy in the land drainage and flood protection field is to protect human life and minimise flood damage, and to maximise food production through draining agricultural land where poor natural drainage impedes crop production. The policy adopted, however, is only one of many possible approaches to these problems and other options are available in both the urban and the agricultural policy fields.

Policy alternatives

The approach to urban flooding involves either *accepting* the risk and consequent flood damage and loss of life when it comes, or seeking to *modify* the magnitude and frequency of flood events and their effects, through structural or non-structural schemes (Smith and Tobin 1979). The acceptance of flood damage may be necessary in areas where flood alleviation schemes are not justifiable in economic terms or are technically difficult. However, this approach to flood problems appears socially unacceptable. This is partly because people affected by floods are considered to have had little choice in

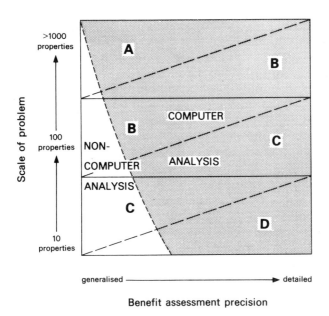

	Field survey	Depth/damage data	Other data
A	none; land use from maps and plans	all: sector averages (including industrial)	mean ground floor heights of properties
B	selected field checks; land use survey from maps/plans	residential: type or type and age averages retail, etc.: type averages industrial: site survey or average data	ground floor heights from maps and plans
C	full field land use survey	residential: type, age and social class (census or questionnaire) retail, etc.: category or sub-category industrial: full site survey	ground floor heights levelled (or from aerial photographs)
D	full field land use survey	all: full site survey methods	levelled ground floor heights

Figure 6.1 Alternative approaches to flood alleviation benefit assessments: generalised and detailed surveys for large and small schemes, with or without computer analysis (from Penning-Rowsell and Chatterton 1977).

their locations, partly because of the stress of flood events and also because certain people may be unable to afford to replace their flood damaged property.

Modifying floods and flood damage can involve structural engineering schemes comprising embankments and levées, channel enlargement, flood relief channels, flood storage reservoirs and washland schemes, the latter involving designating certain areas of flood plains to be deliberately flooded to protect other more damageable locations. In addition property can be flood proofed against the incursion of flood water. Permanent flood proofing, including constructing buildings on raised platforms, is now fairly common on British flood plains. However, considerable scope exists for further contingent flood proofing whereby, for example, specially designed flood shields are erected on receipt of a flood warning.

Non-structural approaches to flood damage reduction involve flood insurance programmes, public relief funds for flood victims, zoning flood plain land to restrict urban development and thereby reduce potential damage, and flood forecasting and warning schemes to minimise damage and loss of life during flood events.

Land drainage engineers have emphasised structural approaches, owing to their training, yet any of these approaches may provide an acceptable scheme depending on local circumstances. For example, a structural scheme based on embankments may be the only appropriate approach where an urban area impinges directly on to the river banks, such as at Exeter. There is insufficient room to create adequate washlands to flood naturally without damage. A structural approach involving flood proofing might be the best policy where property damage is not sufficient to justify civil engineering works to prevent flooding. Here warning schemes such as that in operation at Shrewsbury may also help to reduce damage and save lives (Harding and Parker 1974).

In theory, it is only worthwhile spending on these schemes – whether structural or non-structural – as much as the damage to be averted (Penning-Rowsell and Chatterton 1977, Chatterton, Pirt and Wood 1979). In practice the emotional stress and public feeling aroused by a serious flood does cause schemes to be installed which are not strictly cost-effective, such as the Lynmouth scheme implemented following the disastrous floods in 1952. Also there may well be cases where schemes which are cost-effective may be socially undesirable, owing to their effect on amenity or access to river banks for recreation. This was the case in Pulborough where the Southern Water Authority was willing to provide increased flood protection following serious flooding in 1968, but local opposition led to more minor works and, in effect, the acceptance of future losses (Chatterton and Farrell 1975). Therefore a strict cost-effectiveness or flood plain management approach to urban flood protection is unlikely to be universally appropriate or acceptable, although some reference to the costs and benefits of flood alleviation schemes is necessary to prevent unwise public expenditure.

For agricultural land drainage the policy options are generally fewer. If low-lying land is to be protected from flooding and under-drained to allow greater agricultural productivity then it will inevitably involve engineering works. These may well include channel widening to allow arterial rivers to carry away surplus water, dredging ditches to carry field runoff to arterial watercourses, and field drainage with tile or plastic pipes, permeable back fill, mole drains or subsoiling to promote rapid alleviation of waterlogging (Green 1979). In addition pumps may be necessary to raise water from low-lying ground into arterial watercourses at a higher level, owing to tides or flood conditions, and thereby lower the watertable below the surface in the fields. All such schemes are well tried and the river engineer in Britain has developed extensive skills in this area.

The main policy alternatives are, indeed, mainly outside the sphere of land drainage altogether and involve alternative approaches to the improvement of agricultural productivity. Such policies might involve more extensive use of fertilisers and herbicides to improve grazing on wetland areas or using specialised equipment and crops to obtain the maximum return from the difficult circumstances. Alternatively the finance used for land drainage might be cost-effectively allocated to improving food production elsewhere – perhaps in upland areas or in field amalgamation of lowland England or in developing more allotments in and around urban areas. This type of central-ised agricultural land management is not practised in Britain. Decisions on promoting agricultural production are left to local institutions including land drainage committees rather than taken at a national strategic level. As such true cost-effectiveness is rarely obtained but, arguably, a more balanced agri-cultural economy results.

Statute-based policies and plans

Much of land drainage and flood alleviation policy in Britain is specified in the legislative duties of executive agencies in this field of water planning.

Central government grants for drainage schemes. Grants to farmers from the Ministry of Agriculture, Fisheries and Food cover the improvement of ditches, cutting new ditches and various ancillary items such as pumps, spreading spoil from dredging, constructing culverts to carry water away, moling subsoil, fees to consultants and in certain cases ditch filling and fencing. In return, field drainage must comply with Ministry standards and grant-aid is only paid following satisfactory construction of drainage schemes. Farmers therefore often undertake drainage operations over a period of time, using the grant-aid recouped on one scheme to finance the next, rather than draining large areas at a time. The grant for field drainage is generally 50% of capital costs under the Land Drainage (Scotland) Act 1958 and the Farm Capital Grant Scheme under the Agricultural Act 1970 (which finances other agricultural improvement as well as land drainage).

Arterial drainage schemes are also grant-aided by the Ministry of

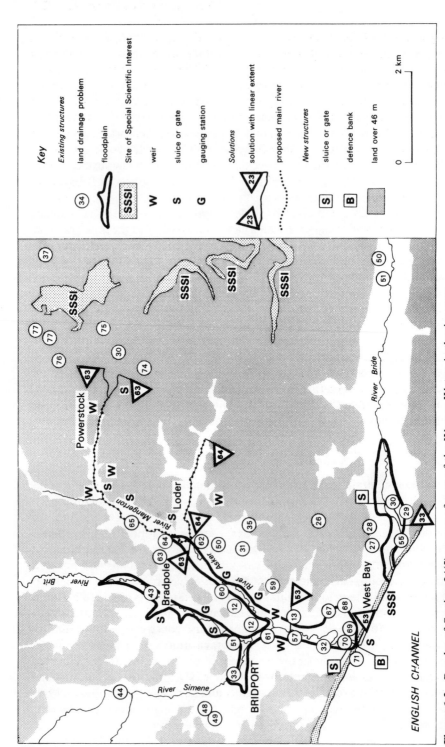

Figure 6.2 Results of Section 24(5) survey of part of the Wessex Water Authority area.

Agriculture, Fisheries and Food or the Scottish Development Department. Again grants are generally only allowable for capital expenditure. In the past this has encouraged a reliance on flood alleviation through engineering schemes, with their pattern of high capital expenditure and low revenue requirements, but more recently grant-aid has been paid on flood warning schemes under the Land Drainage Act 1976 in England and Wales and under the Agriculture Act 1970 in Scotland. Nevertheless other means of reducing flood damage such as flood proofing are not allowable for grant-aid. Therefore while it would be unfair to accuse river engineers in Britain of taking a one-sided view of flood alleviation, as has been the case in the United States (White 1973), nevertheless the grant-aid system tends to encourage engineering-based schemes rather than promoting compulsory flood insurance, encouraging permanent evacuation of flood risk areas and demolishing property or systematising public relief plans. For example, Water Authorities are most reluctant to purchase and demolish property suffering repeated flooding, partly because this can imply Water Authority responsibility for the flooding and partly because the cost would not be grant-aided. As a consequence excessive amounts of capital may be used to protect relatively few properties.

Section 24(5)) land drainage and flood alleviation surveys. An important element of central government policy on land drainage is that Water Authorities – but not the Regional Councils in Scotland – are now required to carry out 'surveys of their areas in relation to their drainage (including flood protection) functions' (Water Act 1973, Section 24(5)). In doing this they must consult every relevant local authority and 'have regard to' their structure and local plans prepared under the Town and Country Planning Act 1971.

These surveys should improve the identification of genuine flooding and land drainage problems. This identification has hitherto been mainly a result of public protest at particular flood events and farmers' concerns at impeded drainage. Government has recognised such an *ad hoc* or crisis-response approach to land drainage planning as insufficient for a rational approach to allocating public expenditure.

To guide implementation of this policy the Ministry of Agriculture, Fisheries and Food (1974) has given the Water Authorities directions on the type of information required in these most comprehensive surveys. Nevertheless some Water Authorities have taken these surveys more seriously than others and, for example, a brief report of a survey by the Thames Water Authority in 1978 was rejected by the Ministry as being insufficiently detailed. Water Authorities, however, have had difficulty in staffing these surveys at a time of financial restraint, and river engineers have appeared reluctant to undertake these surveys which they have seen as somewhat outside their traditional area of expertise. Therefore the initial response to Ministry plans for the scope of the surveys was cautious to say the least (Penning-Rowsell and Chatterton 1976) although progress since 1975 has been more rapid and survey results are appearing (Severn Trent Water Authority 1978, Wessex Water Authority 1979) (Fig. 6.2).

The results that have emerged from Section 24(5) surveys have shown extensive flooding and land drainage problems. Over 1600 urban and field drainage problems have been identified by the Severn Trent Water Authority although many are highly localised, affecting just a handful of properties or a few hectares of agricultural land. Nevertheless it would appear that there is enough drainage work to keep river engineers employed for many years to come, and some have suggested this as the main motive underlying the Section 24(5) surveys. However the cost-effectiveness of many such small schemes, and the conflicts with nature conservation interests from draining the small pockets of wetland which remain today, may cause more problems for the engineers than the implementation of the larger schemes such as on the rivers Lee and Trent in the past.

Non-statutory elements in land drainage policies and plans

Non-statutory elements within land drainage and flood protection policy include the development control liaison procedure between Water Authorities and planning authorities and the requirement for cost-benefit calculations before grant aid is given by central government. In general these policies are set out in government circulars and guidance notes, which advise executive agencies on the approaches and techniques to be used, or are the subject of informal agreements between government departments and river engineers.

Conservation and land drainage guidelines.   Drainage works can create blocks of arable monoculture thus reducing the stability and diversity of wildlife and the variety of landscapes. Sites of Special Scientific Interest and National Nature Reserves may be designated but they may not stop farmers draining their land. Many species which depend on wetland conditions have been threatened by drainage works. In addition to ethical reasons for not destroying such rare species there are scientific reasons for retaining such habitats and educational advantages in their use and enjoyment.

There are statutory obligations under the Countryside Act 1968 (Section 11) and the Countryside (Scotland) Act 1967 that in exercising their functions under any Act every Minister, government department and public body, including of course Water Authorities and Regional Councils, 'shall have regard' to the desirability of conserving the natural beauty and amenity of the countryside. Under Section 22 of the Water Act 1973 a similar and more extensive duty is placed on Water Authorities to protect wildlife and other natural features, including those in urban areas. However, these statutory duties for having regard to conservation considerations are vague and have been ignored on many occasions in the past.

Growing concern for the conflict between land drainage and conservation led the Water Space Amenity Commission to establish a Working Party to prepare guidelines to integrate land drainage policies with the maintenance of nature conservation and amenity interest in the countryside (Drummond 1977, Water Space Amenity Commission 1978). The guidelines comprise procedures for drainage schemes involving sea defence works, and schemes in fenland and marsh areas, rural upland areas, urban and hill areas. The guidelines make recommendations for scheme appraisal, design and maintenance, involving a full environmental impact assessment if major environmental repercussions are likely. In each of these areas full consideration is given to the potential effect of drainage on landowners' rights, on the recreation potential of drainage channels and surrounding land, and the effect on landscape and fisheries. The only omission concerns farm ditches, which is unfortunate since here much of nature conservation interest may be lost through unwise maintenance.

Two examples from the guidelines show the depth of the advice given. First, for protecting sea coast dunes used as a natural sea defence system, the guidelines advocate that where dunes are less than 50 metres thick, or where they are being damaged by uncontrolled access, they should be fenced to reduce access and encourage further sand accretion. Secondly, provision should be made in all capital schemes for replacing the trees, shrubs and hedges removed and where possible these should be augmented. Their siting 'should enhance the landscape and where necessary screen and soften the effect of intrusive elements such as sluices, locks and gauging stations'. In addition to these design and management details, systematic consultation procedures with interested parties are recommended, and financial aspects of conservation work in land drainage schemes are outlined.

Whether these guidelines will be adopted in full by river engineers and Land Drainage Committees is uncertain; they do provide for the first time an important counterbalance to the statutory drainage responsibilities of Water Authorities. They do not, however, present a clear line of analysis which might lead to a decision on conservation grounds *not* to drain an area or protect it from flooding. This is the kind of decision which is the focus of debate about the drainage of key wetland sites in lowland England such as the Amberley Wild Brooks and the Somerset Levels (Nature Conservancy Council South West Region 1977, Williams, R. 1977). In these cases more powerful policy instruments are needed to reconcile the fundamental conflicts between nature conservation and agricultural development.

Three further examples illustrate key land drainage issues. First, a plan by the Severn Trent Water Authority to unify land drainage within their region illustrates how the existing division of statutory responsibilities hinders an integrated approach to drainage problems. Secondly, a proposed scheme at Builth Wells in Wales shows the difficulties of assessing the benefits of flood alleviation and of obtaining agreement on detailed design. The third example details the public inquiry into draining Amberley Wild Brooks in Sussex and shows the conflict which can develop over agricultural drainage between Water Authorities, farmers and nature conservation and amenity interests. The controversial nature of these examples helps to reveal many crucial issues underlying land drainage, but owing to these controversies neither scheme has been implemented.

The Severn Trent Water Authority plan: 'A unified approach to land drainage'

To assist their long-term strategy for improving the drainage of their catchments the Severn Trent Water Authority (1977) has proposed a plan for increasing and systematising liaison between those with drainage responsibilities. This plan seeks to make the best of what is undoubtedly a fragmented division of statutory responsibilities and permissive powers while the long process of consultation prior to new legislation tentatively suggested by the Ministry of Agriculture, Fisheries and Food is in hand.

The background to the approach.   The fragmentation of land drainage responsibilities means that a coordinated approach to reducing land drainage and flooding problems can only be achieved with good liaison between all concerned and there are adequate allocations to land drainage budgets.

Poor liaison in the past has contributed to confusion between the agency sewerage responsibilities of District Councils – whereby they have undertaken work since 1974 at Water Authority expense – and the land drainage duties and responsibilities which Districts still exercise at their own expense. This confusion has delayed drainage improvement and, in addition, the low level of grant from the Ministry of Agriculture, Fisheries and Food has meant that local authority drainage work has been sparse in some areas. For example, only 20% of the administrative costs of land drainage works can be recoverable in grant, and the grant payable to County Councils on small agricultural schemes under Section 100 of the Land Drainage Act 1976 has stayed at £50 per hectare since 1961 during a period of rapid price inflation. Given higher local authority financial priorities elsewhere this low grant level has resulted in relative neglect of minor watercourses especially in urban areas.

However, one of the few *duties* as opposed to *powers* given to Water Authorities under the Land Drainage Act 1976 is the supervisory responsibility for all land drainage in their region, not just over those 'main rivers' on which they have direct responsibility. This duty without full financial control, in that local authorities are financially autonomous and any land drainage is voluntary, poses considerable problems for Water Authorities. This plan aims to solve these problems for the Severn Trent region.

The unified approach: consultation and 'maining'. The strategy adopted is to increase liaison between the Severn Trent Water Authority and local authorities to make Districts and County Councils more aware of the need to plan for future drainage improvements and to link individual schemes into a system of priorities based on the Section 24(5) survey. District Councils will be encouraged to use their land drainage powers to make channel improvements and County Councils are to be encouraged to increase their work carried out for riparian owners on a voluntary and rechargeable basis under Section 99 of the Land Drainage Act 1976. Given the inevitable difficulty of liaising with its 90 District Councils the Water Authority is advocating closer liaison between Districts and Counties concerning land drainage to complement the generally satisfactory liaison between the Authority and the 19 Counties.

The plan also includes increasing the length of designated 'main rivers' within the region so that the Authority has direct powers over the principal watercourses draining the area rather than having to rely on District or County Council drainage work. Currently there are some 3200 km of designated 'main river' in the region and under the plan this would increase by some 25%. Similar policies for increasing the length of 'main rivers' have been adopted by the Northumbrian Water Authority (1978a, 1978b) and the North West Water Authority (1978a) as part of their annual plans.

The Severn Trent policy of increasing 'maining' is based on set principles to ensure the main arteries of the drainage system come within Water Authority control. For example, 'main rivers' would be extended to the outfalls from all Internal Drainage Districts and the drains taking upland water to by-pass these Districts. This would correct the situation whereby the Internal Drainage Boards have no powers to improve channels downstream from their Districts and the Water Authority has no powers there unless the watercourse is 'main river'. If the responsibility here lies with a District Council unwilling to carry out maintenance or improvement works owing to financial restraint then drainage problems can result. Further principles include 'main river' designation for new development areas where future discharges will exceed the existing channel capacity and extension of 'main river' status to the outfalls from regulating reservoirs and major Water Authority surface water and sewage works outfalls. This proposal would solve the problem where effluent from these outfalls flows into a watercourse on which drainage improvement and maintenance is the responsibility of a District Council, before eventually flowing into a 'main river' further downstream, having thereby passed two boundaries dividing drainage responsibility.

The 'maining' policy would result in the Water Authority, as the superior statutory overseeing body in the drainage field, having control over all significant arteries of the drainage system right through to the estuaries so eliminating changes in responsibilities along watercourses. These proposed changes are analogous to the changes in responsibilities for pollution control which took place after 1948 in England and Wales to create catchment-based pollution prevention River Boards. That change was to ensure that local authorities could not pass on pollution to unsuspecting bodies downstream and the Severn Trent Water Authority hopes to ensure that drainage problems cannot be ignored because they do not affect the locality with the responsibilities and powers to solve the problem.

Implementing this plan to 'main' significant stretches of the Severn Trent arterial watercourses will require finance since the Water Authority will require that watercourses to be 'mained' are in a fit condition to carry out their drainage functions. This is because if the Water Authority is to relieve the District Councils of their responsibilities for improvement and maintenance then at least these watercourses should be of reasonable standard before designation; the Water Authority should not be saddled with the cost of rectifying past neglect by the Districts.

A cautious local authority response.   Any extension of Water Authority powers is met with some scepticism and opposition. While most of the District Councils in the Severn Trent area have received the proposed plan favourably, some Councils view with concern the cost of the plan in terms of channel improvements. Some in any case wish to see the maintenance responsibility for improved 'non-main' watercourses retained by the Districts, where they feel local experience and control would result in greater economy. They are also perhaps fearful that further erosion of their engineering responsibilities in the water field might render their works departments and direct labour forces under-employed.

Not all of the County Councils support the view contained within the Severn Trent plan that they have a responsibility for improving arterial land drainage in agricultural areas, preferring to see this as a Water Authority responsibility. Since many of the proposals for 'main river' designations come in such areas and since resources would have to be devoted to bringing them up to 'main river' standard before designation, this comes down to an argument as to who should pay – an argument dear to the hearts of local authorities in somewhat closer contact with their rate paying paymasters than are the Water Authority engineers.

Assessment.   The Severn Trent plan in effect is a proposal for increased 'maining' to solve the Water Authority's difficulties in executing its statutory supervisory role in the land drainage field, rather than an integrated approach to land drainage problems themselves. Such integration may come about when this plan, the Section 24(5) surveys of the Severn Trent Water Authority (1978) and the guidelines prepared by the Water Space Amenity Commission (1978) can be combined, but until this further step is made the unification of approach envisaged in the plan cannot be complete. Nevertheless the Unified Approach undoubtedly represents a useful attempt to improve the region's land drainage planning system. Legislative change is clearly needed, however, to solve problems of divided land drainage responsibility and insufficient finance, particularly as far as District and County Council responsibilities are concerned.

The Builth Wells flood alleviation scheme

Damaging floods have occurred regularly at Builth Wells, located 58 km from the source of the Wye, with properties flooded to depths of 1·75m. However, disagreement on the design and cost-effectiveness of a proposed flood alleviation scheme has stifled progress. A solution may be industrial development on the flood plain to raise the cost-effectiveness of a scheme giving increased flood protection to both this development and existing urban areas. Ironically, however, industrial development has been discouraged in the past partly by the current flood problems and public interest has now waned to the extent that there remains little local pressure for implementing the scheme (Parker and Harding 1978).

The flood alleviation scheme and its formulation. Without a flood alleviation scheme, Builth Wells currently relies on alternative flood hazard adjustments although these present a poor alternative, particularly in Llanelwedd (Fig. 6.3), although structural elevation of new property has been used. Flood damage reduction depends upon flood warnings but the proximity of the source of the Wye means that warnings based on upstream river levels are normally available only a few hours before a flood. During floods many commercial managers and residents have responded to warnings by moving valuables but nevertheless serious damage has still occurred and insurance companies have refused damage cover or insisted on prohibitively high premiums.

Following four serious floods in the 1960s, a request from a local council and a petition signed by inhabitants of Llanelwedd, the Wye River Authority began investigations of permanent flood alleviation measures in February 1967. A variety of flood alleviation techniques was initially considered, including relocating flood prone property, upstream flood control dams, bypass channels and a complete embankment scheme. Relocation was rejected because of its disruptive effects and the lack of alternative suitable level land. Upstream flood water storage would have required uneconomically high dams even if suitable sites could be found. Bypass channels were rejected since they would use up the very areas it was hoped to make flood free. A complete embankment scheme was also rejected as necessitating banks over 5 m high. Subsequent flood levels would have completely filled some arches of the bridge and threatened its stability (Fig. 6.3).

By April 1967 an outline scheme estimated to cost £235 000 was agreed in principle, subject to further agreement with the five local councils involved to pay the 50% of costs remaining after grant-aid. This agreement was eventually signed in February 1970. The scheme finally proposed extends about 4 km down from the Wye's confluence with the Irfon (Fig. 6.3) and below the

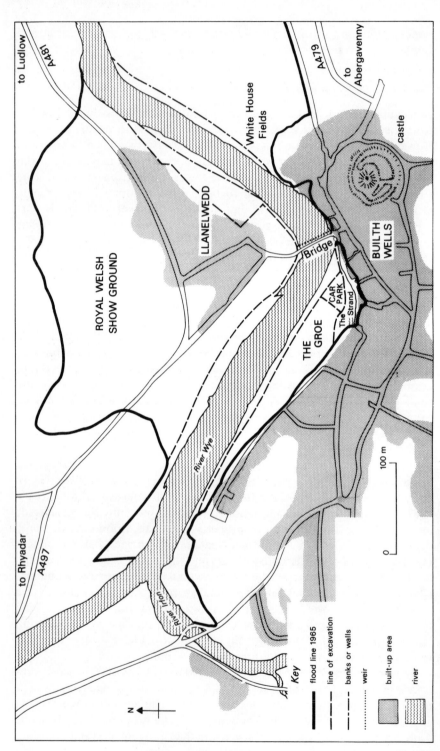

Figure 6.3 Proposed Builth Wells flood alleviation scheme.

bridge the main work is excavation. For nearly a kilometre the river bed will be lowered by some 1·5 m and the channel widened to lower the 50-year design flood about 1·2 m below existing levels. Just downstream of the bridge a weir will avoid undermining the bridge foundations and incorporate a fish pass to preserve important fisheries interests.

In addition to raising river channel capacity, extensive flood walls and embankments will be needed. These would be about 0·6 m high downstream of the bridge but larger upstream where three controversial options exist for protecting Builth itself. The cheapest involves 1·8 m high earth banks or walls around the car park (Fig. 6.3) with extensions to high ground along the north of the Strand. Alternatives consist of an embankment along the southern edge of the car park and along the northern edge of the Strand, with car park access through a flood gate, or a 1·5 m high wall the length of the 'Groe' recreational area. Spoil from excavation will be used for the earth banks and to fill parts of the White House Fields, making them flood-free and suitable for development, although this option is costly.

Problems with scheme implementation. Given the flooding frequency at Builth Wells and the degree of public concern in the recent past, surprisingly little progress has been made in implementing the proposed scheme. Problems have concerned economic viability, disagreements between local councils, and the future of the White House Fields and the Groe. Doubts about the economic viability of the scheme were present from a relatively early stage. A benefit assessment using standard flood damage information (Penning-Rowsell and Chatterton 1977) has not yet been undertaken and even with such information benefit calculations remain complex since substantial indirect benefits might accrue through increasing the area of flood-free land. This could lead to industrial development which would probably have a multiplier effect in improving the town's economy. Partly resulting from these uncertainties, however, a rigorous cost-benefit analysis of the scheme has never been completed (Parker 1976). The existing analysis is based on crude estimates and the resulting benefit-cost ratio for the proposed scheme is low. This does nothing to make the implementation of the scheme by the Welsh Water Authority more likely.

A more favourable ratio might be obtained by giving additional weight to the development possibilities of the town. Alternatively it might be more cost-effective to install a scheme designed to protect only against smaller floods. However, the Builth Wells flood alleviation investigations were based upon only one pre-determined flood magnitude: the 50-year 'design flood', similar in magnitude to the 1960 event at Builth Wells. All subsequent appraisal related to this design flood and no attempt was made to calculate the costs and benefits of schemes designed to protect against floods of alternative magnitudes.

A key problem has also been the failure to reach agreement between the local councils on design options, particularly over the Groe area. In 1970 the Builth Urban District Council would not accept any work on the Groe but later agreed to a proposal with flood wall heights not exceeding 1·2 m, or with these walls erected as a second phase in the scheme after experiencing the effects of the main works. These conditions undermined the whole essence of the scheme and were therefore unacceptable to the Wye River Authority.

A second major obstacle to agreement concerns the farmland known as White House Fields (Fig. 6.3) which would probably become flood free with filling by spoil from the scheme and from flood banks downstream of the bridge. The site might well be valuable for future industrial development. In 1971 the Council was not prepared to proceed with the scheme until this land was publicly owned, since it did not wish to see the major benefits of a publicly funded project going to a private landowner. However, without central government help there were considerable difficulties in the Council purchasing White House Fields.

In response to these disagreements the Wye River Authority felt unable to proceed until the problems had been settled, causing great concern to the Colwyn Rural District Council, which embraces the high flood risk Llanelwedd, who proposed a meeting to resolve the difficulties. The outcome was to present the entire case to the Welsh Office for central government involvement but little came of this approach and the lack of local council agreement was unresolved, despite local government reorganisation which might have reduced such local disputes.

Disagreement over the Groe plans basically concerns the aesthetic and amenity aspects of the flood alleviation scheme. Builth Wells has an important summer tourist trade and the car park acts as a focus for tourist stops. The Groe recreational area and the river itself are considerable amenity assets. Flood walls or embankments to protect property from winter floods might detract considerably from the amenity value of the Groe area, with possible loss of summer trade. Local inhabitants are also reluctant to lose their view of the river.

The flood problem and industrial development.　Attracting population and employment to Builth Wells, and Mid-Wales as a whole, is vital to maintain local services and prosperity; between 1957 and 1971 the town's population fell from 1706 to 1552. To attract significant industrial employment sufficient areas of flat flood free land are necessary yet at Builth Wells this is very scarce: nearly all undeveloped flat land is unprotected flood plain. Even given the proposed flood alleviation scheme one of the sites suitable for industry, at White House Fields, would only be protected if excavated material could be used to raise land levels at a cost (in 1968) of over £5000 per hectare excluding purchase costs.

In 1968 when the proposals for flood alleviation seemed good Builth Wells had already been identified by the Mid-Wales Industrial Development

Association for possible industrial, employment and population expansion which prompted a feasibility study of expansion possibilities in the town. In 1969 the Welsh Office, the development agencies including the Association and five Mid-Wales Counties discussed selecting towns in Mid-Wales for concentrated industrial growth including building advance factories. Builth Wells was not, however, on the list of 'growth towns' selected, the nearest being Rhayader. Although the criteria of growth town selection did not specifically include the availability of flood free land, towns were selected on their capability of generating the necessary urban amenities. Whilst the proximity of Rhayader to Builth Wells was probably a major reason for Builth not being selected, the difficulty of obtaining flood free land would have been a major problem had local technical conditions been in consideration since the Mid-Wales Industrial Development Association is not prepared to use flood prone land.

Assessment.   Public interest in the flood alleviation scheme has now faded, probably because there have been no serious damaging floods here since 1968. Inevitably it takes time to generate a solution to a flood problem and justify a scheme and by the time public agencies have produced designs and are ready to begin works public concern and support for the necessary expenditure may have evaporated.

Builth Wells now finds itself in the unfortunate position of continued flood risk, of needing significant industrial development to improve the benefit-cost ratio but with little immediate prospect of such development partly because of the lack of flood free land. Unless the basic disagreements can be resolved, or unless upstream regulation of the Wye can be developed to protect Builth Wells, ironically only a further severe flood might provide the momentum, once again, for resolving the fundamental conflicts between interested parties concerning a flood alleviation scheme.

The Amberley Wild Brooks drainage scheme and public inquiry

The public inquiry in 1978 into the grant-aiding by the Ministry of Agriculture, Fisheries and Food of a scheme to drain the Amberley Wild Brooks marked the end of an era in land drainage and a period of intense questioning of both policies and schemes in the agricultural drainage field.

Conflict between drainage and amenity and nature conservation reaches a peak in inland fen and marsh areas. Whereas in coastal marshes reclamation costs can be higher than the obtainable benefits, the potential for agricultural enhancement on inland wetlands is generally good. However, unique and rare habitats for specialised fauna and flora abound in these conditions, some of which are of international importance. With the extensive land drainage since 1930 the number of such inland wetlands has steadily decreased and the draining of those remaining is intensely controversial.

Amberley Wild Brooks lie to the easterly bank of the river Arun, comprising a shallow 365-hectare depression forming part of the natural flood plain (Penning-Rowsell and Chatterton 1977). Much of the Brooks is below high tide level and, although largely protected by embankments from river flooding, drainage from surrounding hills floods much of the site almost every winter. Water only escapes to the river through three gravity sluices – tide-locked for 18 out of every 24 hours – one of which was in poor condition. Agricultural use prior to the drainage proposal was low intensity cattle grazing and hay production. A few fields were completely overgrown and parts of the area were deteriorating.

Within the Brooks there is an eighteen-hectare Site of Special Scientific Interest (SSSI) on part of a relict raised bog on a peat deposit. An extensive system of interconnecting dykes demarcates a complex ownership pattern of many small fields. Most of the Brooks is farmed by six farmers but numerous residents of Amberley own small parcels and the Sussex Trust for Nature Conservation owns two fields totalling 4·5 hectares.

The events leading to the public inquiry.   Plans to drain the Wild Brooks date back to 1937 when the then Arun Catchment Board proposed to alleviate flooding at Pulborough and Amberley, a scheme which was never implemented. The West Sussex River Board prepared another scheme in 1960 to prevent summer flooding of agricultural land. This was installed in 1968 through enlarging channel capacity at Pulborough and raising embankments right down the river. Nevertheless winter flooding continued and parts of the Brooks can be flooded for more than a month and waterlogging can prevent grazing for six months each year.

Following the notably wet winter of 1974−5 the farmers complained to the Southern Water Authority (Sussex Rivers Division) that the 1968 scheme had not gone far enough. The Water Authority commissioned research on the likely benefits of a scheme for the Arun between Pulborough and Arundel (Middlesex Polytechnic Flood Hazard Research Project 1976). This indicated that while the whole scheme was not cost-effective the Amberley Wild Brooks might justify improved drainage. A series of meetings was held with interested parties and the Sussex Local Land Drainage Committee approved a scheme, which was endorsed by the Regional Committee, and submitted it to the Ministry of Agriculture, Fisheries and Food for grant-aid in July 1977.

The scheme was to cost £339 000 split between the Internal Drainage Board (£87 000 – eligible for 50% grant) and the Water Authority (£252 000 – eligible for 80% grant, the remainder derived from county rate precept). The scheme was designed to protect the area from flooding for four out of every five years and to control ditch water levels through pumping from the Brooks into the river. A conservation zone of eighty-one hectares was proposed for the area surrounding the SSSI where water tables would be maintained at a high level.

At this time the Amberley residents began to protest to the Water Authority about potential loss of amenity and conservation value of the Brooks and what they saw as a waste of public money if the scheme materialised. An agreement on the scheme in December 1976 between interested parties, including the Sussex Trust for Nature Conservation, was now seen to be a mistake resulting from the belief that there was no means of public examination of the project, as indeed there was not under the Land Drainage Act 1961. The Amberley Society was formed specifically to oppose the scheme and members petitioned the Minister for Agriculture to hold an inquiry under Section 96 of the then new Land Drainage Act 1976. By this time, despite many meetings, considerable antagonism and mistrust had arisen between the objectors and the Southern Water Authority, fuelled by the lateness with which the Amberley Society joined the debate and the Water Authority's determination to proceed once initial agreement had been reached.

Thus was initiated the first public inquiry into a drainage scheme in England and Wales, with an Inspector appointed who was both engineer and town planner, aided by agriculturalist and ecologist assessors. The Inspector's brief was 'to ascertain a) the reason for and the benefits expected to accrue from the proposals, . . . and b) the effect (if any) . . . on the natural beauty of, or amenity in the area or on the flora and fauna' so as to enable the Minister to decide whether to grant-aid the scheme.

Faced with the public inquiry the Water Authority commissioned an updated assessment of the benefits of the scheme. National opposition to the proposal was growing (Hall 1978) and at the eleventh hour the Water Authority commissioned consultants to survey the ecological value of the Brooks. The survey, intended to counter the objectors' contention of unique ecological value for the Brooks, was abortive owing to lack of time. In any case it was the wrong season for ecological assessment and this move highlighted the remarkable lack of ecological expertise within the Authority.

The case presented for the drainage scheme. The case for the scheme was put by the Water Authority solicitor and engineers, the consultants assessing the likely benefits and the National Farmers' Union and the Country Landowners' Association.

The Water Authority argued that the scheme was needed to prevent the winter flooding, that it was cost effective with a benefit:cost ratio of at least 1·01:1 and possibly 1·3:1, and that the Authority had not been notified under Section 23(3) of the Water Act 1973 by the Nature Conservancy Council that the area had special ecological interest. Furthermore the area was not rated as a Grade 1 site in the recent nature conservation review (Ratcliffe 1978), nor specified in the Ramsar Convention list of internationally important sites (Foreign and Commonwealth Office 1976). Indeed the Sussex Pevensey Levels had been drained recently yet had been subsequently both listed in the nature conservation review and designated as an SSSI. The Authority considered that the flora and fauna would regenerate after the proposals had been implemented and that the intended conservation zone more than met its statutory obligations to have regard for nature conservation.

The consultants assessed the benefits using a questionnaire survey of the appropriate farmers to determine likely future agricultural uses for the Brooks if the drainage scheme went ahead. The farmers suggested that some 14% of the Brooks could go to arable cropping and the remainder would carry higher livestock densities so releasing upland grazing for further arable cultivation. The enhanced agricultural return for both the Brooks and associated adjoining upland gave estimates of the capital expenditure allowable for the scheme of between £470 000 and £580 000 to set against the costs of £339 000 plus £119 000 for field underdrainage and other farmers' costs (Penning-Rowsell 1978a).

The National Farmers' Union and the Country Landowners' Association supported the benefit assessment, and indeed considered the figures somewhat low. Both organisations pointed to the deteriorating drainage condition of the Brooks, their members' interests in conservation as demonstrated by the acceptance of the conservation zone, but also their requirement for compensation for lack of improved income if the scheme did not materialise. Privately many of the farmers began to realise that they might undertake some of the drainage works themselves, using mobile pumps to relieve surface water flooding, while publicly still supporting the comprehensive Water Authority scheme.

The case against the proposal.   Not until the day of the inquiry was the position of the County planning department certain, having originally supported the Water Authority. In the event the County opposed the scheme, but the weight of objection came from the Amberley Society, the Council for the Protection of Rural England and the various nature conservation agencies such as the Royal Society for the Protection of Birds and the Friends of the Earth.

The planning department pointed to their general statements of intent in the draft structure plan on the conservation importance of wetlands and the need to retain biological diversity within the County. In reality the County Council had no specific prior policy towards the Brooks, and appeared at the inquiry to follow the lead of the various amenity and conservation interests. The Council for the Protection of Rural England contested the benefit assessment, arguing that part of the benefits, as increased food production, were in fact costs in the form of subsidies to the farmers through artificially high prices maintained by the European Economic Community. Once drained, the area would become an ordinary piece of countryside without the special landscape qualities which warranted its inclusion within the South Downs Area of Outstanding Natural Beauty.

The Amberley Society also contested the benefit assessment, arguing that the benefits had been over-emphasised both by allowing for enhanced productivity away from the Brooks and by using incorrectly high values of agricultural return. The Society pointed out that the Nature Conservancy Council had formally notified the County Council of its intention to designate practically the whole area as an SSSI and argued that the flora of the area was unique owing to close juxtaposition of acid and alkali habitats. The Brooks contained representatives of about 25% of all British flora including 16 species which are national rarities. Elements of the fauna were unique, with the Downey Emerald dragon-fly known to breed only in the acid area of the Brooks and the Hairy dragon-fly only known in the Brooks and on Pevensey Levels. The impact of the drainage works would be to remove habitats through channel widening and to reduce ecological diversity partly owing to greater use of fertilisers with arable cropping leading to eutrophication.

The Nature Conservancy Council emphasised that the Brooks was one of the few surviving marshlands of great value and that once lost it could not be reinstated. The Council supported the evidence given by other nature conservation interests and emphasised its reluctance at the initial agreement on the intended conservation zone, which was considered too small to retain the ecological diversity of the Brooks. The Royal Society for the Protection of Birds pointed to the national or international importance of the Brooks for Bewick Swans, Shovelers and Ruff and the regional significance of the site for all wildfowl such as the Pintail, Teal and Snipe. In an adjacent Brook, now drained, the population of Widgeon had declined from 2000 to zero in eight years and the same was feared for many species now abundant at Amberley.

The Inspector's recommendation and the Minister's decision. Four months after the 4½ day public inquiry the Inspector reported his deliberations. He contested the benefit assessment, although rejecting the low figures presented by the Amberley Society, and therefore recommended against grant-aiding the scheme on cost-effectiveness grounds. He also fully accepted the case for the ecological importance of the area, pointed to recent agreement by the National Farmers' Union and Country Landowners' Association (1977) in encouraging their members to be more aware of shifting emphasis towards conservation of the countryside, and believed that this reflected both government and public opinion. The Inspector was critical of both the Water Authority and statutory conservation agencies for insufficient consultation on the proposed scheme.

The Minister accepted the Inspector's recommendations although partly disagreed with his reasons. The methods used for assessing the benefits of the scheme were upheld by the Minister while accepting that Amberley Wild Brooks constituted a very important site in respect of unique nature conservation interest. However, the Minister rejected the many calls at the inquiry for clearer guidance on how to balance the requirements of agriculture and conservation, preferring these to be established for each individual site. Nevertheless the Minister agreed to look again at the policy guidance notes issued to Water Authorities in the area of benefit appraisal and recommended a more systematic process of consultation and exchange of information between all the parties involved in reconciling the requirements of agriculture and conservation.

Assessment.   This decision not to proceed with the drainage proposals was historic, being the first under new legislation and the first time that grant-aiding had been refused for what in effect were conservation reasons.

In arriving at the decision the Minister undoubtedly proceeded somewhat illogically: while rejecting the Inspector's critique of benefit assessment methods he supported his recommendations to refuse the grant-aiding on cost-effectiveness grounds. Moreover, government decisions later the same year amended the required discount rate – which measures the present value of future benefits – from 10% to 5% for such schemes, which would have virtually doubled the calculated benefits. We can see that high but inexplicit economic value was put on the conservation significance of Amberley Wild Brooks, a lack of clarity which cannot but lead to further similar diputes over future drainage schemes.

The Water Authority can be criticised for insufficient consultations with amenity groups, owing to its slow realisation of the nature conservation and amenity value of the Brooks, and above all for having insufficient staff with knowledge of the ecological significance of its land drainage works. Once roused the energy of the conservation groups was remarkable and the weight of evidence they produced was of great significance to the final decision. Without a public inquiry it is doubtful whether a satisfactory outcome would have materialised since, although willing to compromise, the Water Authority was unwilling to see the scheme dropped completely. Even with the recent guidelines on conservation and land drainage (Water Space Amenity Commission 1978) such cases are likely to remain unresolved without public inquiries but following Amberley all Water Authorities are likely to be more circumspect in their land drainage proposals.

Evaluation

The land drainage and flood alleviation field is complicated by embracing these two somewhat contrasting areas each involving different planning problems. Both involve significant conflicts mainly between those who might gain by a flood alleviation scheme and those who contribute towards its cost. Any evaluation, then, must look closely at the effects of land drainage and flood protection policies on sectional interests.

Does society provide water planners with an adequate framework of legislation, institutions and financial provisions?
The land drainage area occupies a privileged position within water planning mainly through the allocation of central government grant-aid. Land drainage institutions are powerful, both centrally where the Ministry of

Agriculture, Fisheries and Food exerts considerable influence on both policies and scheme decisions and locally where the Regional and Local Land
Drainage Committees have a degree of independence from other Water
Authority work. This institutional power can facilitate planning decisions,
which helps the engineer, but can make public objection appear too difficult
to mount. Financial provisions are certainly adequate to cater for currently
identified problems although mandatory contributions towards drainage
costs from developers and farmers would promote equity. Legislation gives
Water Authorities, local authorities and Internal Drainage Boards sufficient
power to implement schemes although responsibilities are unnecessarily divided. Scottish legislation has lagged behind that in England and Wales but
there is generally no legislative impediment to necessary land drainage work.

To what extent do public attitudes and preferences towards water and
associated land resources affect policies, plans and schemes?
A major problem in the land drainage field is that social goals are very poorly
articulated, particularly concerning design standards, and perhaps do not
exist at all. Public perception of risk and uncertainty is poor and people
appear to see flood alleviation as marginal to basic needs except when
flooding affects them. Agricultural land drainage is hardly understood by the
public and excites little interest so it is difficult to assess whether the water
planner is meeting relevant social goals; the needs of the farming community
and those flooded are being met, although as at Builth Wells there can be
inordinate delays in scheme implementation. The growth of environmental
awareness in the general public was seriously underestimated by drainage
engineers, traditionally so committed to increasing the area of drained land,
with unfortunate consequences for wetland nature conservation.

How do the inherent characteristics of water in Britain influence the choice
of alternative policies, plans and schemes?
The size of British rivers influences the design of flood alleviation schemes. In
particular, the short warning periods available before flood events limit the
usefulness of flood warnings. In agricultural drainage the abundance of low-
lying land and the English lowland clay soils have encouraged field under-
drainage schemes, particularly in fenland areas. The lesser land drainage
problems in Scotland explain the relative inactivity there and the less polished
policy framework. The increasing coastal flooding hazard has necessitated
costly solutions including tidal barages and intensive embankments. Leaving
coastal areas to flood is unacceptable given the population affected and the
amount of threatened agricultural land. Given the decision to protect these
people and land the schemes adopted are logical.

To what extent are resource management principles incorporated into
water policies, plans and schemes?
For over 40 years land drainage planning in England and Wales has been

catchment-based so the management unit is closely related to the resource being planned although drainage responsibilities within catchments are split. Storage reservoirs installed for river regulation for water supply also have a flood control effect, thereby following multi-purpose principles. However, in the agricultural field, emphasis on increasing food production through drainage is creating less diverse and potentially unstable natural habitats.

How well is water planning (in this area) integrated with other forms of public planning?

The relationship between flood alleviation and development control is imperfect. Many cases of unwise development have resulted from insufficient consultation between planning departments and river engineers. Changes in planning legislation may be necessary, or some alternative strategy adopted so that planning departments have greater regard for Water Authority advice.

Is land drainage planning comprehensive and systematic and are all relevant interests adequately involved?

The strengths of land drainage planning include the engineers' skill in perfecting drainage techniques, thereby reducing real costs, and the acceptance of cost-effectiveness criteria in scheme design, although their use needs greater care and fundamental differences on the nature of benefits do occur, as at Amberley and Builth Wells. Two improvements will enhance the planning system: the results of the Section 24(5) surveys of England and Wales, to establish more rational expenditure ceilings, and careful use of the Conservation and Land Drainage Guidelines.

Consultation with interested parties occurs too often *after* critical planning stages, particularly concerning nature conservation and amenity matters. In England and Wales since 1976 public inquiries allow all interests access to decision-making but disagreements can be fundamental, as at Amberley; it would be unwise to conclude because all interests are thereby considered that decisions are necessarily wise and equitable.

British flood alleviation policies have emphasised engineering schemes, partly because grant-aiding encourages capital expenditure, but alternatives have not been ignored. For agricultural drainage the engineer is by tradition committed to embankment and pumping schemes but often no alternative is practicable.

The power of agricultural interests fundamentally influences all decisions, capitalising upon government policy to increase food production by investment in land improvements via the private farmer. Whether this dominant influence is satisfactory for planning urban flood alleviation schemes is questionable, as must be the lack of a betterment levy to recoup for the community some of the increased value of land drained with public grants. The water industry should increase public consultation on land drainage, as embraced within the Severn Trent plan. It is inappropriate to criticise water planning agencies or river engineers for over-emphasising drainage. The Ministry of Agriculture, Fisheries and Food, in promoting food production, balances drainage against alternatives. Here the agricultural domination certainly biases policies towards certain types of capital intensive agricultural techniques, including land drainage, as opposed to more environmentally sensitive alternatives.

Selected further reading (for full bibliography see pp. 254−66)

For a comprehensive description of both hydrological and socio-economic aspects of flood alleviation see:

Ward, R. C. 1978. *Floods: a geographical perspective.* London: Macmillan.

The following papers give a useful background to the physical aspects of agricultural land drainage:

Cole, G. 1976. 'Land drainage in England and Wales.' *Journal of the Institution of Water Engineers and Scientists* **30**, 345−67.
Hill, A. R. 1976. 'The environmental impact of agricultural land drainage.' *Journal of Environmental Management* **4**, 251−74.

For a regional perspective on the scale of flood problems see:

Parker, D. J. and D. M. Harding 1978. 'Planning for urban floods'. *Disasters* **2**(1), 47−57.

For an analysis of London's flood problems and the new tidal barrier see:

Horner, R. W. 1978. 'Thames tidal flood works in the London excluded area.' *Journal of the Institution of Public Health Engineers* **6**(1), 16−24.

The following paper gives an excellent account of the political processes leading to the incorporation in 1974 of land drainage within the Water Authorities:

Richardson, J. J., A. G. Jordan and R. H. Kimber 1978. 'Lobbying, administrative reform and policy styles: the case of land drainage.' *Political Studies* **26**(1), 47−64.

For more details of the cost-benefit techniques central to flood alleviation and land drainage scheme design see:

Penning-Rowsell, E. C., and J. B. Chatterton 1977. *The benefits of flood alleviation: a manual of assessment techniques.* Farnborough: Saxon House.

The nature conservation and amenity aspects of land drainage are fully detailed in:

Water Space Amenity Commission 1978. *Conservation and land drainage guidelines: draft for consultation.* London: WSAC.

7 *The political character of water planning*

In this final Chapter we examine more critically the place of water planning within society; this locates water planning as an unavoidably *political* activity. Many water planners, in contrast, would prefer to see water planning primarily as a technical exercise. This is a view based on positivist thinking (Keat 1979), which emphasises data and facts above values and interpretations and consequently sees decision making as rational if founded mainly on politically neutral data-gathering rather than on genuine political debate. Our analysis draws on the perceptions of those involved in the planning process of the nature of power within society. Many concerned with planning in Britain see society as groups and individuals each with equal opportunity or power to influence decisions through democratic processes. This pluralist view of society appears to find support in certain cases analysed in earlier Chapters, where genuine democratic processes and cooperative effort dominated policy decisions. However, the view is also at odds with other planning situations identified, including both certain overall water planning policies and decisions concerning individual schemes. Here we saw fundamental conflict between groups competing for the same resources. Such evidence supports a view of society as a collection of individuals and groups in often irreconcilable conflict leading to alienation, rather than one emphasising basic consensus among those involved where disagreements are simply temporary aberrations or imbalances in an otherwise satisfactory system. These different views of society affect the way planners plan and, above all, influence their approach to conflict over policies, plans and schemes.

This analysis not only helps to explain certain policies followed by Regional Water Authorities and central government, especially in the water pollution and land drainage fields but also the low financial commitment by society to water recreation and amenity. It can also further our understanding of the evolving structure of water management and the outcome of certain decision making sequences described in previous Chapters.

Who is water planning for?

Water planning has extensive social and economic implications, influencing food production through land drainage policies and schemes and affecting industrial efficiency and profitability through water supply and effluent disposal costing and allocation. The distribution of the substantial public investment involved can affect local and regional economies.

Water planning, therefore, is clearly a political exercise, as it is concerned with allocating scarce financial resources which is one significant dimension of political activity. Since water planning is political are there 'losers' and 'gainers' from the process, as in other political arenas? Is the allocation of these scarce resources equitable and therefore 'fair'; what degree of inequity is tolerated; do certain sectional interests 'win' time after time, and why? Does the water planning system always operate for the common good, or are policies, plans and schemes consciously or unconsciously promoted to benefit certain groups more than others and, if so, why? In short, we have to examine who is water planning for?

To approach this evaluative question, which is more basic than those posed in Chapter 1, we focus on three fundamental aims of water planning: economic efficiency, equity, and environmental and public health protection. Using examples from the four main areas of water planning we can evaluate briefly the reality of policies, to see for whom water planning shows the most concern.

Economic efficiency

Water Authorities give high priority to economic efficiency: to maximising the return on all expenditure. Economic principles are being applied more widely and rigorously to reduce unnecessary expenditure. Leakage reduction, water reclamation and domestic metering experiments with consumption-related charges are all attracting greater attention in the search for more economical operation. However, such approaches to economic efficiency create dilemmas by having equity implications: charges based on metering may adversely affect those least able to pay.

Nevertheless, in significant areas of water planning economic efficiency is not pursued. The continuing emphasis on meeting rather than managing water supply demands is based on an imperfect analysis of the environmental and social costs of new reservoirs and other schemes. Waste management schemes themselves are not based sufficiently upon cost-benefit criteria. The lack of a charging system for direct discharges gives industrialists a loophole for avoiding the real pollution costs of their products. Little attention is given to the social benefits of amenity and recreation policies and schemes, to facilitate choice between schemes competing for particularly scarce resources, and so raise economic efficiency. Therefore, in economic terms, the level of investment on such policies and schemes is at best ill-considered and at worst completely arbitrary, and merely reflects pressure group lobbying, although some might argue this correctly measures the opportunity costs of this expenditure.

In the land drainage field some attempt is made at economic analysis, but here the main deficiencies are that the opportunity costs of land drainage expenditure are ignored, even in terms of alternative policies to promote food production, and the analysis as yet gives insufficient weight to nature conservation value. In the storm sewerage field, accepted design standards are economically extravagant to say the least in that the cost of schemes generally far exceeds the benefits in terms of reducing the flood damage which would otherwise occur; the return on expenditure is demonstrably poor.

In short, while water planning authorities are showing regard to costs, this is not oriented towards maximising the social benefits accruing from schemes promoted but towards balancing the books on a year-by-year basis. The economic efficiency practised appears to focus more on accounting expediency than on a genuine search for cost-effectiveness.

Why is this so? Clearly the reason lies partly in the difficulty of measuring benefits and in the traditional reluctance of engineers to give sufficient focus in scheme design to economic performance by seeking to maximise the difference between benefits and costs. The acceptance of certain standard techniques to measure the economic benefits of land drainage was prompted to facilitate the task of the river engineer, and the rigour of the economic analysis is at least partly illusory. In other areas reliable benefit assessment is highly problematic; the only solution proposed is to let market mechanisms determine social benefits – largely through metering water supplies and charging for recreational use of water space. Such a solution, however, causes problems for assessing future benefits, for example of increased water supply from new schemes. This is because we can only study current markets. However, a new scheme may itself radically affect the market the water planner is attempting to use and thereby predict future social benefits, with which to justify future expenditure. Furthermore the allocation of water recreation resources using market mechanisms may well disadvantage low income groups by totally excluding certain facilities, such as angling water rights. Therefore the mechanisms necessary for promoting economic efficiency can have unforseen and inequitable consequences. To avoid the conflict that these would bring, the water planner chooses to ignore such routes to economic efficiency.

Perhaps a more fundamental reason, therefore, for the absence of a proper search for economic efficiency is that such a notion depends on assigning the same utility to a service or commodity for all consumers. Yet different people clearly benefit from and therefore value the same commodity in different ways. Consequently economic efficiency means different things to different people, depending on their priorities. For the water planner to gauge the social benefits of more reliable water supply systems, and thereby plan cost-effective schemes, requires analysis of individuals' reactions to droughts. As well as being methodologically problematic, this will certainly reveal conflicts about standards rather than a common assessment of future need: one man's reliable water supply is another man's water rate increase. Since the planner needs to believe and convince others that there is a consensus for his plans it is more comfortable to extrapolate existing water demand trends, and assume that social benefits of greater reliability exceed the costs of the necessary schemes, rather than enter the hornet's nest of alternative water supply standards, some of which would undoubtedly be more economically efficient than supply extension.

In similar vein the land drainage engineer incorrectly assumes that if each scheme is cost-effective when based on reliable flood damage data then the total programme of schemes promoted by the Ministry of Agriculture, Fisheries and Food is the most economically efficient allocation of those scarce resources. The assumption is incorrect because while most observers might agree about the value of flood damages averted, considerable disagreement would be revealed by evaluating the opportunity costs of the land drainage budget as a whole if such public debate were initiated by a more thorough search for greater economic efficiency. In both water planning fields public debate is not promoted, true economic efficiency is not pursued and the conflict that such approaches would entail is hidden behind the apparent economic efficiency of balanced budgets.

Equity

In a mass media society people expect an equal standard of service everywhere from nationalised industries (Brown 1978). Approximately the same high standard of water supply is indeed given to over 95% of the population, but in other water planning fields inequity abounds.

Recent statutory requirements have attempted to ensure that water charges are not unduly discriminatory. Water charges, however, represent just one area where discrimination is possible. For example, in the 1975–76 drought industry was given supply priority over domestic consumers, so as to maintain industrial production, and pollution legislation has continually eroded common law riparian rights to receive unpolluted water. The power of industrial lobbies in a profit-oriented society continues to shape water pollution plans and to delay full implementation of the Control of Pollution Act 1974.

Similarly, in the field of water recreation and amenity, market mechanisms have increased provision for private club interests – sometimes at the expense of the general public – given the rising value of the scarce resource. Management expediency or powerlessness rather than any concerted view on the types of people who should benefit from water-based recreation lead water planners to accept such tendencies, but the effect is nevertheless inequitable since these clubs usually embrace a fairly narrow spectrum of society. The farming lobby has successfully maintained the system of land drainage grants and subsidies through which government policies for increased food production are implemented by increasing the profitability of private farming to at least that rate of return obtainable on other capital investment. The result is that many individual farmers have prospered as a consequence of policies based on public expenditure and designed to creater greater national food production.

Various sectional interests clearly have a dominant influence on water planning, which demolishes the claim that democratic processes can accurately measure consensus opportunity costs. These interests are supported by those in government, with their particular view of wealth creation and the mechanisms of economic growth, and they generally represent industrialists, landowners and the wealthy. This does *not* necessarily mean that water planners deliberately seek to promote the interests of these groups, but their policies, and those of government, automatically tend to support those within society with the greater economic strength.

Environmental and public health protection

What is the water industry record in the environmental and public health protection field? There have undoubtedly been substantial improvements in river pollution, but over a very long time. The history of water pollution control legislation shows continual reluctance to curtail industrial pollution, particularly in estuaries and at the coast. The recent review of discharge consent conditions shows government willingness to allow existing river pollution levels to continue. Inadequate finance still limits further improvement but the record of water industry prosecutions for exceeded consents is most unsatisfactory. Consents are inadequately monitored and enforced and there is ample evidence of illegal pollution both from industrial enterprises and from Water Authority sewage treatment plant. The presence of polluting domestic sewage discharges is no reason for tolerating illegal industrial pollution. The implementation of the Control of Pollution Act 1974 has been delayed inordinately in the interests of economic growth or reduced public expenditure, so as to maintain living standards and provide tax reductions. The water supply field sees economic arguments continually winning over environmental considerations, as at Carsington and Cow Green, and environmental diversity has undoubtedly suffered in the drive for greater agricultural production through land drainage. The environmental impacts of recreation schemes are rarely assessed adequately and the amenity opportunities of water schemes are rarely grasped to full advantage.

The level of environmental care, however, is not so much a function of the individual water planner or water planning agency as of government policy and market forces. Increased expenditure on environmental protection has generally only been sanctioned when the profitability of the relevant industrial, agricultural or recreational concerns is not threatened. Such a policy is not surprising given that Britain is an industrial nation based on private enterprise. However, being now one of the nation's principal environmental protection agencies the water industry may find uncomfortable tensions between its statutory duties in this field, if these are taken seriously, and other aspects of government economic policy. This tension is not appreciated by the public for whom water planning agencies have attracted the naïve image of being themselves environmentally insensitive.

Water planning aims, therefore, at policies, plans and schemes which are economically efficient, equitable and designed to promote environmental and public health protection. The reality falls some way short of fulfilling such aims, because strong sectional interests successfully promote the maintenance of their status and prosperity, because water planning professionals are reluctant to alter established practices, because government policy does not always coincide with these aims, but basically because in our society market forces often dictate otherwise.

How is water planned?

Given that water planning at least shows signs of dominance by sectional interests, this calls into question the way decisions are made and the institutional arrangements, including the public accountablity of water planning.

The water planners

Although the role of government and market forces should not be underestimated, part of the explanation for certain interests dominating water planning decisions may be found in terms of the characteristics of the water planners themselves. However, this element of explanation is recognised to be of a lesser order than the more fundamental economic forces determining water policies.

Indeed, analysis which suggests that the engineer or other water planner is to blame for all the deficiencies of water planning is both naïve and dangerous, since public confidence in the skills of specialists and professionals is thereby undermined. A more careful consideration shows that the water planner is seldom a free agent to mould policies and plans to obtain optimal results but is buffeted by market forces and by the whims of his political masters, whether in local government or with the Water Authorities. For example, incorporating highly desired recreation facilities into water schemes may be uneconomic – charges may not cover revenue costs. Charging schemes for pollution discharge may prove inoperable despite their theoretical niceties and environmental benefits. The scope for the local water planner to influence policies will often be minimal when the major focus of budgetary control lies with government departments, and legislation may inhibit new policies, as indeed may the administrative hierarchy within which the water planner is located.

Nevertheless the dominance of the science and engineering specialisms results in a restricted perception of water planning solutions (Ruddoff and Lucken 1971). Perhaps equally important are the social characteristics of water planners. They tend to be professional, well-established members of society. Coupled with their engineering training, this favours a conventional approach to planning and a tendency to favour the *status quo* rather than the search for social change. Thus the interests of the water planner and the industrialist often broadly coincide, as they also do with farmers and land-owners. There is clearly no conspiratorial association here but the detailed analysis of decision-making and policy changes by Richardson, Jordan and Kimber (1978) shows a concerted system of mutual self-support between, in this case, landowners and farmers, civil servants and the water planners themselves, to retain a privileged position for all these interests. In other cases the mix of interests will be different but there is a tendency, encouraged by their positions as government employees, for the water planners to give unquestioning support to government policy – in contrast to other fields such as housing and land use planning where tensions are open and public and where radical alternative policies are more common – and this necessarily leads to the support of industrial profitability and the maintenance of the interests of landowners and the wealthy.

How decisions are made and evaluated

Analysing the water planning process is problematic because decision making is often either relatively private and even secret or strongly post-rationalised making procedures appear falsely systematic and non-political. Major decisions may force public scrutiny but water planning is a continual process and often only clues are available about particular decisions and their reasons. Perhaps only planners themselves are positioned to make searching assessments but such evaluation appears to imply professional incompetence and is avoided or not published.

Some conclusions, however, are possible about water planning processes and procedures. As described in Chapter 1 the idealised comprehensive planning process is iterative, proceeding sequentially through a number of key steps leading from the setting of goals or the identification of a problem through information gathering to the implementation and monitoring of the effectiveness of a policy, plan or scheme (Mitchell 1971). In this context an encouraging feature of recent water planning is the production by Water Authorities of publicly accessible annual, medium-term and specific plans containing explicit goal statements and policy alternatives. Prior to the Water Act 1973 such plans were notably absent – as is still general in Scotland – although occasional factual surveys normally devoid of policy statements were published. The water planning process therefore could be becoming more systematic, with goals used to set planning objectives and strategies and form the basis of performance monitoring and more informed public debate.

Recognising water planning as a political process, goals should ideally be formulated through extensive rational debate between those making decisions and those affected. However, the professional composition of the water planners – and the local participation and accountability problems of the

Water Authorities – provide barriers in the way of thorough goals debates. Such obstacles are not insurmountable, nor does local participatory planning inevitably result in rational or equitable decisions. However water planning goals often lack public acceptance. Consultation with interested parties often comes too late in the planning process, as at Amberley Wild Brooks, and existing public inquiry procedures, as at Carsington, inhibit open discussion of overall government policy.

Good planning requires adequate information, both for the planners and the planned. A positive aspect of the Water Act 1973 is the statutory requirement for detailed Section 24 surveys. Basic planning data were previously missing but there are still important social, economic, environmental and legal areas where information is inadequate and techniques need investigation (Sewell 1973). Assessing public preferences and shifts in social goals is doubly important for the Water Authorities, given their lack of adequate local accountability. In addition there is a host of technical areas needing research, including medical aspects of water quality, methods of renovating aged sewers, leak prevention, water treatment and the control of trace pollutants.

Water planners, however, already rely too heavily upon data to make decisions for them and technical data gathering should not be at the expense of other planning techniques. The reliance upon 'objective' quantitative data reflects the scientific and engineering background of water planners, and their poor appreciation of water planning as a political rather than a technical process. Engineers involved in water planning will often avoid situations where public debate and participation is necessary, preferring to see planning as a design process for which mathematical formulae provide acceptable answers. Consultation therefore often follows after the scheme is 'perfected', according to traditional engineering designs, instead of embracing political debate about scheme aims or policy goals. Any 'subjective' data are eliminated leaving the planning process comfortably neutral but, unfortunately, incomplete. The concept of the neutrality of data is indeed central to engineering-based water planning, ignoring that 'objective' measurements reflect underlying values and that design reflects engineers' views on the desirability of particular policies, plans and schemes.

In addition to clear goal setting and adequate data gathering the extent to which alternative means of solving problems and achieving goals are reviewed comprehensively is a further indicator of the comprehensiveness of decision-making. Water supply planning has certainly suffered from poor consideration of demand management options, although trends are towards a more comprehensive approach. Urban flood protection plans have over-emphasised structural solutions but as schemes become economically more marginal and environmentally or politically unacceptable the unprotected sites which remain should see a combination of non-structural and structural solutions.

The degree to which the performance of plans is monitored to evaluate achievements is a further test of comprehensive planning. Systems for monitoring river water quality certainly appear thorough, although consents are inadequately enforced and the river pollution classification is based on excessively wide class intervals so that the real deterioration as a result of revised consent conditions may be masked. In other non-technical fields, however, the consequences of policies or plans are not often systematically analysed. Examples include the take-up of land drainage benefits and the realisation of water demand forecasts; capital expenditure, once made, is often assumed to have been worthwhile without systematic checks or experimentation with alternative policies.

Water planning, therefore, is slowly becoming more systematic in evaluating alternatives and the consequences of plans. More rigorous and wider use of cost-benefit analyses in land drainage during the 1970s is one example but less progress has been made in evaluating the alternatives to increased per capita water consumption and in environmental impact analysis. Here, as with water quality improvement, more comprehensive planning awaits advances in appraisal methods and the willingness for the water planner to enter areas of enquiry which are explicitly political or controversial. However, a word of caution is needed here. Further search for more comprehensive or 'rational' decision making may not result in better planning. Approaches to planning which favour apparently rational decision making may be excessively inflexible. In addition they may well serve to elevate the planning *process* above a concern for the problem being tackled and to encourage both water planners and the public to see planning as essentially technical and therefore politically neutral instead of being fundamentally concerned with human values.

How the water planning system is structured

Recent British administrative reforms have characterised a search for improved rationality and efficiency (Johnson 1976). Greater efficiency has been seen by government as attainable with larger organisations – an assumption which in reality is highly dubious – and as a consequence centralisation has increased in the water field and local accountability has declined.

The Water Authorities.   Through integration, delocalisation and managerialisation the Water Act 1973 (Jordan, Richardson and Kimber 1977) has given central government in England and Wales more power, has caused public accountability problems, and inevitably raises questions as to the desired style of water planning and a debate about efficiency versus participation.

Although partly a consequence of integration the government considered delocalisation necessary to improve water service efficiency. Regionalisation was intended to avoid over-centralisation and still retain links with local opinion through local authority membership of Water Authorities.

However, the Authorities are basically technically oriented organisations within which there is little conflict over planning goals, which themselves are seen as non-controversial. Therefore there is a tendency to seek efficiency rather than participation and Authorities, therefore, have created a predominantly non-participatory form of planning (O'Riordan 1976b). The 1974 reorganisation largely reflects the view that water planning is primarily a scientific, technical and technological matter to be managed, therefore, by professionals competent in appropriate specialisms. Management by experts necessarily implies limited scope for local participation and democracy and that technical criteria dominate political criteria; indeed this concept of planning is positively encouraged, so as to maintain the style of management by experts even when non-technical matters are under consideration.

Being a capital-intensive industry facing complex engineering, hydrological, chemical and biological problems the argument for an important scientific and technical presence in the management structure of the water industry is overwhelming. However, it is also clear that the form of managerialisation adopted has its costs in the form of loss of public involvement as well as its technical benefits. With the removal of water services from local government the water industry since 1974 in England and Wales has taken a strikingly different path here to other major fields of British public planning. British town and country planning changed in the 1970s towards participatory planning (Goodall and Kirby 1979), apparently as a reaction to 1960s' 'system planning' when planners adopted 'scientific' techniques assuming thereby that their actions were value-free. Following local authority complaints, Water Authority membership was marginally adjusted in 1979, slightly increasing local authority representation from large cities and appointing one member to represent consumer interests on some Boards. Water planning, however, remains based more upon the model of scientific planning or managerial control adopted for other public utility industries such as gas and electricity, yet these have developed their own forms of accountability via consultative councils.

The case for local public accountability and participation in water planning rests, first, on the need for strong links between water and local land use planning to promote efficient integration of the two fields – a purely technical consideration. Secondly, schemes which depend for their viability upon the public as purchasers of freely marketed goods and services – such as certain water recreation facilities – require some public participation at design stages to ensure the eventual marketability of those commodities; again this is a purely technical matter. Thirdly, the water industry's position as a monopoly supplier of other commodities, such as water for drinking or effluent disposal capacity, requires public accountability to ensure that no section of society is unduly disadvantaged by the effects of water planning. Fourthly, there may well be considerable conflict in reality between those affected by water planning, and public participation and representation within decision-making agencies may help to resolve this conflict. These latter elements in the case for accountability and participation are essentially moral considerations in that they presuppose the essential 'rightness' of equity or the absence of conflict and others may disagree with these presuppositions.

As an alternative to local accountability, central parliamentary accountability offers some scope for democratic control of water planning. Water Authorities are responsible now to Ministers who are themselves accountable to Parliament but this form of accountability is far more indirect and remote than the previous local government forms and the adequacy of current parliamentary scrutiny is questionable.

The Water Act 1973 did not provide an adequate system for redressing grievances, as the Daymond case illustrated. Proposed Regional Consultative Councils to represent local opinion were not included in the 1974 reorganisation (Department of the Environment and Welsh Office 1972). The net result of a lack of both full parliamentary or direct local accountability is the potential for water planners to devise and implement policies with little scope for public opposition, and indeed for little opposition at all if the policies have government and therefore financial support.

However, although close participation between Water Authorities and all local interests may be important to the success of water planning public participation is certainly no panacea. Formal consultative procedures typically receive limited public response. Pressure groups may be unrepresentative of the larger population, they may sometimes take opposing viewpoints and their success in influencing policy depends less on the rationality of their arguments and more on the economic power and political skills of their members. Furthermore, participation may slow the planning process to a point of gross inefficiency. Nevertheless, measures to make liaison with local interests a statutory requirement as opposed to a permissive power – suggested in the 1977 White Paper on the water industry – are necessary to strengthen local participation. Changes in public inquiry procedures should allow debate of government policy as well as local issues (Levin 1979). However, while such improvements ensure all relevant interests have a roughly equal opportunity to contribute, all interests will still not have an equal influence on decisions. This is because the traditionally strong and politically astute interests, such as the agricultural and angling lobbies and the professions, can make better use of these opportunities and generally present arguments with which government is more likely to agree since government is largely in power to support these interests.

The Scottish comparison

The Scottish dimension is interesting in raising the question why in the small space of Britain two completely different water planning systems exist, and also because it allows comparative evaluation of each.

Scotland's more abundant water resources and its different legal and governmental traditions, are major reasons why water management structures in Scotland are unique. A large relatively pollution-free resource base and a small population means that Scotland has ten times as much water available per head than England and Wales. Furthermore, flood problems are few and water space for recreation far exceeds demands. In Scotland, therefore, competition between different water demands and interests is significantly less problematic than in England and Wales.

Therefore planning is geared less to conflicting use management because conflict can often be avoided. Furthermore the number of water planners in Scotland is relatively small compared with England and Wales, increasing the likelihood of mutual understanding and cooperation. With the exception of angling and fishing proprietors, interest and pressure groups are less active in Scotland, given the lesser conflict levels, and environmental interests tend to be less vociferous than south of the border because schemes which threaten environmental quality are less numerous. The relative cheapness of Scottish water, its rate support grant subsidy and the anonymous charging system through local authority rates – and the consequent absence so far of a Scottish dimension to the water charges equalisation issue – all make Scottish water planning less controversial.

Separate legal and governmental traditions provide Scotland with opportunities for administrative reforms which are different from England and Wales. Central government has been less dominant than local government in the water field in Scotland than in England and Wales. The Scottish Office has often viewed water in the particular context of Scottish social and economic development, including rehousing and industrial development (Coppock and Sewell 1978). This view has favoured a service role for water, which has fitted comfortably with other local authority services, rather than a commodity role which would favour a nationalised industry approach as in the Water Authorities.

As a consequence, although there are similarities in the 1974 and 1975 administrative reforms notably in the amalgamation of water undertakings and the regionalisation of water planning, strikingly contrasting management structures have developed. The merit of the Scottish system lies in the potential for full local democratic control and participation to promote 'fair' resolution of conflict. However, there is more conflict between water interests in England and Wales to be resolved and therefore more genuine need for participation from local, environmental and recreational interests for whom the internalisation of conflicts within Water Authorities is hardly helpful. Perhaps the very presence of greater conflict in England and Wales promotes the style of non-participatory water planning, whereas the relative absence of conflict in Scotland allows participation because it threatens nothing. The Scottish system has greater potential for close liaison between water planning and other areas of local planning and for the full range of local services to be planned in a unified manner. Finally, the independence of the River Purification Boards is often claimed in Scotland to be superior to the system in England and Wales, where the Water Authorities are both 'poachers' and 'gamekeepers'. How far this claim is valid is difficult to ascertain. However, a notable difference in pollution prevention in Scotland is the stricter control over discharges to estuaries, and without the Boards as independent watchdogs some of the recent river water quality improvements attained in Scotland would not have occurred. Nevertheless it is clear that overall standards of sewage treatment and industrial pollution control require raising both in Scotland and England and Wales and the power and success of Purification Boards faced with determined industrial opposition is still untested.

Some international comparisons

British water planning systems commonly receive high praise (Okun 1977) and there are many technical and managerial advantages in multi-functional catchment-based planning. However, water planning systems can be structured in many ways (Fox 1976) and international comparison reveals marked differences (Howe 1977). Other systems have merits, not least for larger countries with different resource bases or social contexts (Sewell 1978) and Britain can learn from others and vice versa.

International comparisons confirm water management structures in England and Wales as remarkably integrated. Only two ministries here have major water responsibilities whereas in France, for example, seven are involved necessitating an Inter-Ministerial Water Commission. Belgium and the Netherlands both involve four major ministries although each gives one prime responsibility (Palmer 1976). In West Germany, the United States, Canada and Australia responsibilities are further divided between states or provinces and the federal government. Britain, Finland and Japan are all characterised by centralised financial control with some regional delegation. Local and regional authorities have greater financial independence in the United States, Canada, West Germany and France (Organisation for Economic Co-operation and Development 1976, 1977).

England and Wales are unusual in having country-wide, multi-functional, regional, catchment-based institutions. In federal countries, such as the United States, West Germany and Canada, power is decentralised but state plans are increasingly coordinated by the federal government and states often combine to form regional organisations, sometimes catchment-based. Therefore, in the United States water pollution control by the Environmental Protection Agency is increasingly felt at state level. Increasingly common are river basin commissions coordinating water supply and pollution across state boundaries (Okun 1977). River basin planning is weakly developed in some countries, such as Sweden, although in southern Sweden some river management organisations have been established to coordinate river-based water interests (Ministry of Agriculture 1977).

Efforts have been made to decentralise water services in France, Japan and Finland where government is traditionally centralised. France has country-wide, river basin planning with six Basin Agencies (*Agences Financières de Bassin*) although their responsibilities and powers are more restricted than British Water Authorities. The Agencies have a financial role in water supply, waste water and pollution control fields, leaving water users to plan, commission and undertake schemes.

Although water management is commonly part-regionalised, fragmented local responsibilities are widespread and reminiscent of England and Wales before 1974. In the Netherlands some 600 mainly single-function water boards – *Waterschappen* – remain (Van Soest 1973) and water administration in West Germany is split amongst 25 000 local authorities and water associations. The United States has 40 000 authorities concerned with community public water supplies alone (Greenberg and Hordon 1976).

Other countries might learn from the British integrated, regional, catchment-based water institutions but concerning public accountability and elected local and user representation Britain might learn from others. The French system combines the merits of regional catchment-based management with well developed local and user participation. The Basin Agencies' finance is determined by tripartite Basin Committees with equal representation from central government, elected local authority representatives and water users. These users are elected from basin-wide or nationwide bodies such as Chambers of Commerce. Such representation also exists on France's advisory National Water Committee (Tenière-Buchot 1976). Water planning institutions in Germany, the Netherlands, Belgium, Japan and the United States all have elected user representation. In the Ruhr area of West Germany, for example, the water associations are composed of all users who elect directors to run commercially the effluent control and water supply works.

Water planning policy also differs in other countries, no more so than in the pollution field. Many countries suggest that they have adopted the polluter-pays principle but are applying it to varying degrees. France and the Netherlands have pioneered the charge-based incentive approach (McIntosh and Wilcox 1978); tax concessions for industrial investment in pollution abatement plant are available in Finland and West Germany. Canada, like Britain, continues with flat rate charges for domestic sewage treatment whereas most other countries link charging systems to volume. Penalties based on polluters compensating those damaged by pollution are levied in Finland. Most other countries only attempt regulation of direct discharges and this aspect of the polluter-pays principle remains untackled. The particular conditions and traditions in each country determine the choice of policy and method of implementation. Nevertheless it is significant to note that strategies considered 'impossible' in one country – such as direct discharge charges – may be found working reasonably well in others, and such international comparisons may usefully illuminate future policy options in Britain.

Conclusion

This Chapter has adopted a critical stance concerning both how decisions are made and the composition and structure of the water planning system. This criticism should not detract from the considerable merits in British water planning systems, both in Scotland and in England and Wales, particularly when set in their wider international context and with respect to the development of technical solutions to water planning problems. Nevertheless the analysis of future water plans should involve critical evaluation of the economic efficiency, equity and environmental and health protection considerations so as to isolate the real intended or unintended effects of particular policies.

Such an evaluation recognises water planning as a political activity which has both economic and social consequences, intended or otherwise. Within this political activity certain interest groups dominate decision making, particularly in the land drainage, amenity and recreation and the pollution control fields. There is clear evidence that the outcome of policies, plans and schemes favours certain sections of society – particularly the wealthy, landowners and certain private recreation interests. Future studies of water planning which ignore these factors will not provide a correct analysis of the forces promoting particular policies, plans and schemes.

Pertinent here is the role of public education in the complexities of water planning. As society becomes more complex and uncertain so the need grows to raise public consciousness of the issues involved in resource planning, to further understanding of the planning system and its biases and to promote democratic influence on decision making.

Responsible and successful water planning must respect and reflect the goals and preferences of the whole of society. An informed and educated public is likely to contribute more to the success of policy making and implementation than if it is misinformed and ignorant. Water planners must provide factual information and the rationales behind their decisions – although this may be uncomfortable for the planners and reveal basic divisions between sections of society – and explain to the public their dependence upon public expenditure to achieve social goals.

It is often claimed that the public is disinterested in water matters, but it is also true that public consciousness will not be raised without careful education and explanation. Regrettably in the past the water industry has provided little information and often remained distant from the public. The Water Authorities have made a start in this education process, although often only to justify increasing water charges. Moves towards a still less guarded and more open water industry will be to the benefit of all, even if in the short term the task of the water planner has to change to meet this need.

Selected further reading (for full bibliography see pp. 254–66)

Useful material on decision-making in water planning and research needs can be found in:

Sewell, W. R. D. 1973. 'Broadening the approach to evaluation in resources management decision-making.' *Journal of Environmental Management* 1, 33–60.

For further details on alternative international approaches to water planning institutions and policy see the following and the individual reports from which it was compiled (Organisation for Economic Co-operation and Development 1976):

Organisation for Economic Co-operation and Development 1977. *Water management policies and instruments*. Paris: OECD.

Bibliography

Agricultural Development and Advisory Service 1974–7. *Getting down to drainage.* Drainage leaflets Nos. 1–21. London: Ministry of Agriculture, Fisheries and Food.

Andrews, C. D. 1976. *We didn't wait for the rain* . . . London: National Water Council.

Andrews, C. D. 1979. 'The mosaic that turned into a unified industry.' *Water* **25**, 24–8.

Anglian Water Authority 1976. *Annual report and accounts.* Huntingdon: AWA.

Ardill, J. 1974. 'Watchdog for nationalised water.' *Water and Sewage Works* **121**, 64–5.

Arvill, R. 1976. *Man and environment: crisis and the strategy of choice.* 4th edn. London: Penguin.

Association of Scottish District Salmon Fishery Boards 1977. *Salmon fisheries of Scotland.* Farnborough: Fishing News Ltd.

Baldwin, A. 1977. 'Give us this day . . .' *Geographical Magazine* **49**, 498–501.

Barr, L. R. 1973. *Areal reorganisation of water management in England and Wales.* Unpublished MA thesis. British Columbia: University of Victoria.

Baumann, D. D. 1969. *The recreational use of domestic water supply reservoirs: perception and choice.* Dept. of Geog. research paper 121. Chicago: University of Chicago.

Beaumont, P. 1977. 'Resource management: a case study of water.' *Progress in Physical Geography* **1** (3), 528–36.

Bell, W. J. 1978. 'Water quality and public health.' *Water Pollution Control* **77** (3), 360–9.

Bennet, G. 1970. 'Bristol floods 1968. Controlled survey of effects on health of local community disaster.' *British Medical Journal* **3**, 454–8.

Biggs, A. I. 1977. 'Effects on industry.' In *Procs. of the one-day seminar on the operational aspects of the drought 1975–76*, held on 29 March. London: Institution of Water Engineers and Scientists and the Institution of Civil Engineers.

Blythe, R. 1969. *Akenfield: Portrait of an English village.* London: Penguin.

British Waterways Board 1965. *The facts about the waterways.* London: BWB.

British Waterways Board 1978. *Annual report and accounts 1977.* London: BWB.

Broads Consortium Committee 1971. *Broadland study and plan.* Norwich: Broads Consortium.

Broady, M. 1977. 'Welsh water: the politics of water supply.' In *Water planning and the regions*, P. J. Drudy (ed.) Discussion paper 9, 19–30. London: Regional Studies Association.

Brown, J. C. 1977. 'Sludge disposal: a specialised operation.' *Water* **15**, 2–9.

Brown, J. C. 1978. *Social and political objectives of the Water Authorities.* Water services policy seminar, 13–14 July. York: University of York.

Brown, R. M., N. I. McClelland, R. A. Denninger and R. G. Toyer 1970. 'A water quality index – do we dare?' *Water and Sewage Works* **117**, 339–43.

Burke, R., and J. P. Heaney 1975. *Collective decision making in water resource planning.* Massachusetts: Lexington Books.

Capner, G. 1979. Untitled reply to paper on the planning role of Water Authorities. *The Planner* **65** (1), 22.

Central Water Planning Unit 1975. *Household use of water.* Technical Note 7. Reading: CWPU.

Central Water Planning Unit 1976a. *The significance of synthetic chemicals in rivers used as a source of drinking water.* Technical Note 14. Reading: CWPU.

Central Water Planning Unit 1976b. *Analysis of trends in public water supply.* Reading: CWPU.

Central Water Planning Unit 1976c. *Regional distribution of water demand by the food industry.* Technical Note 15. Reading: CWPU.

Central Water Planning Unit 1976d. *The Wash water storage scheme, report on the feasibility study.* London: HMSO.

Central Water Planning Unit 1976e. *Some empirical information on demands for water-based recreation activities.* Technical Note 13. Reading: CWPU.

Central Water Planning Unit 1977. *Public water supply in 1975 and trends in consumption.* Technical Note 19. Reading: CWPU.

Chartered Institute of Public Finance and Accountancy 1978. *Water service charges statistics 1978–79.* London: CIPFA.

Chatterton, J. B., and S. J. Farrell 1975. *Proposed flood alleviation scheme for Pulborough: benefit assessment.* Enfield: Middlesex Polytechnic.

Chatterton, J. B., J. Pirt and T. R. Wood 1979. 'The benefits of flood forecasting.' *Journal of the Institution of Water Engineers and Scientists* 33 (3), 237–52.

Clawson, M. 1959. *Methods of measuring the demand for and value of outdoor recreation.* Reprint No. 10. Washington: Resources for the Future.

Clawson, M., and J. L. Knetsch 1966. *Economics of outdoor recreation.* Resources for the Future. Baltimore: Johns Hopkins.

Clyde River Purification Board 1976a. *Report for the year ending 31 December 1975.* Glasgow: CRPB.

Clyde River Purification Board 1976b. *Water quality: a baseline report.* Glasgow: CRPB.

Clyde River Purification Board 1978. *Report for the year ending 31 December 1977.* Glasgow: CRPB.

Cole, G. 1976. 'Land drainage in England and Wales.' *Journal of the Institution of Water Engineers and Scientists* 30 (7), 345–67.

Collins, N. R. 1975. 'The Cotswold Water Park.' *Water Space* 5, 12–17.

Conlon, B. 1977. 'From Tyne to Tees – Kielder water.' *Water* 12, 20–2.

Consumers' Association 1975. 'Seaside sewage revisited.' *Which?*, July, 206–8.

Control of Pollution Act 1974. London: HMSO.

Coppock, J. T., and B. S. Duffield 1975. *Recreation in the countryside.* London: Macmillan.

Coppock, J. T., and W. R. D. Sewell 1978. *Water management policies in Scotland.* Final report on research project No. HR3108/2. London: Social Science Research Council.

Cordle, P. and C. Willetts 1976. 'Links between regional water authorities and local authorities.' *Corporate planning* 3 (3), 39–50.

Cotswold Water Park Joint Committee 1970. *Cotswold Water Park master plan.* Gloucester: Gloucestershire County Council.

Coughlin, R. 1975. *The perception and valuation of water quality: a review of research methods and findings.* Regional Science Research Institute, Report No. 80. Philadelphia: RSRI.

Council for the Protection of Rural England 1974. *Submission to the Secretary of State for the Environment and National Water Council on the report of the Water Resources Board 'Water resources in England and Wales'.* London: CPRE.

Council for the Protection of Rural England 1975. *Landscape – the need for a public voice.* London: CPRE.

Council for the Protection of Rural England 1977. *Quarterly Bulletin* 10 (6), June. London: CPRE.

Craine, L. E. 1969. *Water management innovations in England*. Baltimore: Johns Hopkins.

Dart, M. C. 1977a. 'Charging principles for effluent and sewage disposal.' In *The economics of charging structures for the water services*. Water Research Centre (ed.) Paper 6. Stevenage: WRC.

Dart, M. C. 1977b. 'Industrial effluent control and charges.' *Water Pollution Control* **76** (2), 192–204.

Dartington Amenity Research Trust 1973. *Llangorse lake: a recreation survey*. Totnes: DART.

Dartington Amenity Research Trust 1975. *Llandegfedd and Siblyback reservoirs*. A study prepared for the Sports Council and the Countryside Commission. London: Sports Council.

Davidson, J., and G. Wibberley 1977. *Planning and the rural environment*. Oxford: Pergamon.

Department of the Environment 1973. *The new water industry: management and structures* (the 'Ogden report'). London: HMSO.

Department of the Environment 1974. *The water services: economic and financial policies*. Third report to the Secretary of State for the Environment. London: HMSO.

Department of the Environment 1976. *Pollution control in Britain: how it works*. Pollution report 9. London: HMSO.

Department of the Environment 1977a. *Guidance on Water Authorities' annual plans and programmes to be submitted under section 24 of the Water Act 1973*. London: HMSO.

Department of the Environment 1977b. *Sport and recreation*. Cmnd. 6200. London: HMSO.

Department of the Environment 1978. *Digest of environmental pollution statistics*. Pollution report 4. London: HMSO.

Department of the Environment and Welsh Office 1971. *Report of a river pollution survey of England and Wales* 1. London: HMSO.

Department of the Environment and Welsh Office 1972. *Consultation paper on public participation in water management*. London: HMSO.

Department of the Environment and Welsh Office 1973. *A background to water reorganisation in England and Wales*. London: HMSO.

Department of the Environment, Welsh Office, Ministry of Agriculture, Fisheries and Food 1976. *Review of the water industry in England and Wales: a consultative document*. London: HMSO.

Department of the Environment, Welsh Office, Ministry of Agriculture, Fisheries and Food 1977. *The water industry in England and Wales: the next steps*. London: HMSO.

Department of the Environment Water Data Unit 1974. *The surface water year book of Great Britain 1966–70*. London: HMSO.

Department of the Environment Water Data Unit 1975. *Groundwater year book 1968–70*. London: HMSO.

Department of the Environment Water Data Unit 1976. *Water demand in England and Wales 1974*. Technical memo. 9. Reading: WDU.

Department of the Environment Water Data Unit 1977. *Water data 1975*. London: HMSO.

Department of Health and Social Security 1969. *The bacteriological examination of water supplies*. Report 71. London: HMSO.

Ditton, R. B. 1969. *Recreation and water resources: a critical analysis of selected literature*. Ph.D. University Microfilms, Ann Arbor: University of Illinois.

Doornkamp, J. C., and K. J. Gregory (eds) 1980. *Atlas of drought in Britain 1975–76*. London: Institute of British Geographers.

Dower, M. 1965. *The challenge of leisure*. London: Civic Trust.

Dracup, S. B. 1973. Water supply in Great Britain 1690–1950, a brief history in six parts. *British Water Supply* Jan.–June. London: British Waterworks Assoc.

Driver, B., and R. Knopf 1976. 'Temporary escape, one product of sport fisheries management.' *Fisheries* 1, 24–29.

Dror, Y. 1964. 'Muddling through – science or inertia?' *Public Administration Review* 24 (3).

Drudy, P. J. (ed.) 1977. *Water planning and the regions*. Discussion paper 9. London: Regional Studies Association.

Drummond, I. 1977. 'Conservation and land drainage.' *Water Space* 11, 23–30.

Dugdale, W. 1975. 'Universal metering, the case against.' *Water* 4, 9–10.

Economic Intelligence Unit 1977. *The drought of 1975–76 in England and Wales*. Prepared for Anduff Car Wash Ltd. London: EIU.

Ellis, J. B. 1979. 'The nature and sources of urban sediments and their relation to water quality.' In *Man's impact on the hydrological cycle in the UK*, G. E. Hollis (ed.), 199–216. Norwich: Geobooks.

ENDS 1979. *The water industry. 1: Are the water authorities fudging the books?* Report 17. London: Environmental Data Services.

Eno, J. M., and D. C. Pollington 1975. 'Washington sewage works: design and operation.' *Water Pollution Control* 74 *(5)*, 571–83.

Faludi, A. 1973. *A reader in planning theory*. Oxford: Pergamon.

Fielding, M., and R. F. Packham 1977. 'Organic compounds in drinking water and public health.' *Journal of the Institution of Water Engineers and Scientists* 31 (4), 353–75.

Fish, H. 1973. *Principles of water quality management*. London: Thunderbird Enterprises.

Fish, H. 1975. 'Scientific services in Regional Water Authorities.' *Water Pollution Control* 74 (3), 291–302.

Fish, H., and S. Torrance 1978. *Control of specific industrial pollution of water sources*. Paper presented to the International Water Supply Association, Kyoto Congress.

Foreign and Commonwealth Office 1976. *Convention on wetlands of international importance especially as waterfowl habitat*. Treaty series 34. Cmnd. 6465. London: HMSO.

Fox, I. K. 1976. 'Institutions for water management in a changing world' *Natural Resources Journal* 16 (4), 743–58.

Fox, I. K., and L. E. Craine 1962. 'Organisational arrangements for water development.' *Natural Resources Journal* 2, 1–44.

Freeman, A. M., R. H. Haveman and A. V. Kneese 1972. *The economics of environmental policy*. London: John Wiley.

Freeman, L. 1977. 'Trade effluents: the charges and the consequences.' *Water* 17, 13–16.

Friedmann, J. 1959. 'The study and practice of planning.' *International Social Science Journal* 11, 327–39.

Garland, J. H. N. 1979. 'River pollution and people.' *Water* 25, 46–8.

George, M. 1977. *Water, navigation and drainage authorities in England and Wales (with special reference to the situation in Broadland)*. Unpublished paper.

Gilg, A. W. 1978. *Countryside planning, the first three decades 1945–76*. London: Methuen.

Goodall, B., and A. Kirby (eds) 1979. *Resources and planning*. Oxford: Pergamon.

Green, F. H. W. 1976. 'Recent changes in land use and treatment.' *Geographical Journal* 143 (1), 12–26.

Green, F. H. W. 1979. 'Field under-drainage and the hydrological cycle.' In *Man's impact on the hydrological cycle in the UK*, G. E. Hollis (ed.). Norwich: Geobooks.

Greenberg, M. R., and R. M. Hordon 1976. *Water supply planning: a case study and systems analysis*. State University, New Jersey: Center for Urban and Policy Research.

Greenfield, M. 1975. 'NWC: watchdog or lapdog?' *Municipal Journal* **83** (14, supplement), 21–2.

Greer, W. T. 1976. 'The reorganisation of water services in Scotland: water and sewage.' *Water Pollution Control* **75** (2), 266–71.

Gregory, R. 1975. 'The Cow Green reservoir.' In *The politics of physical resources*, P. J. Smith (ed.), 144–201. London: Penguin/Open University.

Gregory, S. 1957. 'Annual rainfall probability maps of the British Isles.' *Quarterly Journal of the Royal Meteorological Society* **83**, 543–9.

Hall, C. 1978. 'Amberley Wild Brooks.' *Vole* **7**, 14–15.

Hanson, M. 1975. 'Water for recreation.' *Municipal Journal* **83** (14, supplement), 15–18.

Harding, D. M. 1977. 'The case for conservation at Llyn Brianne.' *Nature in Wales* **15** (4), 212–7.

Harding, D. M., and D. J. Parker 1974. 'Flood hazard at Shrewsbury, UK.' In *Natural hazards local national global*, G. F. White (ed.), 43–52. New York: Oxford University Press.

Harrison, J. G., and P. Grant 1976. *The Thames transformed – London's river and its waterfowl*. London: Deutsch.

Hender, J. D. 1975. 'Corporate management for regional water authorities.' *Water Pollution Control* **74** (3), 248–61.

Herrington, P. R. 1973. *Water demand study, final report*. Dept. of Economics. Leicester: University of Leicester.

Herrington, P. R. 1976. 'The economics of water supply and demand.' *Economics* **12** (2), 67–84.

Herrington, P. R. 1979. *Broad Oak (Canterbury) reservoir proposal. Proof of evidence*. London: Council for the Protection of Rural England.

Highland Regional Council, Department of Water and Sewerage 1978. *Regional report*. Inverness: HRC.

Highland River Purification Board 1977. *Third annual report 1977*. Inverness: HRPB.

Hill, A. R. 1976. 'The environmental impact of agricultural land drainage.' *Journal of Environmental Management* **4**, 251–74.

Hollis, G. E. 1978. 'Water for London.' In *Changing London*. H. T. Clout (ed.), 118–27. Slough: University Tutorial Press.

Hollis, G. E. 1979. *Agriculture and the hydrological regime: recent research in the UK*. Paper presented at International Institute for Applied Systems Analysis conference, 23–7 April, Smolenice.

Horner, R. W. 1978. 'Thames tidal flood works in the London excluded area.' *Journal of the Institution of Public Health Engineers* **6** (1), 16–24.

Howe, C. W. 1977. *The design and evaluation of institutional arrangements for water planning and management*. UN Water Conference, Mar Del Plata 14–25 March.

Hunt, P. C. 1977. 'Fisheries in relation to other Water Authority activities.' *Water Pollution Control* **76** (4), 481–92.

Huxley, T. 1976. 'Recreation and conservation in the Scottish wetlands'. In *Proceedings of Royal Society of Arts conference, Recreation and conservation in water areas*. London: RSA.

Ingham, M. 1975. 'Freightwaves '75 turns the tides.' *Waterways News* Sept. London: British Waterways Board.

Inland Waterways Amenity Advisory Council 1971. *Remainder waterways*. A report to the Secretary of State for the Environment. London: IWAAC.

Inland Waterways Amenity Advisory Council 1974. *Scottish waterways, Forth and*

Clyde, Union Canal. A report to the Secretary of State for the Environment. London: IWAAC.

Inland Waterways Amenity Advisory Council 1977. *Observations on the review of the water industry in England and Wales.* London: IWAAC.

Institution of Water Engineers 1963. *Final report to the council on the recreational use of waterworks.* London: IWE.

Institution of Water Engineers 1972. 'Reorganisation of water services: England and Wales.' *Journal of the Institution of Water Engineers* **26** (6), 291– 310.

Jenking, R. C. 1973. *Fylde metering.* Blackpool: Fylde Water Board.

Jenking, R. C. 1976. 'Financing the water cycle.' *Water Pollution Control* **75** (2), 244–56.

Johnson, E. A. G. 1954. 'Land drainage in England and Wales.' *Proceedings of the Institution of Civil Engineers* Part III, **3** (3), 601–51.

Johnson, N. 1976. 'Recent administrative reform in Britain.' In *The management of change in government*, A. F. Leemans (ed.). Amsterdam: Martinus Nijhoff.

Jordan, A. G., J. J. Richardson and R. H. Kimber 1977. 'The origins of the Water Act 1973.' *Public Administration* **55**, 317–34.

Keat, R. 1979. 'Positivism and statistics in social science.' In *Demystifying Social Statistics*, J. Irvine, I. Miles and J. Evans (eds). London: Pluto Press.

Kinnersley, D. J. 1976. 'What price water quality?' *Journal of the Institution of Water Engineers and Scientists* **30**, 368–77.

Kooyoomjian K., and N. Clesceri 1974. 'Perception of water quality by selected respondent groupings in inland water-based recreational environments.' *Water Resources Bulletin* **10** (4), 728–44.

Lambert, N. 1977. 'Underground assets worth £35 000millions – to replace'. *Water* **15**, 23–4.

Lancashire County Council 1976a. *Anglezarke recreation area local plan. Survey and Issues.* Preston: LCC.

Lancashire County Council 1976b. *West Pennine Moors plan. Public participation report.* Preston: LCC.

Lancashire County Council 1978. *West Pennine Moors plan. Approach to a plan.* Preston: LCC.

Land Drainage Act 1976. London: HMSO.

Lester, W. F. 1977. 'Whither pollution control?' *Water Pollution Control* **76** (3), 327–31.

Levin, P. H. 1979. 'Highway inquiries: a study in governmental responsiveness.' *Public Administration* **57**, 21–49.

Liddell, P. 1978. 'Towards better recreational access to North West reservoirs.' *Water Space* **13**, 35–7.

Lindblom, C. E. 1959. 'The science of "muddling through"'. *Public Administration Review* **19**, 79–88.

Lingard, J. 1975. 'Universal metering, the case for.' *Water* **4**, 6–9.

Lloyd, J. 1975. 'What is resource planning?' *Municipal Journal* **83** (14, supplement), 7–13.

Local Government Operational Research Unit 1973. *The economics of flood alleviation.* Report No. C155. Reading: LGORU.

Local Government Operational Research Unit 1977. *The value of water-based recreation: a background study.* Report No. C257. Reading: LGORU.

Local Government Operational Research Unit 1978a. *The value of water-based recreation.* Report No. C268. Reading: LGORU.

Local Government Operational Research Unit 1978b. *The economics of pumped drainage.* Report No. C271. Reading: LGORU.

Local Government (Scotland) Act 1974. Edinburgh: HMSO.

Lowe, P. D. 1975a. 'Political resources of the environmental lobby.' *Built Environment Quarterly* **1**, 73–6.

Lowe, P. D. 1975b. 'Formation and structure of the environmental lobby.' *Built Environment Quarterly* **1**, 158–61.

Lowe, P. D. 1977. 'Amenity and equity: a review of local environmental pressure groups in Britain.' *Environment and Planning* **9**, 35–58.

Macrory, R., and B. Zaba 1978. *Polluters pay: the Control of Pollution Act explained*. London: Friends of the Earth.

McGeoch, J. A. N. 1977. *Was reorganisation an effective treatment?* Paper presented at Institute of Water Pollution Control, Scottish Branch, 15 March. Perth.

McIntosh, P., and J. Wilcox 1978. 'Water pollution charging systems and the EEC.' *Water* **23**, 2–6.

McLoughlin, J. 1975. 'The Control of Pollution Act 1974–2.' *Journal of Planning and Environmental Law*, 77–85.

Middlesex Polytechnic Flood Hazard Research Project 1976. *Proposed embankment scheme, Middle Arun: benefit assessment*. Enfield: Middlesex Polytechnic.

Miers, R. H. 1967. 'A wide view of land drainage.' *Association of River Authorities Yearbook*, 56–71.

Ministry of Agriculture 1977. *Water in Sweden*. National report to the UN Water Conference, prepared by the Swedish Preparatory Committee for the Water Conference. Stockholm: Ministry of Agriculture.

Ministry of Agriculture, Fisheries and Food 1974. *Guidance notes for Water Authorities*, Water Act 1973 section 24. London: MAFF.

Ministry of Housing and Local Government 1948. *Gathering grounds*. Sub-committee of the Central Advisory Water Committee (the 'Heneage report'). London: HMSO.

Ministry of Housing and Local Government 1967. *Report on safeguards to be adopted in the operation and management of waterworks*. London: HMSO.

Ministry of Housing and Local Government 1970. *Taken for granted. Report of the working party on sewage disposal* (the 'Jeger report'). London: HMSO.

Ministry of Land and Natural Resources and Department of Education and Science 1966. *Use of reservoirs and gathering grounds for recreation*. London: HMSO.

Mitchell, B. 1971. *Water in England and Wales. Supply, transfer and management*. Dept. of Geog. research paper 9. Liverpool: University of Liverpool.

Mitchell, B. 1979. *Geography and resource analysis*. London: Longman.

Mukhopadhyay, A. K. 1975. 'The politics of London water.' *The London Journal* **1** (2), 207–24.

Munton, R. C. 1974. 'Agriculture and conservation in lowland Britain.' In *Conservation in practice*, A. Warren and I. B. Goldsmith (eds), 323–36. London: John Wiley.

National Anglers' Council 1978. *Newsletter No. 25*. Peterborough: NAC.

National Farmers' Union and Country Landowners' Association 1977. *Caring for the countryside: a statement of intent for farmers and landowners*. London: NFU and CLA.

National Water Council 1976. *Paying for water*. London: NWC.

National Water Council 1977a. *Desalination*. Standing Technical Committee on Water Treatment Report No. 6. London: NWC.

National Water Council 1977b. *The 1975–76 drought*. London: NWC.

National Water Council 1977c. *Sewers and water mains: a national assessment*. Standing committee on water mains and sewers Report No. 4. London: NWC.

National Water Council 1977d. *Review of discharge consent conditions: consultation paper*. London: NWC.

National Water Council 1977e. *Annual report and accounts 1976/7*. London: NWC.

National Water Council 1978a. *Water industry review 1978*. London: NWC.

National Water Council 1978b. *River water quality, the next stage: review of discharge consent conditions.* London: NWC.

National Water Council 1979. *Annual report and accounts 1978/9.* London: NWC.

Natural Environment Research Council 1975. *Flood studies report* (Vols I–V). London: NERC.

Nature Conservancy Council 1977. *The future of Broadland.* London: NCC.

Nature Conservancy Council South West Region 1977. *The Somerset wetlands project.* Taunton: NCC.

Naughton, J. 1974. 'The water planners'. *Surveyor* **144** (4288), 13–16.

Nelson, A., and K. D. Nelson 1973. *Dictionary of water and water engineering.* London: Butterworth.

Newbury, D. 1977. 'Accounting and accountability'. *Water* **17**, 9–11.

Northumbrian Water Authority 1976. *Second annual report and accounts.* Gosforth: NWA.

Northumbrian Water Authority 1978a. *Annual plan 1978.* Gosforth: NWA.

Northumbrian Water Authority 1978b. *Annual plan 1978: report of survey.* Gosforth: NWA.

North West Sports Council 1972. *Leisure in the North West.* Manchester: NWSC.

North West Water Authority 1975. *Report on the pollution of Cowm reservoir.* Warrington: NWWA.

North West Water Authority 1976a. *Liaison with planning authorities.* 3rd edn. Warrington: NWWA.

North West Water Authority 1976b. *Annual report and accounts.* Warrington: NWWA.

North West Water Authority 1977a. *Annual report and accounts.* Warrington: NWWA.

North West Water Authority 1977b. *Recreational access to gathering grounds.* Paper for Minister of State's meeting with Chairmen and Directors of Government Agencies. Warrington: NWWA.

North West Water Authority 1978a. *Report on planning.* Warrington: NWWA.

North West Water Authority 1978b. *Underground dereliction in the North West.* Warrington, NWWA.

Okun, D. A. 1977. *Regionalization of water management.* London: Applied Science Publishers.

Organisation for Economic Co-operation and Development 1976. *Study on economic and policy instruments for water management.* Series of 8 national monographs. Water management in: Canada, Federal Republic of Germany, Finland, France, Japan, Netherlands, UK and USA. Paris: OECD.

Organisation for Economic Co-operation and Development 1977. *Water management policies and instruments.* Paris: OECD.

O'Riordan, T. 1971. *Perspectives on resource management.* London: Pion.

O'Riordan, T. 1976a. 'Policy making and environmental management: some thoughts on purposes and research issues.' *Natural Resources Journal* **16**, 55–72.

O'Riordan, T. 1976b. *Environmentalism.* London: Pion.

O'Riordan, T. and R. D. Hey 1976. *Environmental impact assessment.* Farnborough: Saxon House.

O'Riordan, T., and G. Paget 1978. *Sharing rivers and canals.* A study of the views of coarse anglers and boat users on selected waterways. Study 16. London: Sports Council.

Osborne, C. A. 1974. *Water-based recreation in the UK – a review of literature.* Working Paper 109, School of Geography. Leeds: University of Leeds.

Palmer, A. M. 1976. *The planning and management of water resources within selected countries of the EEC.* Unpublished M.Sc. thesis. Newcastle: University of Newcastle-upon-Tyne.

Parker, D. J. 1976. *Socio-economic aspects of flood plain occupance.* Unpublished Ph.D. thesis. Swansea: University of Wales.

Parker, D. J., and D. M. Harding 1978. 'Planning for urban floods'. *Disasters* **2** (1), 47–57.

Parker, D. J., and D. M. Harding 1979. 'Natural hazard evaluation, perception and adjustment'. *Geography* **64** (4), 307–16.

Parton, D. 1978. 'Statutory control and planning in relation to water recreation and freshwater fisheries.' In *Recreational and freshwater fisheries, their conservation, management and development,* J. S. Alabaster (ed.), Papers and proceedings of a Water Research Centre conference, Oxford, 85–98. Stevenage: WRC.

Patmore, J. A. 1972. *Land and leisure.* London: Penguin.

Payne, B. J. 1978. *Water Authorities and planning authorities: a study of developing relationships.* Dept. of Town and Country Planning, Occ. Paper 1. Manchester: University of Manchester.

Penning-Rowsell, E. C. 1978a. *Proposed drainage scheme for Amberley Wild Brooks, Sussex: benefit assessment.* Enfield: Middlesex Polytechnic.

Penning-Rowsell, E. C. 1978b. *The effect of salt contamination on flood damage to residential properties.* Enfield: Middlesex Polytechnic.

Penning-Rowsell, E. C., and J. B. Chatterton 1976. 'Constraints on environmental planning: the example of flood alleviation'. *Area* **8** (2), 133–8.

Penning-Rowsell, E. C., and J. B. Chatterton 1977. *The benefits of flood alleviation: a manual of assessment techniques.* Farnborough: Saxon House.

Penning-Rowsell, E. C., and J. B. Chatterton 1980. 'Assessing the benefits of flood alleviation and land drainage'. *Proceedings of the Institution of Civil Engineers* Part 2 **69**, 295–315.

Penning-Rowsell, E. C., J. B. Chatterton and D. J. Parker 1978. *The effect of flood warning on flood damage reduction: a report for the Central Water Planning Unit.* Reading: CWPU.

Penning-Rowsell, E. C., and D. J. Parker 1974. 'Improving flood plain development control.' *The Planner: Journal of the Royal Town Planning Institute* **60**, 540–3.

Perry, A. H. 1976. 'The long drought of 1975–76'. *Weather* **31**, 328–34.

Pitkethly, A. S. 1979. *The development of water supply administration in the UK: Scotland compared to England and Wales.* Paper given at 1st British–Bulgarian Geographical Seminar.

Plaid Cymru 1976. *It's Wales' water.* Cardiff: PC.

Porter, E. A. 1973. *Pollution in four industrialised estuaries.* London: HMSO.

Porter, E. A. 1978. *Water management in England and Wales.* Cambridge: Cambridge University Press.

Potter, S. 1978. *The capability of lochshores for recreation.* Planning Research Group, Occ. Student Paper 3. Enfield: Middlesex Polytechnic.

Pullin, J. 1975. 'The unacceptable face of the British seaside'. *Surveyor* **146** (4346), 22–4.

Pullin, J. 1976a. 'Multifunctionalism – pursuing the logic of water reorganisation.' *Surveyor* **147** (4373), 15–16.

Pullin, J. 1976b. 'Scotland – water and drainage services in a regionalised system.' *Surveyor* **147** (4380), 11–14.

Pullin, J. 1976c. 'Leak detection – maximising an untapped resource.' *Surveyor* **147** (4377), 13–15.

Pullin, J. 1977. 'Poachers and gamekeepers move towards a cleaner Clyde'. *Surveyor* **149** (4419), 9–11.

Ratcliffe, D. E. (ed.) 1978. *A nature conservation review.* Cambridge: Cambridge University Press.

Redknap, B. V., and W. I. K. Scott 1976. 'The local authority agency function for sewerage'. *Water Pollution Control* **75** (2), 257–65.

Rees, J. A. 1969. *Industrial demand for water: a study of south east England*. London: Weidenfeld and Nicolson.

Rees, J. A. 1976. 'Rethinking our approach to water supply provision.' *Geography* 61 (4), 232–45.

Rees, J. A. 1977a. 'The economics of environmental management.' *Geography* 62, 311–24.

Rees, J. A. 1977b. 'Money down the drain.' *Geographical Magazine* 49, 493–5.

Rees, J. A. 1978. *The management of urban domestic water services: studies in Australia and in England and Wales*. Unpublished Ph.D thesis. London: University of London.

Rees, J. A., and R. Rees 1972. 'Water demand forecasts and planning margins in south east England.' *Regional Studies* 6, 37–48.

Reeve, D. A. D. 1975. 'Operations in the RWAs.' *Water Pollution Control* 74 (3), 277–90.

Rennison, R. W. 1979. *Water to Tyneside*. Newcastle-upon-Tyne: Newcastle and Gateshead Water Company.

Richardon, J. J., and A. G. Jordan 1979. *Governing under pressure. The policy process in a post-parliamentary democracy*. Oxford: Martin Robertson.

Richardson, J. J., A. G. Jordan and R. H. Kimber 1978. 'Lobbying, administrative reform and policy styles: the case of land drainage.' *Political Studies* 26 (1), 47–64.

Richardson, J. J., and R. Kimber 1974. 'The British Waterways Board: a neglected asset?' *Public Administration* 52, 303–18.

Roberts, F. W. 1974. 'The jubilee of the Royal Commission Standard'. *Water Pollution Control* 73 (2), 129–37.

Rodda, J. C., R. A. Downing and F. M. Law 1976. *Systematic hydrology*. London: Newnes-Butterworth.

Ross. S. L. 1977. 'An index system for classifying river water quality.' *Water Pollution Control* 76 (1), 113–22.

Royal Commission on Environmental Pollution 1971. *First report*. London: HMSO.

Royal Commission on Environmental Pollution 1974. *Fourth report: pollution control progress and problems*. London: HMSO.

Royal Commission on Environmental Pollution 1979. *Seventh report: agriculture and pollution*. London: HMSO.

Royal Commission on Local Government in Scotland 1966–69. *Report*. London: HMSO.

Royal Commission on Sewage Disposal 1912. *Standards and tests for sewage and sewage effluents discharging into rivers and streams*. Eighth Report, 1. London: HMSO.

Royal Town Planning Institute 1976. *Planning and the future*. London: RTPI, Institution of Civil Engineers and Royal Society of Chartered Surveyors.

Ruddoff, A., and D. Lucken 1971. 'The engineer and his work: a sociological perspective.' *Science* 172, 1103–8.

Russell, C. S. 1974. 'Restraining demand.' In *The management of water resources in England and Wales*, B. M. Funnell and R. D. Hey (eds). Farnborough: Saxon House.

Scherer, U., and R. Coughlin 1971. *The influence of water quality in the evaluation of stream sites*. Report 27. Philadelphia: Regional Science Institute.

Scottish Development Department 1973. *A measure of plenty, water resources in Scotland: a general survey*. Edinburgh: HMSO.

Scottish Development Department 1976. *Towards cleaner water 1975*. Report of a second river pollution survey of Scotland. Edinburgh: HMSO.

Scottish Information Office (undated). *Water in Scotland*. Edinburgh: HMSO.

Seeley, I. H. 1973. *Outdoor recreation and the urban environment*. London: Macmillan.

Select Committee of the House of Lords 1973. *Sport and leisure*. Second report. London: HMSO.

Severn Trent Water Authority 1977. *A unified approach to land drainage*. Birmingham: STWA.

Severn Trent Water Authority 1978. *Land drainage survey: section 24 (5) Water Act 1973. Interim report*. Birmingham: STWA.

Sewell, W. R. D. 1971. 'Environmental perceptions and attitudes of engineers and public health officials.' *Environment and Behavior* 3 (1), 23–59.

Sewell, W. R. D. 1973. 'Broadening the approach to evaluation in resources management decision making'. *Journal of Environmental Management* 1, 33–60.

Sewell, W. R. D. 1978. 'Water resource planning and its future societal context.' *Water Supply and Management* 1, 387–97.

Sewell, W. R. D., and L. R. Barr 1978. 'Water administration in England and Wales: impacts of reorganisation.' *Water Resources Bulletin* 14 (2), 337–48.

Silver, R. S. 1974. 'Desalination – past, present, future'. *The Chemical Engineer* 281, 35–40.

Simkins, A. 1974. 'Links with local government.' *Municipal Journal* 82 (10), 266–73.

Smith, A., and A. Simkins 1975. 'Collaboration, consultation.' *Municipal Journal* 83 (14, supplement), 23–4.

Smith, K. 1972. *Water in Britain. A study in applied hydrology and resource geography*. London: Macmillan.

Smith, K. 1977. 'Water resource management in Scotland.' *Scottish Geographical Magazine* 93 (2), 66–79.

Smith, K. 1979. 'Trends in water resource management.' *Progress in Physical Geography* 3 (2), 236–54.

Smith, K., and G. A. Tobin 1979. *Human adjustment to the flood hazard*. London: Longman.

Smith, R. J. 1970. *Measuring recreational benefits: the Clawson method applied to a sailing club*. Discussion paper series B, No. 19 Faculty of Commerce and Social Science. Birmingham: University of Birmingham.

Smith, R. J., and N. J. Kavanagh 1969. 'The measurement of benefits of trout fishing: preliminary results of a study at Grafham Water, Great Ouse Water Authority, Huntingdonshire.' *Journal of Leisure Research* 1 (4), 316–32.

Southern Water Authority 1976. *Annual report and accounts*. Worthing: SWA.

South West Water Authority 1978. *Development plan*. 2 vols. Exeter: SWWA.

South Western Council for Sport and Recreation 1976. *A regional strategy for sport and recreation in south west England*. Somerset: SWCSR.

Stott, P. F. 1976. 'The new national industry: a review.' *Water Pollution Control* 75 (2), 238–43.

Sutcliffe, J. V. 1978. *Methods of flood estimation: a guide to the Flood Studies Report*. Report 49. Wallingford: Institute of Hydrology.

Swainson, N. A. (ed.) 1976. *Managing the water environment*. Vancouver: University of British Columbia Press.

Tanner, M. F. 1973a. *Water resources and recreation*. Sports Council Water Recreation Series Study 3. London: Sports Council.

Tanner, M. F. 1973b. 'The recreational use of inland waters.' *Geographical Journal* 139, 456–61.

Tanner, M. F. 1976. 'Water resources and wetlands in England and Wales.' In *Proceedings of Royal Society of Arts conference, Recreation and conservation in water areas*. London: RSA.

Tayside Regional Council 1978. *Regional report*. Dundee: TRC.

Tenière-Buchot, P. F. 1976. 'The role of the public in water management decisions in France.' *Natural Resources Journal* 16 (1), 159–76.

Thames Water Authority 1978. *Annual report and accounts 1976/7*. London: TWA.

Thames Water Authority 1979. *Plan 1979* (3 volumes: Development Plan, Strategic Issues and Summary and Overview). Reading: TWA.

Thomas, D. L. 1976. *The operating of section 16 of the Water Act 1973*. Mimeograph. Warrington: North West Water Authority.

Tinker, J. 1975. 'River pollution: the Midland dirty dozen.' In *Pollution: the professionals and the public*, A. Porteus *et al.* (eds). Milton Keynes: Open University Press.

Tivy, J. 1974. *Loch Lomond: report on the intensity of shoreside environmental damage and management recommendations*. Unpublished. Glasgow: Glasgow University.

Tobin, G. A. 1979. 'Flood losses: the significance of the commercial sector.' *Disasters* 3 (2), 217–23.

Truesdale, G. A., and M. R. G. Taylor 1975. 'Sewage treatment to meet tomorrow's needs.' *Water Pollution Control* 74 (4), 455–64.

Turner, K. 1978. 'The recreational response to changes in water quality: a survey and critique.' *Int. Journal of Environmental Studies* II, 91–8.

Twort, A. C., R. C. Hoather and F. M. Law 1974. *Water supply* 2nd edn. London: Edward Arnold.

Van Oosterom, H. 1977. 'The structure and functions of the RWAs.' In *Water planning and the regions*, P. J. Drudy (ed.), Discussion Paper 9. London: Regional Studies Assoc.

Van Soest, J. J. 1973. 'Water management in the Netherlands.' *Planning and Management in the Netherlands* 7 (2), 88–97.

Ward, R. C. 1975. *Principles of hydrology* 2nd edn. London: McGraw Hill.

Ward, R. C. 1978. *Floods: a geographical perspective*. London: Macmillan.

Water Act 1973. London: HMSO.

Water Research Centre 1977. *The economics of charging structures for the water services*. Papers and proceedings of a seminar organised by the WRC, Oxford 5–6 July. Medmenham: WRC.

Water Research Centre 1979. *Proceedings of a conference on river pollution control*. Keble College, Oxford. Medmenham: WRC.

Water Resources Board 1972. *Desalination*. London: HMSO.

Water Resources Board 1973. *Water resources in England and Wales*. 2 volumes. London: HMSO.

Water Space Amenity Commission 1977a. *Who we are and what we do*. London: WSAC.

Water Space Amenity Commission 1977b. *The recreational use of water supply reservoirs in England and Wales*. Research report 3. London: WSAC.

Water Space Amenity Commission 1977c. *The potential of towpaths as waterside footpaths*. Research report 1. London: WSAC.

Water Space Amenity Commission 1977d. *Water recreation in country parks*. Research report 2. London: WSAC.

Water Space Amenity Commission 1978. *Conservation and land drainage guidelines: draft for consultation*. London: WSAC.

Webb, M. G. 1977. 'Charging principles for water supply.' In *The economics of charging structures for the water services*. Papers and proceedings of a seminar, Oxford 5–6 July. Medmenham: WRC.

Welsh National Water Development Authority 1977. *Annual report and accounts*. Brecon: WNWDA.

Welsh Office 1975. *Committee of inquiry into water charges in the area of the Welsh National Water Development Authority* (the 'Daniel report'). Report submitted to the Secretary of State for Wales. Cardiff: WO.

Welsh Water Authority 1978a. *Annual report and accounts*. Brecon: WWA.

Welsh Water Authority 1978b. *A strategic plan for water space recreation and amenity*. Consultation edition. Brecon: WWA.

Wessex Water Authority 1978a. *The Wessex plan 1978–1983*. Bristol: WWA.
Wessex Water Authority 1978b. *Annual report and accounts*. Bristol: WWA.
Wessex Water Authority 1979. *Somerset land drainage district, land drainage survey report*. Bridgwater: WWA.
Westmacott, R., and T. Worthington 1974. *New agricultural landscapes*. Cheltenham: Countryside Commission.
White, G. F. 1969. *Strategies of American water management*. Ann Arbor: University of Michigan.
White, G. F. 1973. 'Natural hazard research'. In *Directions in geography*, R. J. Chorley (ed.), 193–216. London: Methuen.
White, G. F. *et al*. 1958. *Changes in urban occupance of flood plains in the United States*. Dept. of Geog. research paper 57. Chicago: University of Chicago.
White, S. F. 1974. 'Water reorganisation at the centre.' *Public Health Engineer* 11, 151–4.
Williams, A. 1977. 'The relationship between Regional Water Authorities and local authorities.' In *Water planning and the regions*, P. J. Drudy (ed.). Discussion paper 9. London: Regional Studies Assoc.
Williams, R. 1973. *The country and the city*. London: Chatto and Windus.
Williams, R. 1977. 'The Somerset Levels: a case for conservation?' *Water Space* 12, 15–18.
Wiseman, R. 1974. 'Sewage works: a legacy of neglect.' *New Civil Engineer* Aug. 22, 28–31.
Woodward, G. M. 1976. 'The reorganisation of water services in Scotland: rivers.' *Water Pollution Control* 75 (2), 272–85.
Wootton, G. 1970. *Interest groups*. New Jersey: Prentice Hall.
Yorkshire Water Authority 1978a. *Water and trade effluent charges in Yorkshire arising from the Water Act 1973 and the Control of Pollution Act 1974, their effect on the competitive position of industry particularly opposite the European Common Market with particular reference to the wool industry*. Leeds: YWA.
Yorkshire Water Authority 1978b. *Guidelines for the storage and disposal of animal wastes from intensive livestock units (in particular from piggery units)*. Leeds: YWA.

Index

Legislation from 1945 onwards only is cited in this index.